Jane Butel's Southwestern Grill

▲▲▲▲▲▲▲▲▲▲▲▲▲▲▲▲

Jane Butel's Southwestern Grill

▼▼▼▼▼▼▼▼▼▼▼▼▼▼▼▼

Jane Butel with Gordon McMeen

Illustrations by Michelle Burchard

May 10, 2004

To Jay —

J Butel

HPBOOKS

HPBooks
Published by The Berkley Publishing Group
200 Madison Avenue
New York, NY 10016

Copyright © 1996 by Jane Butel
Book design by Irving Perkins Associates
Interior illustrations by Michelle Burchard
Cover design by James R. Harris
Cover photograph by Steven Mark Needham/envision

First edition: June 1996

Published simultaneously in Canada.

The Putnam Berkley World Wide Web site address is
http://www.berkley.com

Library of Congress Cataloging-in-Publication Data
Butel, Jane.
    Jane Butel's Southwestern grill / Jane Butel with Gordon McMeen.—1st ed.
        p.   cm.
    ISBN 1-55788-242-8
    1. Barbecue cookery. 2. Cookery, American—Southwestern style.
I. McMeen, Gordon. II. Title.
TX840.B3B92   1995
641.5'784—dc20   95-37879
                                                                                        CIP

Printed in the United States of America

10   9   8   7   6   5   4   3   2

I dedicate this book to my parents—Dorothy and Sidney Franz, who always loved grilling and smoking foods and taught me that appreciation. And, to my husband, Gordon, who so patiently helped with the creation, tending and timing of the recipes in this book. Last but not least, to Anna (our German shepherd) and Puddin' (our Yorkshire terrier), who licked every last bone and patiently stood by during all the testing and tasting.

▼▼▼▼▼

Acknowledgments

I wish to thank all those who helped me get this book into print, who, in one way or another, we could call upon while we grilled and smoked to create these delicious recipes.

Marlene Steinberg, who voraciously researched the entire universe for grill manufacturers and accessories so that we could give you a very full review. Jan Smith, who patiently helped research all the recipes, assisted with creating new ideas and did a lot of testing. Also, I wish to thank those who overall assisted whenever called upon . . . Deborah Reid, Sarah Larson and Amy Butel.

And not the least—to my publisher, John Duff, who has always been so enthusiastic and supportive. And to Jeanette Egan, my editor, who always had time to assist with questions as well as ideas. And to my patient agent, Sidney Kramer, who so thoroughly reviewed all the paperwork necessary before we could develop this book.

Contents

▼▼▼▼▼

Introduction   1
    Grilling   3
    Smoking   15
    Rottisserie Cooking   21
Appetizers   23
Soups & Stews   43
Salads from the Grill   61
Grilled Beef & Lamb   79
Grilled Pork   93
Grilled Poultry   103
Grilled Seafood   119
Smoked Meats   131
Smoked Poultry   143
Smoked Seafood   157
Quick Smoking   169
Round 'n' Round She Goes   179
Sauces, Salsas, Marinades, Bastes & Rubs   201
Vegetables & Side Dishes   219
Breads & Spreads   231
Desserts from the Grill   249
Guide to Manufacturers   258
Mail-Order Sources   269
Metric Conversion Charts   270
Index   271

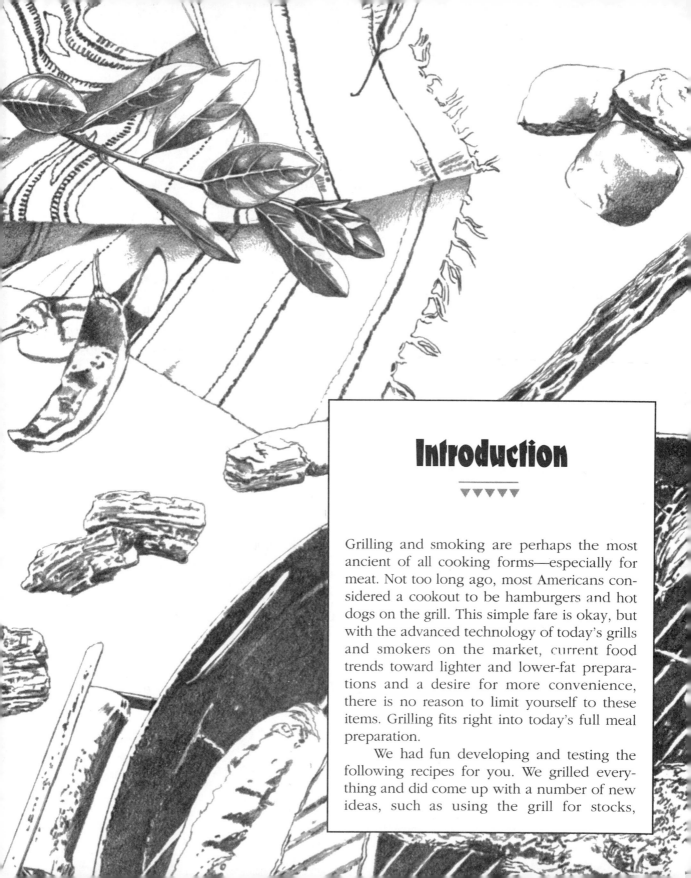

Introduction

▼▼▼▼▼

Grilling and smoking are perhaps the most ancient of all cooking forms—especially for meat. Not too long ago, most Americans considered a cookout to be hamburgers and hot dogs on the grill. This simple fare is okay, but with the advanced technology of today's grills and smokers on the market, current food trends toward lighter and lower-fat preparations and a desire for more convenience, there is no reason to limit yourself to these items. Grilling fits right into today's full meal preparation.

We had fun developing and testing the following recipes for you. We grilled everything and did come up with a number of new ideas, such as using the grill for stocks, grilling tomatoes for preserving in the freezer and creating new flavor combinations for main dishes—all with a Southwestern accent. We grilled all kinds of vegetables and fruits for side dishes, salads and desserts. We even grilled breads and pancakes! One of our goals was to fully use the fuel and time spent in front of the grill. When grilling two small steaks on most grills, there is a load of extra space. Use it! Make stocks; cook appetizers, side dishes and even desserts. It is more fun, too. Everyone can cook together, and no one is a galley slave.

Everyone can enjoy the fun of grilling and smoking. The basic difference between the two is that grilling is much faster, but not necessarily easier. The temperature for grilling is hotter than that for smoking, so the cooking time is much shorter. It is necessary to watch foods that are grilling more closely, because except for larger cuts of meat or whole poultry, most foods cook in a few minutes.

Smoking is slow, low-temperature cooking, which is best for larger pieces of meat such as roasts, brisket, or ham as well as racks of ribs. Don't forget vegetables when smoking. My favorite potatoes are smoked. Other vegetables smoke well, too. When smoking, the fire must be well started to begin with. The wood must be smoking hot along with the main fuel source, whether it be charcoal, electric or gas. The correct temperature must be achieved before the foods are loaded for cooking. Then the fire needs only periodic tending every hour or so but doesn't need continuous watching. You need to ensure that there is still fuel in the firebox and that the meat or vegetables are cooking evenly. Do remember, each time you open the smoker, you add at least 15 minutes to the overall cooking time. With experience, you will learn that you can cook with a minimum of looking.

For this book, barbecuing is defined as grilling and then applying a barbecue type of sauce; grilling is cooking over hot coals on a rack.

Rotisserie cooking, or spit cooking, is another way to cook outdoors. This is an old form of cooking that has been revived with new technology and gadgets that make it easier than ever to cook using this method. Rotisserie cooking is somewhere between grilling and smoking in both time required to cook and temperatures used. Don't just think of large cuts for spit cooking; small items can be cooked on skewers.

As with all cooking, safety is important, but even more so outside. Often the outdoors is where children and pets play, and they need to be kept away from hot cooking equipment. Those who are not familiar with grilling and smoking can burn themselves on the hot surfaces.

For aid in selecting a new grill or smoker, see the listing (pages 258–268) of most of the major manufacturers and the features each offers, complete with the addresses and phone numbers.

GRILLING

Before starting to cook, review the rest of this introductory chapter. You do not need to have expensive or sophisticated equipment to enjoy grilling. Note the different types that follow. There are certain basic tools that do make outdoor cooking much more enjoyable; check that section (page 6).

FUEL SELECTION

There are three basic types of fuels: charcoal, electric and gas—either LP or natural gas. Every grilling cook has a preference, and if you have already decided, go for it. However, if you are just starting or rethinking your current unit, here are the basic benefits and pitfalls of each.

Charcoal We have Henry Ford to thank for the charcoal briquettes we take for granted today. Being an entrepreneur, he did not wish to waste the sawdust and trimmings from the hardwoods left from his famous Model Ts, so he developed a charcoal briquette that is still being made today by many folks.

Charcoal grilling is the most popular: According to a recent study by the Barbecue Industry Association, 58 percent of all grills owned are charcoal. Many swear by the flavors produced. Charcoal grills are probably the least expensive equipment but probably the most expensive fuel. In addition to the hardwood or coal briquettes, dry hardwoods can be used—but never pine or other softwoods. Charcoal-fired grills and smokers need watching to determine if the fire is holding. Also, they do require a bit of know-how to start the fire (see the section on Starting Charcoal Fires, pages 7–8).

Charcoal itself does produce hot fires—up to 2,000F at the tip of the heat. However, the wood smoke has already been burned out when the briquettes are made, so if a smoky taste is desired, wood chips, sawdust or wood chunks need to be used.

There are two basic types of charcoal: hardwood or coal. The hardwood types are generally easier to start, but those containing some coal burn longer and are heavier, meaning you should use fewer briquettes to achieve the same fire. When buying charcoal, always look at the list of ingredients. Does it have sodium nitrates or petroleum products in addition to the charcoal? Personally, I do not like either. I never use any petroleum-based product in the charcoal nor do I use it for starting. Also, examine the charcoal for density; the denser types burn longer and hotter.

Hardwood chunks can be used in a charcoal grill if desired. They generally take much longer than charcoal to get an established bank of coals.

There are a number of woods that are great for grilling. My favorites are fruit woods and hickory. What, not mesquite? To my taste, mesquite is too oily and strong flavored. However, for strong-flavored meats and foods such as steaks or duck, mesquite can be very good. Also, mesquite burns very hot and smokier than other woods and so is excellent for smoking. Alder is popular in the Northwest and has always been a favorite for salmon. Grape cuttings supply a subtle, somewhat sweet flavor that is reminiscent of wine.

A new favorite is to toss on a handful of herbs such as dried bay leaves or the woody stems of thyme, rosemary or sage. Some even use spices such as cinnamon or cloves, soaked in water, to enhance the flavor. These can definitely add to the flavor in smoking—by simply placing them in the water pan.

One of charcoal's pitfalls is cost. Over a year's time, with frequent grilling and smoking, the fuel cost can be sizably more than that incurred with a gas or electric grill.

Another negative is the time required to start the fire. Generally a gas grill or electric grill is ready for cooking in less than 10 minutes, whereas, depending on several factors, charcoal can take up to 30 minutes to get the coals just right. Another is the convenience: You must remember to buy the charcoal and keep a supply for last-minute grilling. Also, storing it is a consideration. You do need a dry, convenient place to store the briquettes, as they are very dirty.

Gas—LP or Natural Gas grills, particularly if they have some form of permanent briquettes, cook with almost the same flavor as charcoal does. They are easy to light and can be used year-round as they are so quick to perform and will supply enough heat to cook even in subzero weather. They preheat to grilling or broiling temperature in less than 10 minutes on average. They also cool down rather quickly and are easily cleaned with a wire brush after use.

The choice between LP or natural gas is often based more on necessity than on actual preference. LP grills are portable. They operate on portable tanks that must be filled when empty at a service station or recreational vehicle center that sells LP or propane gas. A general rule of thumb is that you get an hour of grilling for each gallon the tank holds. Most are 5-gallon tanks, so 5 hours of cooking will be available. The gauge, if available, must be watched to determine when to buy more fuel. For convenience, I've always bought a spare tank and kept it filled so I wouldn't run out in the middle of grilling a meal.

If no natural gas is available for piping to the installation, then LP must be the answer. Generally, for permanent installations natural gas is preferred as it is considered safer and more dependable. You never have to refill a tank, and it is generally less costly and produces consistent heat. You must know which you want when you buy your unit, as the fittings for each are different.

One disadvantage of gas is that the unit must have a supply of gas. You must check on this regularly if using LP gas. Generally, except for small camping models, gas grills also are more expensive than charcoal units.

Electric Electric units generally need 220 volts to reach a hot broiling temperature—the same as that for an electric range. Most that are made to plug into regular household current of 110 volts cannot generate enough heat to reach 550F (275C). These are the tabletop models.

When selecting an electric unit, be sure to get one with pumice-type rocks, a heavy-duty 220-volt heating unit and a lid. Otherwise, you will probably be disappointed in the slow heating and low-temperature cooking.

For a more functional unit, however, you will need to have installed a 220-volt outlet and to buy what is called a pigtail or heavy electrical connecting cord, both of which can be somewhat costly. Some find the cord an inconvenience to wrap up when not in use. The portable 110-volt electric units are not high performing.

WHICH TYPE OF GRILL TO CHOOSE?

If you are inexperienced with grilling and are in the market for a grill, start with a simple model that can easily be exchanged for a more capable, full-featured model after you learn what your preferences are. The former model can always be retired as a grill for camping or as an auxiliary unit for big parties or relegated to a garage sale. But try a simple model before really investing. Nothing is more disappointing than to spend quite a bit of money only to discover that you do not like the features on your grill and want another.

I do recommend a grill with a lid for more functional usage. By supplying slow, circulating heat, this grill is good for cooking tough cuts of meat as well as for baking and for imparting smoky flavors to foods. Some even have a feature to allow for smoking when grilling. The grill can also be used without the lid. Following is a review of the general features of the most popular types.

CHARCOAL GRILLS

Brazier Grills These are the simplest type of grill and range in size from a portable tabletop unit to a half barrel or a huge 5-foot or longer grill for mega cookouts and catering. Some have lids, spits and even wheels. Larger versions have cranks to adjust the height of the grill rack and also the cooking temperature.

Hibachis Generally small, they are quite efficient for appetizers and small meals. Usually with adjustable racks, air dampers and no lids, they have open racks for the charcoal so that the ashes can fall through. They are designed for fuel efficiency.

Covered Kettle or Wagon Grills These have lids and offer a range of sizes and features. Air dampers in the lid and under the charcoal rack allow for the adjustment of the flow of air that controls the cooking temperature. The more open, the hotter and more brazierlike the grill is. They may be used uncovered for quick-cooking foods such as hamburgers. Covering the grill also helps prevent flare-ups and makes the grill more ovenlike for larger cuts of meat.

GAS OR ELECTRIC GRILLS

Either of these offers the convenience of not having to start a fire, and either is much faster to preheat and easier to clean after use than a charcoal model. Ceramic briquettes are desirable for adding a smoky flavor to grilled foods. If not available, wood chips can be used. The engineering and technological advances in today's grill manufacturing have made these much more high performing and useful than they formerly were. If interested, see a demonstration of one at your local dealer's or cooking school, if possible.

EQUIPMENT FOR GRILLING & SMOKING

Long, Heavy, Heat-Resistant Gloves Select gloves that are at least long enough to go halfway to your elbows and that are treated to not catch fire.

Fire-Control Material Keep handy a mister, heavy foil and a lid for the grill, if available.

Long-Handled Tools Select tools with wood or insulated handles. Test for durability. They should not be flexible, because if they bend, they will not be strong enough to turn, lift or handle large roasts.

Sharp Knives Keep knives sharp and available for cutting, trimming, checking doneness, etc.

Wooden Cutting Boards Wooden boards will not melt when they get too close to the side of the grill as the plastic or nylon ones will.

Stiff Metal Cleaning Brush This brush is the best for brushing the rack to remove cooking residue.

Heavy Skewers Select skewers that will not buckle when loaded. Also, look for ones with small pointed ends so that the food will not be broken when skewered. These are handy for small foods, because they make turning easier and prevent some items from falling through the grill.

Specialty Holders Fish, ribs, skewered foods, roasts and vegetable holders and racks are available and are handy for maximizing the space on the surface of the grill. Remember, however, that they can present a storage problem.

Starting Charcoal Fires

There are a number of ways to start a fire. In general, place the briquettes in a pyramid and open the vents if you have a covered grill. Do use caution. Do not use a combustible liquid such as gasoline or alcohol, which can flare up too much and start a fire that you never intended. Frankly, I do not like any combustible petroleum-based fuel. I do not like my potential meal sitting over the fumes.

Chimney starters You can buy a chimney starter where grills are sold or you can make your own. Once you purchase or make one, you do not have any further expense, because they last for several years. You use newspaper as a starter. They are fast, efficient and work to contain the charcoal briquettes with adequate ventilation to fuel the fire. Also, there is no worry about burning off the starter odor. To use, place newspaper below the grate and briquettes above. One match is sufficient to light the newspaper, and the briquettes will quickly catch in minutes. For a large fire, generally two batches need to be lighted to get the fire off to a good start.

To make a chimney starter, a large can, such as a 3-pound coffee can with both ends opened, is needed and a grate or something similar must be soldered or welded about an inch up from the bottom to hold the newspapers for igniting the briquettes above. Use a beverage opener to make a row of holes about an inch above the grate.

Liquid fire starters Stores that sell briquettes will also carry liquid fire starters. This is my least favorite way to start a fire, and they must never be used on a smoldering fire to make it catch. If you choose this method, be careful to not use any more than just enough to start the fire, letting it soak in for a few minutes before lighting. The grill should be no closer to the house or the overhang of the roof than 4 feet. Always wait for at least 15 minutes or longer for the fuel to be all burned out so that the residue of the petroleum products does not flavor the foods you will be cooking.

Electric fire starters This type of starter is easy to use. You just lay it on the grill and place charcoal over it, leaving it there until the briquettes have caught fire. The only drawback is that often, especially for a bigger fire, some of the briquettes will not catch.

Starter blocks Made from paraffin and sawdust, starter blocks are another alternative. They are odor free and efficient.

Starter bags Expensive but convenient, starter bags do, however, smell heavily of petroleum products. You light the entire bag and disperse the charcoal once it adequately catches fire. They are great for camping and cookouts.

To achieve a good charcoal fire with white coals, allow 30 minutes to be certain it will be hot enough when you want it. A frequent problem of those inexperienced with grilling or smoking is that they frequently waste briquettes. Consult your user's manual for the manufacturer's recommendation of the quantity to ignite for various uses.

In general, the larger the amount of briquettes and the deeper they are stacked the hotter and longer the fire will be. The circle of briquettes does not need to be larger than the surface area of the foods that are being cooked.

RULES OF THUMB

- 15 to 25 briquettes—take an average of 15 minutes after igniting to reach 350F (160C) and will reach 420F (215C) after about 30 minutes.

- 50 briquettes—take an average of 20 minutes after igniting to reach 600F (300C) in the center of the grill. Toward the outside, the temperature is 450F (225C). This amount of charcoal will remain in the searing range for 1 hour.

- 70 briquettes—take an average of 20 minutes after igniting to reach 600F (300C) and will maintain this temperature 1 to 1-1/2 hours. The temperature around the outside of the briquettes in the grill will range just under 100F (40C).

If the grill does not have a thermometer (both an oven and an internal roasting thermometer are good to have), you can use the following hand tests to determine heat levels. All are for how long you can hold your palm steady over the coals.

- 3 seconds—for beef and lamb
- 4 seconds—for poultry and fish
- 5 seconds—for pork

WIND FACTOR

Wind can make a grill or smoker up to 100F (40C) cooler on the windy side. When the weather is very windy, select a secure outdoor spot where you can space the grill a safe distance from the side of the house and the roof overhang, generally 4 to 6 feet.

SAFETY TIPS

Warn all guests to keep their distance from the grill to avoid the intense heat and potential for burns. Be sure to keep children and animals away from the cooking area.

Keep fire-control material on hand. A water mister and heavy-duty foil are both excellent for controlling flare-ups. It's a good idea to keep the lid handy even if not covering the food while cooking. Some cooks even like to keep a water hose nearby. For grease or fat fires, a small fire extinguisher or bucket of sand is effective. Prevention and caution are best.

When using gas, be sure the gas has been adequately installed and properly connected. Understand the procedure by reading the manufacturer's instructions about how to turn the gas on to grill and off when not grilling. Keeping a spray bottle of soapy water near the gas-supply valve will allow you to spray soapy water onto the connection and watch while turning on the grill to be sure there are no leaks.

For electric grills, be sure there is no water on or near the plug or socket.

GENERAL COOKING TIPS

Every time you open the lid, you lose about 35 to 50 degrees per minute the lid is off. The recovery time can be up to 20 minutes to regain the heat. So be prepared to baste quickly when the lid is off and to allow adequate cooking time for foods, such as barbecued ribs, that are basted frequently.

The best woods for smoking and grilling for an aromatic flavor are hardwoods, namely hickory, fruit woods or mesquite. Grape cuttings are popular with some. Chips last longer than sawdust, and chunks last longest of all but take the longest to ignite.

DIRECT AND INDIRECT GRILLING

Direct grilling For this method the fire is placed directly below the grill rack. It is the method most often used for hamburgers, steaks, chops and most grilled foods.

Indirect grilling For this method a foil pan (disposable type for easy cleanup) is placed in the center of the firepit of the grill and the fire built on either side of the pan. This way the drips will catch in the pan, thereby preventing flare-ups. Indirect heat is slower than direct, allowing the heat to penetrate deeper, which is best for large roasts, turkeys and the like.

CONTROLLING TEMPERATURE

When grilling, use the following methods to control the temperature:

- Change the distance of the heat from the food by adjusting the rack: The closer the rack is to the heat, the hotter and faster the cooking will be.

- Adjust the amount of heat directly below the food being cooked. Rake a portion of the coals to the side if too hot.

- Cover bony portions, such as wing tips or tips on a roast, with heavy foil after they are done to prevent further cooking.
- Spray a little water on the coals to slow the heat down for a while.

GENERAL GRILL-RACK HEIGHTS FOR CHARCOAL GRILLING

Beef and lamb: Set the rack 3 inches above the coals.
Poultry and pork: Set the rack 4 inches above the coals.
Large roasts or turkeys: Set the rack 5 inches above the coals.

DONENESS

Doneness is most accurately determined by a meat-roasting thermometer. Consult the charts on pages 11 to 15 for information.

If camping or without a thermometer, then the hand test is worthy of note. For any chops or steaks, pressing the meat with one's finger to determine doneness is called the *hand test.* If the meat moves easily and feels similar to the muscled portion of the palm leading to the thumb, then it is rare. If the meat is somewhat firm, similar to the palm closer to the wrist, it is medium. If the meat feels firm and is similar to the bony portion of the wrist where the muscle portion attaches to the wrist, it is well done.

Beef, lamb, and some fish steaks can be cooked rare. Pork used to be cooked very well done, to an internal temperature of 170F (75C). Now food-safety experts have learned that without the fear of trichinosis, pork can be cooked to 160F (60C), which results in much juicier meat.

DONENESS TEMPERATURES FOR BEEF

Meat thermometer will register 140F (55C) for rare.
Meat thermometer will register 150F (65C) for medium rare.
Meat thermometer will register 160F (70C) for medium.
Meat thermometer will register 170F (75C) for well done.
Meat thermometer will register 160F (70C) for hamburgers.

NOTE: These temperatures were supplied by the National Livestock and Meat Board Test Kitchens, 1993.

Doneness Guide for Grilling Beef

Cut	Heat	Time
Steaks (1 inch thick)	Direct	10 to 12 minutes for rare 16 to 18 minutes for well done
Roasts (4-1/2 to 6 lbs.), tender cuts such as sirloin, rib eye tenderloin, eye of round	Indirect	1-1/4 to 2 hours or more for rare
Brisket (5 to 6 lbs.)	Indirect	2-1/2 to 3 hours

NOTES: On all the doneness times, use a meat thermometer or cut with a knife into the thickest, leanest portion to check for doneness. The times are total grilling times; turn at half the time. All meat should be thawed and at room or refrigerator temperature. (If at refrigerator temperature, allow more time for cooking.)

Doneness Guide for Grilling Pork

Cut	Heat	Time
Chops or steaks (1/2 inch thick)	Direct	10 to 12 minutes for medium 12 to 14 minutes for well done
Chops or steaks (1 to 1-1/2 inches thick)	Direct	16 to 20 minutes for medium 25 to 35 minutes for well done
Roasts, loin, sirloin, picnic	Indirect	30 to 35 minutes per lb. for medium 40 to 45 minutes per lb. for well done
Tenderloin (1/2 to 1 lb.)	Indirect	20 to 25 minutes for medium (well done too dry)
Spareribs (2-1/2 to 3 lbs.)	Indirect	1 to 1-1/4 hours for medium (well done too dry)
Country-style ribs (over 3 to 4 lbs.)	Indirect	1 to 1-1/2 hours for medium 1-1/2 to 1-3/4 hours for well done

NOTES: Pork should always have lost its pink color when done. It must be cooked at least medium or 160F (70C).

On all the doneness times, use a meat thermometer or cut with a knife into the thickest, leanest portion to check for doneness. The times are total grilling times; turn at half the time. All meat should be thawed and at room or refrigerator temperature. (If at refrigerator temperature, allow more time for cooking.)

Doneness Guide for Grilling Lamb

Cut	Heat	Time
Chops, loin or rib (3/4 inch thick)	Direct	7 to 9 minutes for rare, 140F (60C) 10 to 12 minutes for medium, 160F (70C) 13 to 16 minutes for well done, 170F (75C)
Chops (1-1/4 inches thick or more)	Direct	Add 2 to 3 minutes to above times
Leg, bone-in (5 to 6 lbs.)	Indirect	20 minutes per lb. for rare, 140F (60C) 25 to 30 minutes for medium, 160F (70C) 35 minutes for well done, 170F (75C)
Leg, butterflied	Direct	12 to 14 minutes per lb. for rare, 140F (60C) 15 to 18 minutes per lb. for medium, 160F (70C) 20 to 25 minutes per lb. for well done, 170F (75C)
Leg, butterflied, rolled	Indirect	Add 1/2 to 3/4 hour more cooking time to above times

NOTES: On all the doneness times, use a meat thermometer or cut with a knife into the thickest, leanest portion to check for doneness. The times are total grilling times; turn at half the time. All meat should be thawed and at room or refrigerator temperature. (If at refrigerator temperature, allow more time for cooking.)

Doneness Guide for Grilling Veal

Cut	Heat	Time
Chops, rib or loin (3/4 inch thick)	Direct	8 to 10 minutes for rare, 140F (60C) 9 to 11 minutes for medium, 160F (70C) 11 to 13 minutes for well done, 170F (75C)
Chops (1 inch thick)	Direct	Add 1 to 2 minutes to above times
Chops (1-1/2 inches thick)	Direct	Add 2 to 4 minutes to above times
Leg, bone-in (7 to 8 lbs.)	Indirect	15 to 20 minutes per lb. for medium, 160F (70C) 22 to 25 minutes per lb. for well done, 170F (75C)
Leg, boned and tied (3 to 4 lbs.)	Indirect	28 to 30 minutes for medium, 160F (70C) 32 to 35 minutes for well done, 170F (75C)

NOTES: On all the doneness times, use a meat thermometer or cut with a knife into the thickest, leanest portion to check for doneness. The times are total grilling times; turn at half the time. All meat should be thawed and at room or refrigerator temperature. (If at refrigerator temperature, allow more time for cooking.)

Doneness Guide for Grilling Poultry

Cut	Heat	Time
Chicken		
Breast halves, bone-in	Direct	15 to 20 minutes or until no longer pink, 185F (85C)
Breast halves, boned and skinned	Direct	10 to 12 minutes
Thighs or drumsticks	Direct	35 minutes or until no longer pink, 185F (85C)
Halved or quartered	Direct	40 to 50 minutes or until no longer pink, 185F (85C)
Whole chicken (3 to 4 lbs.)	Indirect	1 hour to 1 hour 20 minutes, or until joints move easily and meat is no longer pink, 185F (85C)
Turkey		
Breast halves, bone-in	Indirect	1 to 1-1/2 hours, or until no longer pink, 185F (85C)
Turkey steaks (3/4 inch thick)	Direct	7 to 9 minutes or until no longer pink, 185F (85C)
Whole turkey (8 to 14 lbs.)	Indirect	15 minutes per lb. or until no longer pink and joints move easily, 185F (85C)
Whole turkey (15 to 20 lbs.)	Indirect	12 minutes per lb.
Duck		
Cut up	Direct	40 minutes or until joints move or desired doneness is reached Medium rare, 150F (65C) Well done, 185F (85C)
Whole, with skin pricked	Indirect	2 hours for medium, 160F (70C) 2-1/2 hours for well done, 185F (85C)

NOTES: On all the doneness times, use a meat thermometer or cut with a knife into the thickest, leanest portion to check for doneness. The times are total grilling times; turn at half the time. All poultry should be thawed and at room or refrigerator temperature. (If at refrigerator temperature, allow more time for cooking.)

DONENESS GUIDE FOR GRILLING FISH AND SEAFOOD

Cut	Heat	Time
Fish steaks and fillets	Direct	4 to 6 minutes or until fish flakes
Whole fish (up to 1 lb.)	Indirect	12 minutes or until fish flakes
Whole fish (1 to 5 lbs.)	Indirect	25 to 35 minutes or until fish flakes
Scallops, medium to large	Direct	5 to 7 minutes or until opaque
Shrimp	Direct	3 to 5 minutes or until they turn pink
Lobster tails	Direct	5 to 7 minutes or until flesh is opaque
Whole lobster, thorax butterflied	Direct	10 minutes or longer, depending on size

NOTES: On all the doneness times, use a meat thermometer or cut with a knife into the thickest, leanest portion to check for doneness. The times are total grilling times; turn at half the time. All seafood should be thawed and at room or refrigerator temperature. (If at refrigerator temperature, allow more time for cooking.)

SMOKING

Smoking spells summertime, the lazy joys of personal pleasures and relaxation, when everything is a bit easier, fresher with just-picked flavor, and offers a time for each of us to sit back and create more happy memories.

Let's start with just what smoking really is. Smoking as we've defined it here is slow cooking over a hardwood fire, generating smoke that slowly cooks food. Many, particularly in the South, call this process "barbecuing." Just to be clear, we've consistently called it "smoking."

Smoking is a very old form of both roasting and preserving. In former times, smoking kept meats or fish edible for a longer time with better flavor than most of the alternative cooking methods. With all the new, relatively inexpensive smokers on the market, the joys of smoking are being rediscovered.

Added to the benefits of the smoke flavor are the convenience of little tending and low- or no-fat cooking. You do not need to add any fat to the meats or vegetables when you smoke them. Actually, a great deal of residual fat is rendered out. You might want to add seasonings, herbs, rubs and the like.

In addition to imparting a wonderful smoky taste, smoking produces juicy, low-fat and unbelievably tender foods if they are cooked slowly enough. There are two basic types of smoking—wet and dry. Wet is the standard method, in which water is added to the water pan to keep the foods moist while smoking. For dry smoking no water is added and wood chips are placed in the water container, creating dark, outer browning and a juicy center. Dry smoking is necessary for thin cuts or small pieces of meats or fish. It is usually reserved for moist, tender, smaller cuts that are generally grilled.

A chapter on quick smoking is included for those who want a smoky flavor but don't have the time for traditional smoking.

EQUIPMENT

The type of smoker you have will dictate the way you smoke. A very popular unit, made by several manufacturers, is a simple, inexpensive one with a firebox at the bottom, a window for tending the fire, a pan for water, two or more racks and a vented cover. It does work well. The larger the firebox window, the easier, more convenient and faster you can smoke.

This type of smoker uses hardwoods for smoking and requires time for getting the fire well started before smoking. (See below for more fuel information.)

Electric or gas smokers are much quicker and easier to start up, and gain their smokiness from soaked or green wood chips. It is a personal judgment whether the reduced smokiness from gas and electric smokers is a worthwhile tradeoff for the time, effort and cost of building hardwood fires.

You can smoke in many of the larger gas or electrically fired grills, but the results are not nearly as smoky and juicy as when they are slow smoked in a real smoker.

WHICH TYPE SMOKER TO CHOOSE?

Some home smokers like to purchase commercial smokers because they can smoke a large quantity of food at a time and are usually much quicker due to the fact they smoke under pressure. Also, smokers are relatively easy to build if you have some tools and access to a cutting torch for making a fire-tending window.

CHARCOAL SMOKERS

These are the simplest. Look for models with easy access to the firebox where the briquettes will be placed as they have to be frequently resupplied and will cause difficulties if there is very limited access. A heavy porcelain exterior coating is best. Look for multiple shelves and a water pan.

Kamados These Japanese clay smokers do an excellent job of smoking, but they are heavy and cumbersome, making them difficult to clean. Also, the one we had developed a crack when we moved. They are difficult to move due to their weight. However, they do cook well, providing a slow, smoky environment perfect for smoking meats and other foods.

GAS OR ELECTRIC SMOKERS

Similar benefits apply to gas and electric smokers as to gas and electric grills. They are much more convenient than charcoal because they don't have to be continuously refueled every hour or so. However, electric smokers don't have some of the disadvantages of electric grills, in that the electric smokers can maintain the desired lower temperatures and work well on 110 volts or standard household current.

Gas smokers tend to heat faster and hotter than the electric ones. However, they do need to be hooked up to a gas supply, either LP or natural gas.

SMOKING TECHNIQUES

Basically, smoking takes much more time than grilling, but it is not concentrated time. The only task requiring real concentration is that of properly building the fire if you are using a charcoal or wood fire. You must get the fire off to a good start, or you will never quite catch up and the dinner will be a disaster—it won't get done when you want it and will not have reaped the benefits of smoking.

With an electric or gas unit, you will not have this problem. For those who believe that hardwood smoking is the only way, excellent results can be obtained every time by building the fire so that it starts every time without using a petroleum or chemical based fire starter.

The two best methods we have found for starting fires are to use either a metal charcoal starter called a chimney starter (see Starting Charcoal Fires, page 7), which is a container that uses a bit of newspaper and holds the charcoal nested above for easy lighting, or an electric fire starter, which lies under a bed of hardwood or charcoal until it ignites. Either starts the fire rapidly and totally eliminates the petroleum odor and the danger of flare-ups. Always allow at least 30 minutes to start the fire. All the times in the smoking recipes allow for this as well as for additional time to accommodate the normal time variations in getting the food done.

The average charcoal briquette fire lasts 4 hours if densely built in at least a double layer. A fire built from hardwood chunks can last longer, depending on circumstances, even up to 7 or 8 hours.

There is a large variety in the quality and type of charcoal and/or hardwood available. Usually the supermarket variety of charcoal has a large percentage of coal rather than the charred remains of hardwoods. Coal burns more slowly and is usually harder to ignite. Check the contents label of the next charcoal briquettes you buy to be sure the briquettes are made of 100 percent hardwood charcoal. Also, hardwood chunks are available from various specialty stores, from mail-order catalogues and perhaps from your local nurseryman or landscape maintenance operator.

It is important that once the charcoal begins to ignite and really catches fire, you fill the water pan with hot water. Next, for maximum smoke, you must use soaked dried hardwood chips or green chunks of hardwood.

Be methodical when you place the foods in the smoker. Always place the largest, densest food, such as a roast, with the fat side up and centered over the hottest part of the fire.

Peek rarely! Each look slows down the heat and adds at least 15 minutes to the cooking time. This is why creating a very hot, smoky fire at the beginning of smoking is very important.

Vegetables and smaller cuts of meat or seafood should be placed on the second or third shelf and positioned so that they can catch a good circulation of smoke. Smaller cuts, fish and vegetables can also be smoked in your oven (see Quick Smoking, pages 169–178).

As you can see, for most of the time, you can sit and rock or swing and sip a favorite beverage while your next meal smokes away. Leftover smoked foods freeze well when properly packaged in airtight, vaporproof packaging.

WEATHER

When it is cold, windy or rainy, select a place for smoking that is the most protected your home can supply. Place the starting fire at least 4 feet from the closest portion of any structure, including the eaves' overhang.

Look for a location out of the strong wind; an ell of the house would be a good site. The wind can make it very difficult to maintain the proper low temperature for smoking. When it is cold or windy the cooking times will be longer. As a rule of thumb, add an hour to times less than 4 hours and 2 hours to longer cooking times.

SMOKING TIPS

- Always read your manufacturer's instructions.

- Allow enough time to start an adequate fire in the smoker, whatever the fuel.

- Have on hand a meat thermometer to check the temperature accurately to ensure proper doneness.

- Keep a pair of comfortable, heat-protected mitts on hand for use when smoking.

- For larger meat cuts and more perishable foods, be sure to do the following: Start a substantial, large fire and marinate the meat, poultry or seafood in either a pickling or brining solution to retard possible development of bacteria during smoking.

A basic brine can be made by combining the following in a nonreactive container: 2 quarts water, 1 cup salt, 1 cup sugar, 2 cloves garlic and a generous pinch of black peppercorns or 1 small whole red chile. Stir to dissolve well, then soak in brine as follows: game birds or poultry under 1 pound, soak 1 hour at room temperature; larger cuts of meat, such as a whole chicken or turkey breast up to 3-1/2 pounds, 2 hours at room temperature; and a 3- to 10-pound roast needs to soak in the brine at least 8 hours in the refrigerator, covered and turned occasionally.

When the meat has been brined, lightly rinse with plain water, rub dry and immediately smoke. Or refrigerate, loosely covered, to keep surface dry.

- Always place the skin or fattier side up to ensure a moist product and to allow the smoke to penetrate the fleshiest portion first. Large portions of meats or fish should be placed on the first rack directly above the water and firebox; smaller seafood, such as shrimp or scallops, and vegetables that cook more quickly should always be placed on the second rack.

- Always dry the foods that you are smoking as much as possible. Patting the exterior with a dry cloth or paper towel is a good idea. Drier foods collect the smoke and acquire a more desirable color.

- If you want a soft rather than chewy skin, lightly oil the skin or outside surface, especially that of big birds, such as turkeys, and meats with no outer fat.

- Keep the vents open when starting the fire or encouraging the fire to burn faster. When smoking, only crack the vents. Always use heavy gloves for protection against the heat when adjusting the vents.

- Do not peek except once every hour or so. You can tell if the smoker is working if you see a small stream of smoke coming from the vent and if the exterior of the smoker is very hot.

- Keep the cover on whenever smoking.

- The water pan will be easier to clean if it is covered with foil before the water is added. For variety, aromatic herbs, spices, beer or wine can be placed in the water pan along with the water. Check the water pan and keep it full. Always refill with hot water.

- If using hardwood briquettes or charcoal, keep them dry before igniting, so they will burn easier.

- If for some reason the fire in a charcoal-fired smoker starts to wane, fix it immediately. Try removing the door from the front, which should help the fire to burn faster. If the level of burning briquettes is low, ignite at least 12 to 20 briquettes until covered with white ash and place atop the briquettes in the firebox.

- You can substitute a similar meat, poultry or seafood item for the ones called for. If the cut is larger, add proportionately more time; if smaller, allow less time.

SUGGESTED SMOKING TIMES*

Beef

3- to 4-lb. roasts or brisket	4 to 5 hours for rare
	4 to 6 hours for medium
	6 to 8 hours for well done
Ribs, full side	3 to 4 hours for well done

Pork

3- to 4-lb. roast	5 to 6 hours
Thick chops (1-1/2 to 2 inches thick)	2 to 3 hours
Ribs	4 to 6 hours
Fresh whole ham	8 to 12 hours
Cooked ham	3 to 4 hours

Lamb

5- to 7-lb. leg of lamb	5 to 6 hours

Large Game

7- to 9-lb. roasts	6 to 8 hours

Poultry (unstuffed)

Quartered/halved chicken	3 to 4 hours
3- to 4-lb. whole chicken	4 to 5 hours
5 to 7-lb. capon/roaster	5 to 6 hours
8 to 12-lb. turkey	7 to 8 hours

13- to 20-lb. turkey	8 to 10 hours
3- to 5-lb. duck	4 to 6 hours
8- to 10-lb. goose	7 to 8 hours
3- to 5-lb. pheasant	4 to 6 hours
Under 2-lb. game birds	2 to 4 hours
Fish and Seafood	
Fish fillets	1-1/2 to 3 hours
1- to 2-lb. whole fish	1-1/2 to 3 hours
3- to 6-lb. whole fish	3 to 4 hours
Shellfish, shrimp or lobster	2 to 4 hours

*All the suggested cooking times include extra time for starting a charcoal fire along with the wood chunks for smoking. You can shorten the time by up to 30 minutes if you have a fast-heating electric or gas smoker.

ROTISSERIE COOKING

Rotisserie cooking, or cooking on a spit, is probably the most romantic and historic of all methods of cooking meats and the most favored. The challenge is to get good heat circulation so that the temperature is easily controlled; with this control comes succulence. The crispy skin surrounds a juicy, flavorful roast in which the juices have circulated throughout, rather than dripped out, yielding a moist product. It is low fat too, fitting right in with today's food preferences.

Rotisserie cooking was by far the most preferred method of roasting meats of Escoffier, the renowned chef extraordinaire and the author of the world's culinary bible, *The Escoffier Cookbook*. In his 1941 edition, published by Crown Publishers, he stated, "Of the two [oven or spit] usual methods of roasting, the spit will always be used in preference to the oven, if only on account of the conditions under which the cooking is done, and whatever be the kind of fuel used—wood, coal, gas or electricity.

"The reason of this preference is clear if it be remembered that, in spite of every possible precaution during the progress of an oven roast, it is impossible to avoid an accumulation of vapor around the cooking object in a closed oven. And this steam is more particularly objectionable inasmuch as it is excessive in the case of delicately flavored meats, which are almost, if not entirely, impaired thereby.

"The spitted roast, on the contrary, cooks in the open in a dry atmosphere, and this means it retains its own peculiar flavor. Hence the unquestionable superiority of spitted roasts over the oven kind, especially in respect of small game birds."

The reference to small game birds reminds me of Cornish game hens, which are definitely much more delicate and flavorful when spit roasted.

Many of the grilling recipes featured in the grilling sections can be done easily on the rotisserie. A recipe that immediately comes to mind is the butterflied lamb in the Grilled Leg of Lamb à la Grecque (page 86).

There are some very good rules of thumb to keep in mind. First, balance the meat as evenly as possible on the spit itself, so it will cook evenly. If the roast has been boned securely tie the roast all around. To promote the most even roasting, boning is always a good idea but not critical; you can, for example, thread a leg of lamb on the spit with the bone in. Just thread the spit as directly as possible through the leg from one end to the other, twirling the spit as you go to double-check the balance. Always do that to make sure the meat is as balanced as possible.

Once you are satisfied that you have the meat well balanced, push in the adjustable forks very securely at right angles to each other. In other words, first secure the set of forks that fit on the rotisserie rod on the left side. Then position the forks on the right at right angles to those on the left, press them in as securely as possible, and tighten.

There are a number of grilling accessories especially designed for rotisseries to aid in balancing, holding kabobs, cooking small items and the like. For legs of lamb, fresh ham and legs of most anything, a counterbalance accessory is a very good idea.

When building a fire for rotisserie roasting, build it toward the back. Create a fire bed about 2 inches out from the back of the firebox, extending it in a band that is about 6 inches wide and runs the entire length of the spit and beyond for about 4 inches on each end. Place a drip pan adjacent to the coals and extending the length of the roast. When using charcoal, replenish the briquettes continuously, six to ten every 30 minutes.

In well-designed outdoor gas grills, the fire bed is parallel to the meat on the rotisserie rod, not directly beneath it. Often this is an add-on feature. For more complete feature information on the rotisseries available, see the section listing manufacturers and features (pages 258 to 268).

Many of the manufacturers of the vertical burners behind the rotisseries recommend that a pan be placed to catch the drippings and that aromatics be placed under the roasting meat. As the drippings hit the aromatics, the aroma is increased. Examples of aromatics are garlic cloves, herbs, spices, wines, etc.

For heat control and estimating doneness, here are some general pointers: If the meat is less than 4 inches in diameter, use a high heat. If the roast is larger than 4 inches, use a medium heat. The diameter of the meat, not the weight, determines the rate of roasting and doneness. Always be sure that the rotating food clears the source of heat by at least 1 to 4 inches or as the manufacturer suggests. Ideally, the fire grate should be about 4 to 6 inches from the surface of the meat.

Watch the meat as it cooks to be sure it is roasting properly. If it is browning too fast, reduce the heat; if it is not browning well at all, increase it. Covering the barbecue will allow the heat to flow around the roasting meat and will promote more even cooking. A general rule of thumb is that roasting on the rotisserie takes about the same length of time as roasting in the oven.

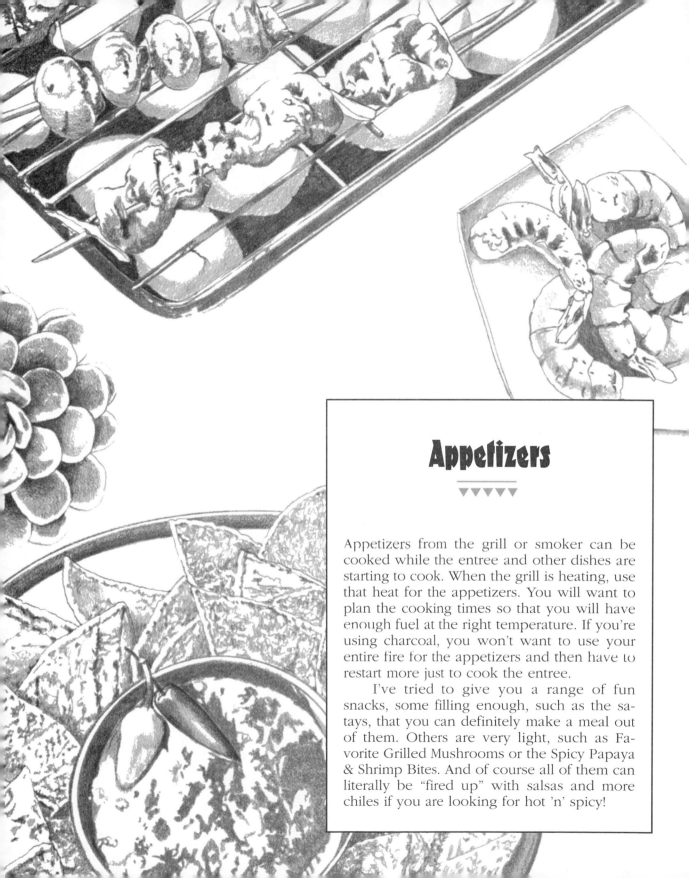

Appetizers

▼▼▼▼▼

Appetizers from the grill or smoker can be cooked while the entree and other dishes are starting to cook. When the grill is heating, use that heat for the appetizers. You will want to plan the cooking times so that you will have enough fuel at the right temperature. If you're using charcoal, you won't want to use your entire fire for the appetizers and then have to restart more just to cook the entree.

I've tried to give you a range of fun snacks, some filling enough, such as the satays, that you can definitely make a meal out of them. Others are very light, such as Favorite Grilled Mushrooms or the Spicy Papaya & Shrimp Bites. And of course all of them can literally be "fired up" with salsas and more chiles if you are looking for hot 'n' spicy!

Come Along Little Doggies

▼▼▼▼▼

These mini-franks take on a Southwestern touch when served with your choice of salsa. We like most any spicy salsa, in particular the Black Bean & Corn Salsa (page 206). These are quick to make while the grill is heating for the entree.

1 (12-oz.) can beer
1 (about 10-oz.) package baby franks
1 to 2 packages mini-size flour tortillas (if unavailable, get the smallest size and halve,
    allowing 1 tortilla or tortilla piece per frank)
1 to 2 recipes salsa (pages 202 to 209)
Guacamole (see below)
1/2 cup shredded Cheddar or Cheddar and Monterey Jack cheese, mixed (optional)

Guacamole

2 avocados
1/2 teaspoon salt
1 clove garlic, minced
1 teaspoon freshly squeezed lime juice
1/4 cup chopped tomato
1/4 cup finely chopped Spanish onion
1 medium jalapeño chile, minced
1/4 cup coarsely chopped cilantro (optional)

Preheat grill to medium or 350F (175C) if not already hot. Place a shallow baking pan on the rack. Add beer and bring to a simmer. Add franks and rotate in beer to cook evenly. Simmer until heated through, about 10 minutes. When almost done, heat the tortillas on the grill and then keep warm in a tortilla holder or napkin-lined basket. Wrap each "doggie" in a tortilla and top with some salsa and Guacamole. Add a sprinkle of cheese, if desired. *Makes 8 to 12 servings.*

Guacamole

Cut avocados in half and remove seeds. Scoop out flesh and cut into small squares. Toss avocados with remaining ingredients in a medium bowl.

SMOKED CHICKEN ROLL-UPS WITH CABERNET CREAM

▼▼▼▼▼

This is one of my personal favorites! You can serve the Cabernet cream as a dipping sauce or use it under meats such as grilled steak (see Variation).

3 to 4 dried chipotle chiles (see Note)
1 teaspoon cider vinegar
1 cup water
2 cups shredded smoked chicken, about 4 legs and thighs or 2 breasts (see page 172)
3/4 cup regular or light sour cream
1-1/2 teaspoons freshly squeezed lime juice
1 tablespoon Cabernet wine
Salt and freshly ground black pepper
4 to 6 thin (10- to 12-inch) flour tortillas
1 teaspoon crushed caribe chile
Few leaves mesclun or leaf lettuce

If a microwave oven is available, combine chipotle chiles, vinegar and water in a glass bowl. Cover and simmer on HIGH power 5 minutes. Or, combine chipotle chiles, vinegar and water in a small saucepan and simmer 30 minutes or until flesh and skin are soft. Set aside.

Meanwhile, mix chicken, sour cream, lime juice and wine in a medium bowl. Mince chipotle chiles and stir into chicken mixture. Taste and adjust seasonings if needed.

Lightly heat a tortilla over a surface unit, grill or steamer or in the microwave oven in a plastic bag until steamed and softened. Then, spread with some of the chicken mixture and sprinkle with some of the caribe chile. Roll and cover with a clean cloth or waxed paper. Repeat with remaining tortillas and chicken mixture. Store in refrigerator overnight or up to 2 days before serving. (These are difficult to cut right after making and need to set before slicing.)

To serve, cut crosswise into 1/2-inch slices and garnish with mesclun. *Makes 6 to 8 servings.*

VARIATION

To make just the sauce, omit chicken and combine sour cream, lime juice and wine with minced chipotle chiles. If serving in a bowl, use only a pinch of crushed caribe chile as a garnish.

NOTE: Chipotle chiles are dried ripe jalapeño chiles that have been smoked; they are available from Mexican specialty stores and by mail order.

SMOKED CHILE-SPARKED GAME JERKY

▼▼▼▼▼

Game is often strong flavored and generally dry. To make flavorful jerky, marinate the strips of game before smoking in chile honey, which is wonderful both for taming the gaminess and for holding in a bit of sweet moisture. This truly makes a big difference.

2 tablespoons crushed caribe chile or to taste
3 pounds antelope or venison steaks
1 cup honey, slightly warmed (see Note)

To make hot honey, simmer caribe in water to cover in a small heavy saucepan 20 to 30 minutes or until chile pulp will slide off peel.

Meanwhile, cut meat into thin slices across the grain for greater tenderness. Trim off any sinew or fat and discard. Place meat in a large glass bowl and set aside.

Strain chile liquid into a bowl large enough to hold meat and mix in honey. Add meat strips and stir well. Cover and refrigerate overnight.

Make a good bed of coals in the smoker to produce a low-temperature heat. (Or turn on the electric or gas smoker to a low-smoking setting.) Spread meat strips over the top shelf of the cooker, allowing some room between strips. Cover smoker and smoke with a low fire 6 to 8 hours or until jerky is very dry. Store in freezer for next party or camping trip. *Makes 12 to 20 servings.*

NOTE: If a microwave oven is available, remove lid and heat honey a few seconds right in jar.

JAN'S CHILE CHEESE PUFF

▼▼▼▼▼

Jan Smith, who frequently and capably assists me at the cooking school, worked with me to create this snack for an open house for which we wanted a flavorful appetizer that would not wilt or dry out while waiting.

10 eggs
1/2 cup all-purpose flour
1 teaspoon baking powder

1/8 teaspoon salt
1/2 cup butter, melted
1 cup chopped, peeled, parched green chile
2 tablespoons mixed minced red and green jalapeño chiles (about 2 large or 3 medium chiles)
1 pint cottage cheese
2 cups (8 oz.) shredded mixed Monterey Jack and Cheddar cheeses

Preheat grill to 425F (220C) if not already hot. Butter a 13 x 9-inch baking pan. Using an electric mixer or a whisk, beat eggs in a large bowl until lemon-colored. Add remaining ingredients and mix well. Pour into prepared pan and place on grill. Cover grill (if grill does not have a lid, use a piece of foil over puff) and cook 15 minutes. Reduce heat to 350F (175C) and grill 30 minutes. If grill does not have a thermostat, reduce heat by moving pan further to the front and leaving grill open until heat lowers. Cut into squares. Serve warm. *Makes 8 to 12 servings.*

GRILLED CLAMS WITH GREEN CHILE, LIME & CILANTRO BUTTER

▼▼▼▼▼

This dish can be served as either an appetizer or a light meal when accompanied by hearty grilled vegetables and crusty bread. It is a perfect appetizer to serve while the grill is heating or another food is cooking.

48 clams in the shell, rinsed
About 1 tablespoon oatmeal, cornmeal or bread crumbs
1/3 cup butter, melted
1/4 cup parched (page 161), peeled and minced green chile
1 teaspoon grated lime zest
3 tablespoons cilantro, coarsely chopped

Soak clams in cold water with a sprinkle of oatmeal for 30 minutes to remove sand—clams exchange sand for oatmeal. Mix together butter, chile, lime zest and cilantro.
Preheat grill to medium or 350F (175C) if not already hot. Place rack 4 to 5 inches above heat. Place clams on rack and grill until they open. Discard any that do not open. It's best to just eat these with the butter, as they open, right off the grill. *Makes 6 to 8 servings.*

MINI-FRANKFURTER REUBENS

▼▼▼▼▼

Since the franks are precooked, they only need to blister and heat through, making them a perfect appetizer to prepare over a fire that is just heating.

1 (about 10-oz.) package mini-frankfurters
1 cup sauerkraut
1 small loaf party rye bread
1 tablespoon Thousand Island dressing
2 teaspoons Dijon mustard
6 ounces thinly sliced Swiss cheese, cut into squares slightly smaller than the bread slices

Preheat grill to medium or 350F (175C) if not already hot. Place rack 3 to 5 inches above heat. Place franks on 1 or 2 long skewers for grilling. Place frankfurters on grill until heated through.

Meanwhile, place sauerkraut in a small pan and place on grill to heat. Spread 8 to 12 bread slices with Thousand Island dressing and 8 to 12 bread slices with mustard. Drain sauerkraut. To serve, halve each frank and place 1 on each mustard-topped bread slice, top with a spoonful of drained sauerkraut, then a square of cheese and a dressing-topped bread slice. Spear with a wooden pick or bamboo skewer and briefly place on grill to melt cheese or at least heat it thoroughly. Serve immediately. *Makes 8 to 12 servings.*

PORTUGUESE MINI-PIZZAS

▼▼▼▼▼

I first enjoyed these in West Vancouver at a party given in my honor to celebrate the cooking classes I was presenting at Caren's Cooking School. Caren and her husband, José, had a big adobe *horno* (a beehive-style oven with the firebox about a yard off the ground) in the backyard. Caren's husband is Portuguese and he enjoys being the grill master. They built a wood fire and when it got hot, they pulled the logs out, leaving coals upon which they cooked the pizzas.

1 package instant dry yeast
About 2 cups warm water
1 teaspoon salt

1 teaspoon sugar
4-1/2 cups unbleached all-purpose flour (1/2 cup semolina flour can be substituted for
    1/2 cup of all-purpose flour)
2 tablespoons good-quality olive oil, preferably Spanish
Your choice of toppings (see pages 31–32)

Dissolve yeast in 1/4 cup of the warm water in a small bowl. Let stand 5 to 10 minutes or until frothy. Add salt and sugar; blend well.

Using an electric mixer with a dough hook, add flour to bowl, then add 1-1/4 cups warm water and mix until flour is moistened. Add oil and mix 1-1/2 minutes or until oil is combined. Then add dissolved yeast and mix 2 minutes. Add a few tablespoons of water if dough is too dry. Mix about another 2 minutes or until dough is well mixed and springy, adding water as needed to make a soft, workable dough that will hold its shape.

Turn out dough onto a lightly floured surface and knead until smooth and satiny. To test, place a small ball of dough between your fingers. If "threads" develop as you pull ball into 2 pieces, it has been kneaded enough.

Cover dough with a damp towel and allow to rest about 30 minutes. Preheat grill to medium-hot or 400F (205C), or build a hot fire with charcoal. To use, divide dough into 3 pieces. Roll each piece into a 2-1/2-inch ball. Hand shape by using your fingers to make an edging around the outside, then forcing or stretching the center of dough to the outside until a 6- to 7-inch round is formed. Repeat with remaining pieces.

Cover pizza rounds with desired topping. Arrange pizzas on rack. Cook about 5 minutes in a covered grill or until crust is golden brown and cheese is bubbly on an open grill. If preferred, a griddle can be preheated and pizzas placed on the griddle rather than directly on the grill rack. *Makes 3 (6- to 7-inch) pizzas.*

NOTE: When transferring pizzas to the grill, use a large pancake turner.

VARIATIONS

If preferred, these can be baked in a preheated 425F (220C) oven for the same length of time.

Make a double or triple recipe and freeze dough in balls for easy pizza snacks.

FAVORITE GRILLED MUSHROOMS

▼▼▼▼▼

These are so easy that once you've done them, you'll wonder why you haven't been doing them forever. Any fresh, firm mushroom works well. Personal favorites are shiitake or portobello.

4 to 6 mushrooms, depending on size and desired number of servings
2 teaspoons good-quality olive oil, preferably Spanish
Freshly ground black pepper
1/4 teaspoon ground thyme
1/4 teaspoon minced or crushed rosemary leaves

Preheat grill to medium or 350F (175C) if not already hot. Clean mushrooms with a damp cloth; do not soak or wash in water. Combine oil with remaining ingredients in a shallow bowl. Toss mushrooms in oil mixture. Arrange mushrooms on skewers. Place mushrooms on rack. Grill until lightly browned and soft to the touch, about 15 minutes.

Keep warm until serving time or serve from grill. If desired, mushrooms can be cut into serving portions, depending on size of mushroom. Serve with wooden picks. *Makes 4 to 6 servings.*

NOTE: If serving from the grill, use a small skewer for each mushroom for easier serving.

Spring Asparagus Pizza Topping

▼▼▼▼▼

12 stalks slender asparagus
1-1/2 cups thinly sliced tomatoes
6 green onions with tender green tops, minced
3 to 6 minced anchovies (optional)
1 cup (4 oz.) shredded Jarlsberg cheese
3 tablespoons freshly grated Romano cheese

Boil asparagus until color deepens, 4 to 5 minutes, then chill in iced water. Drain well.

To assemble pizza, place 1/3 of tomato slices on each round of pizza dough. Then top each round with 1/3 of asparagus, arranging asparagus like spokes, with tips to edge. Divide green onions, anchovies, if using, and cheeses among rounds.

Grill as directed in Portuguese Mini-Pizzas (page 28). *Makes enough topping for 3 (6- to 7-inch) pizzas.*

Pesto Pizza Topping

▼▼▼▼▼

1/3 cup prepared pesto
3/4 cup (3 oz.) shredded mozzarella cheese
3 tablespoons freshly grated Parmesan cheese
1/4 cup chopped onion
1/2 cup chopped fresh tomato

Spread pesto evenly over 3 pizza rounds. Then top each with 1/3 of each cheese, onion, and tomato.

Grill as directed in Portuguese Mini-Pizzas (page 28). *Makes enough topping for 3 (6- to 7-inch) pizzas.*

GRILLED MUSHROOM PIZZA TOPPING

▼▼▼▼▼

1 cup whole button mushrooms
2 tablespoons good-quality olive oil, preferably Spanish
2 tablespoons Italian oil-cured ripe olives, sliced
2/3 cup reconstituted sun-dried tomatoes, chopped
6 green onions, cut into very thin 2-inch-long slivers
1/2 lemon
3/4 cup (3 oz.) shredded mozzarella cheese

Clean mushrooms with a moist cloth. Heat oil in a heavy skillet over medium-high heat. Add mushrooms and cook until soft, turning occasionally. Cool mushrooms and thinly slice. Evenly divide mushrooms among 3 pizza rounds. Top rounds evenly with olives, sun-dried tomatoes and green onions. Squeeze a little lemon juice over each round and top each with 1/3 of the cheese.

Grill as directed in Portuguese Mini-Pizzas (page 28). *Makes enough topping for 3 (6- to 7-inch) pizzas.*

OYSTERS, IXTAPA STYLE

▼▼▼▼▼

These hot, spicy oysters are wonderful when you have very, very fresh ones. I first sampled them prepared this simple delicious way on the Pacific coast of Mexico in the inlets near Ixtapa.

You may wish to serve some warm flour tortillas cut into triangles to "curb" the heat.

1 tablespoon good-quality olive oil, preferably Spanish
8 cloves garlic, minced
1/4 cup freshly squeezed lime juice
1 teaspoon grated lemon zest
1 teaspoon grated lime zest
2 tablespoons crushed pequin quebrado chile
48 oysters, freshly shucked, with liquor reserved

Preheat grill to medium or 350F (175C) if not already hot. Place rack 4 to 5 inches above heat source.

Add oil, garlic, lime juice and lemon and lime zest to a thin, large baking pan. Place pan on grill and cook a few minutes until garlic is softened. Add pequin quebrado, then taste and adjust seasonings. Add oyster liquor and heat until hot. Add oysters and cook 3 to 5 minutes or until edges begin to curl. Serve from grill, using cocktail forks and small plates. *Makes 6 to 8 servings.*

SPICY SHRIMP & PAPAYA BITES

▼▼▼▼▼

These are light and easy, with a taste of the tropics. They are terrific for hot, steamy nights or before a Polynesian or even Asian menu. We like them anytime.

1 cup pineapple juice
3 tablespoons lime or lemon juice
2 tablespoons crushed caribe chile
1 tablespoon sesame oil
Hot pepper sauce to taste
4 cloves garlic, minced
1/4 cup grated fresh coconut
1 pound large peeled shrimp (15 to 20 count)
2 papayas, preferably watermelon variety, peeled and cut into 1/2- to 3/4-inch chunks

Combine pineapple juice, lime juice, caribe chile, sesame oil, hot pepper sauce, garlic and coconut in a medium bowl. Add shrimp and stir to combine. Cover and marinate 2 hours in the refrigerator, stirring at least twice.

Preheat grill to medium or 350F (175C). Place rack 4 to 5 inches above heat source. Just before grilling, lightly brush rack with oil.

Place a chunk of papaya and a shrimp on each skewer. Drizzle with marinade. Place skewers on hot oiled rack and grill 1-1/2 to 2 minutes on each side or until shrimp are pink. *Makes 4 to 6 servings.*

GRILLED QUESADILLAS AS YOU LIKE 'EM

▼▼▼▼▼

Quesadillas are one of the most popular Southwestern restaurant appetizers. There are many, many variations that can be made, making them a wonderful do-it-yourself appetizer while awaiting a barbecued entree.

2 teaspoons unsalted butter, melted
1 (10- to 12-inch) flour tortilla
1/2 cup mixed shredded Monterey Jack and Cheddar cheeses
1 tablespoon pickled or fresh jalapeño chile slices

FILLING CHOICES (CAN BE COMBINED):

Cooked, crumbled chorizo sausage
Smoked poultry—chicken, duck or turkey
4 or 5 grilled deveined and butterflied shrimp with Cilantro Pesto (opposite)
Cooked bowl of red chili
Cooked chilied ground beef, such as that for tacos
Grilled fish, such as salmon or tuna
Chopped fresh or reconstituted sun-dried tomato
Chopped onion

GARNISHES

Salsa(s) of choice
Lettuce leaves
Sour cream
Chopped tomato
Caribe or crushed chile

Preheat grill to medium-high or 425F (220C). It is easier to use a griddle or other flat surface for cooking.

Assemble all ingredients you wish to use on a tray and set in a place convenient to the grill. Place griddle on grill rack. When griddle is hot, lightly brush with butter in a semicircle half the size of the tortilla being used. Place tortilla over buttered area and place some cheese on the half of the tortilla that is on buttered area. Top cheese with some jalapeño slices and desired fillings. Grill until cheese starts to melt, then fold over half that does not have fillings on it and lightly press down. Brush top of tortilla half with melted butter and turn over. Grill until cheese is melted and tortilla is a light golden brown on both sides.

To serve, quarter, cutting from center out. Either place salsa on a plate or place lettuce leaves in center of plate, and place quesadilla pieces over lettuce or salsa and top with salsa or sour cream, chopped tomatoes and caribe chile. *Makes 1 quesadilla.*

CILANTRO PESTO
▼▼▼▼▼

Fresh cilantro substitutes for basil in this Southwestern favorite.

2 cups firmly packed cilantro leaves
1/3 cup good-quality olive oil, preferably Spanish
2 tablespoons piñon nuts, toasted
2 large garlic cloves
Pinch of salt or to taste
2 green chiles, parched (page 161), peeled and chopped or 1 (4-oz.) can chopped
    green chiles
1/3 cup grated Parmesan cheese
1/3 cup grated Romano cheese
2 tablespoons butter, softened

Place all ingredients in a blender or food processor; process until pureed. *Makes 1-1/2 to 2 cups pesto or 6 servings.*

NOTE: This mixture can be prepared ahead of time and refrigerated for several days or frozen up to 6 months. It is also good over seafood and over pasta.

A Range of Satays—
Chicken, Pork or Shrimp

▼▼▼▼▼

Borrowed from Asian kitchens, these appetizer satays are a very streamlined version of the yummy barbecue on skewers. We like to make two to three kinds of meat and all three sauces, and serve them fondue-style as a main course with quinoa.

1 tablespoon peanut oil
2 cloves garlic, minced
1/2 cup chopped fresh or canned tomato
1/4 cup smooth peanut butter
1 tablespoon light, low-sodium soy sauce
1 tablespoon minced fresh gingerroot or 1/2 teaspoon ground ginger
1 tablespoon sherry
2 teaspoons crushed caribe chile
1 pound boneless, skinless chicken breasts, cut into 3/4-inch cubes or 1 pound
    boneless pork, cut into 3/4-inch cubes or 1 pound medium to large shrimp,
    shelled, butterflied and deveined
Quick 'n' Easy Satay Dipping Sauce (opposite)

In a shallow glass or stainless steel bowl or baking dish, mix together all ingredients except chicken, pork or shrimp and dipping sauce. Place chicken, pork or shrimp in marinade and stir around to evenly coat all sides. Place on skewers and return to marinade. Refrigerate in marinade at least 5 to 6 hours or overnight.

Preheat grill to medium or 350F (175C) if not already hot. Just before grilling, lightly brush rack with oil. Place skewers sideways on oiled rack and cook until lightly browned, rotating to ensure even cooking. Grill chicken 5 to 10 minutes or until cooked through. Pork will require at least 10 minutes or more. Grill shrimp about 5 minutes or until pink. Serve hot with dipping sauce. *Makes 6 to 8 appetizer servings or 3 or 4 main-course servings.*

Variation

If cooking more than a pound of chicken or meat at one time, brush a fish basket with oil, then place skewers in basket and grill and rotate until done.

QUICK 'N' EASY SATAY DIPPING SAUCE

▼▼▼▼▼

Not very authentic, but it has an exotic flavor. This is a good spur-of-the-moment satay sauce to offer.

2 tablespoons ketchup
2 tablespoons plum or apricot jam, minced or blended
1/2 cup light or regular soy sauce
2 to 3 small green onions, white and light green parts only, finely minced
2 teaspoons sesame oil

    Combine all ingredients in a small bowl and whisk or stir with a fork until well mixed. Keeps well in refrigerator. *Makes enough for 1 pound of satay.*

THAI SWEET HOT SAUCE

▼▼▼▼▼

This will keep in the refrigerator several days.

1-1/2 cups apricot or plum preserves
6 cloves garlic, peeled
1-1/2 to 3 teaspoons crushed pequin quebrado chile or to taste
1 teaspoon molasses
2 tablespoons rice or white vinegar

    Place all ingredients in a blender or food processor; process until pureed. *Makes enough for 3 to 4 pounds of satay.*

Peanut Sauce

▼▼▼▼▼

This Americanized version of the Indonesian original is quickly prepared.

1-1/2 tablespoons tamarind pulp
1/4 cup warm water or as needed
1 cup fresh, frozen or canned pineapple chunks, drained and pureed
1 teaspoon sesame oil
1 teaspoon crushed pequin quebrado or other hot red chiles
2 cloves garlic, minced
1 green onion, white part only, minced
1-1/2 teaspoons freshly squeezed lime juice
1 tablespoon minced gingerroot
1 teaspoon sugar
1/4 cup chunky peanut butter
1/2 cup water

Soak tamarind in water until softened, about 15 minutes. Remove seeds and strings, and strain liquid. Add pulp to a food processor or blender bowl; reserve liquid. Add remaining ingredients except peanut butter, water and reserved soaking liquid to processor and process until well blended.

Combine tamarind liquid, peanut butter and water in a small heavy saucepan; place over medium-low heat. Add pureed mixture and simmer, stirring occasionally, until thick, 15 to 20 minutes. Serve warm or at room temperature. This can be refrigerated for several days or frozen. *Makes enough for 3 to 4 pounds of satay.*

Smoked Hay & Straw

▼▼▼▼▼

These easy-to-make snacks are excellent. They're also a snap to make when the smoker is already going—just fill nooks and crannies with wire trays of nuts, Chinese noodles, or breakfast cereal, such as bite-size shredded wheat, rice or corn, or your favorite snack. We've even tried triangles of corn tortillas . . . naturally.

Any kind of nuts such as English walnuts, pecans, hazelnuts or peanuts
Sunflower or pumpkin seeds
Breakfast cereal, such as bite-size shredded wheat, corn or rice, or Cheerios cereal
Chinese noodles

Place nuts or cereal on a wire screen on top of smoker shelf. If you aren't already smoking with wood chunks, place 3 to 4 water-soaked chunks of your favorite wood in smoking pan. Do not use water.

Smoke over low heat for about 1 hour or until a sample of nut or cereal tastes as smoky as desired. Allow 1/4 cup per serving.

SMOKED JACK WITH SALSA & TORTILLA CRISPS

▼▼▼▼▼

This easy-to-do appetizer is one that you will have to time; it takes about an hour of "cool smoke." However, if you are smoking an entree, then this is a perfect accompaniment. I prefer to use a wedge of cheese at least 3 inches across the back and at least 1 inch thick. If it comes thicker, slice to about a 1-inch thickness so that the cheese will be smoky flavored. A chipotle-accented salsa (page 202) or Black Bean & Corn Salsa (page 206) will best stand up to the smoky flavor of the cheese.

A FEW IMPORTANT TIPS:

- Always smoke cheese on a pan such as a pie pan or shallow foil pan.
- Place 3 to 4 chunks of wet wood on coals.
- Do *not* use water in water pan.
- Always watch to be sure the fire is not too hot and the cheese does *not* melt!

12 ounces to 1 pound Montercy Jack cheese or Muenster or Colby cheese
Tortilla Crisps (page 40)
Salsa (pages 202–209)

About an hour before you want to serve, place cheese on rack in your smoker at least 8 to 10 inches from heat source, which should be a slow one—not too hot. Follow tips above.

Check after a few minutes to be sure fire is not too hot. Smoke about 1 hour for best flavor, checking occasionally to be sure that cheese is not melting. *Makes 6 to 8 servings.*

TORTILLA CRISPS

▼▼▼▼▼

These can be prepared ahead at the same time you are using the oven to bake another dish.

12 corn or flour tortillas or any combination of the two
1 teaspoon vegetable oil

Preheat oven to 400F (205C). Cut tortillas into quarters and spread on an ungreased baking sheet. Lightly brush with oil and bake 8 to 12 minutes or until crisp and lightly golden. *Makes 6 to 8 servings.*

SMOKED DILLED SALMON WITH MUSTARD DILL SAUCE

▼▼▼▼▼

Influenced by Scandinavian ways with salmon, this smoked gravlax is fabulous. It is wonderfully easy if you are planning on serving a smoked meal, such as a brisket or chicken. The salmon can be placed on a top rack when guests are due, and you can take advantage of the same smoke you are using for the rest of the meal. Any leftovers are terrific with pasta, eggs or bagels.

2 pounds fresh salmon fillet
1 bunch fresh dill
1 tablespoon salt
1 tablespoon sugar
1 tablespoon freshly ground black pepper

MUSTARD DILL SAUCE

1/4 cup Dijon mustard
2 tablespoons sugar

1/4 cup apple cider vinegar
1/4 cup vegetable oil
2 to 3 tablespoons dill from inside fish

Cut salmon in half crosswise. Rinse dill. Combine salt, sugar and pepper in a small bowl. Sprinkle inside of both salmon pieces lightly with salt mixture. Top 1 piece with dill. Place on a plate, top with second piece and top with another plate. Cover with plastic wrap and refrigerate for at least half a day or up to 2 days.

To smoke, use a cool fire, placing 3 to 4 soaked wood chunks, such as apple or other fruitwood, on top of the coals. Smoke on top shelf about 30 minutes or until salmon flakes with a fork. It can be slightly rare, depending on your taste preference.

While salmon is smoking prepare mustard sauce. Serve salmon with the sauce. *Makes 8 to 12 appetizer servings or 6 to 8 as a light meal.*

Mustard Dill Sauce

Mix together mustard, sugar and vinegar until thoroughly combined. Beating with a small whisk or fork, slowly add oil a little at a time until blended. Fold in dill.

Genuine Texas Armadillo Eggs

▼▼▼▼▼

These have become popular in restaurants throughout the South. One Southwestern restaurant in Nashville serves them in an egg carton! Grilling or smoking lowers the fat content; however, they are still not a low-fat food.

1 pound chorizo, Mexican-style or homemade (see Note)
2 pounds pork sausage
15 pickled whole jalapeño chiles
1/2-pound chunk Monterey Jack, Muenster or Cheddar cheese cut into about 36
    squares
Salsa of choice

Lightly fry chorizo in a skillet over medium heat, stirring to break up meat. Remove from skillet and drain well; set aside to cool.

Preheat grill or smoker to medium or 350F (175C). Cut jalapeño chiles in half, remove seeds and then halve larger ones again. Place a square of cheese inside each chile. Combine the two sausages and form into 36 small patties. Place a chile with cheese filling on center of sausage patty, then form sausage up around chile filling, sealing well. Place on a baking sheet in covered grill or smoker. Grill about 20 minutes or until browned. Drain and serve warm with salsa.   *Makes 6 to 8 servings*.

NOTE: If chorizo is difficult to find, you can use all pork sausage or enhance hot Italian sausage to make chorizo by adding 1/2 teaspoon each ground cumin and Mexican oregano. If hot Italian sausage is *not* used, add 2 to 4 tablespoons crushed caribe or pequin chile.

Soups & Stews

▼▼▼▼▼

Soups and stews are a wonderful application for your outdoor grill. You can have them bubbling away when the rest of the grill is otherwise occupied with the main course. All too often we heat a large grill just to prepare chops, steaks or burgers. This is a good opportunity to use the excess capacity for preparing homemade soups and stews.

Soups and stews are not very temperature sensitive and can simmer along at whatever heat you need for the other dishes you are preparing. Also, what better use of the grill than to brown the meats and vegetables for your own stocks?

GRILLED BLACKENED TOMATO CREAM SOUP

▼▼▼▼▼

Grilling or searing the tomatoes and baking them until they are quite soft, charred and blackened on the outside heightens the flavor of the pulp, recalling summer's goodness. Sear the tomatoes when you are cooking something else or doing a whole grillful for the most efficiency.

This soup is great for a light meal with a hearty bread or salad. Or, serve it preceding an outdoor grilled or smoked dinner.

4 to 6 tomatoes to equal 2 cups cooked
2 slices onion
1 teaspoon olive oil
1/4 cup unsalted butter
1/4 cup all-purpose flour
4 cups whole or skim milk
Salt and freshly ground black pepper
1 teaspoon ground mild chile for garnish

Preheat grill to 400F (205C). Place tomatoes and onion slices on a piece of foil or easily cleaned baking pan. Lightly brush with oil. Place on grill and cook until the tomatoes are charred and blackened, about 45 minutes.

Meanwhile, prepare the soup base: Melt butter in a medium to heavy saucepan over low heat. Then stir in the flour and cook, stirring, until bubbly and light golden. Gradually stir in the milk. Cook, stirring, until slightly thickened. Season with salt and black pepper. Set aside.

Peel tomatoes and place in a blender with onion slices. Process until pureed. Add to soup base and bring to a simmer over low heat. Serve in warmed bowls or mugs sprinkled with ground chile.   *Makes 6 (3/4-cup) servings.*

VARIATION

Stir 1/2 cup chopped green chiles into the soup base with the pureed tomato mixture. Just before serving, stir 2 tablespoons coarsely chopped cilantro into soup.

NOTE: Blackened tomatoes can be cooled, packed into freezer containers and frozen up to 2 months. Thaw and peel before using.

GRILLED GARLIC SOUP

▼▼▼▼▼

Grilled garlic, like baked garlic, imparts a more mellow, in-depth flavor to foods that are blessed with it! This classic Mexican soup dons a whole new personality when prepared outdoors with grilled garlic.

Grilling the garlic in bunches saves last-minute preparation time.

2 heads garlic
1/2 teaspoon olive oil
8 corn tortillas
6 cups vegetable, beef or chicken stock (pages 59, 57, or 55)
2 tablespoons ground hot chile
1/2 cup mixed shredded Cheddar and Monterey Jack cheeses
1 teaspoon crushed caribe chile or to taste

Heat a grill to 400F (205C). Place garlic heads on a piece of foil or in a garlic baker. Brush with some of the olive oil. Place garlic on grill and cook until soft, about 30 minutes.

Cut 2 of the tortillas into about 1/4-inch-wide strips; brush with oil and place on foil. Place tortilla strips on grill and cook until crisp, about 10 minutes. Set crisp tortilla strips aside. Tear remaining 6 tortillas into medium pieces and set aside.

Using a chef's knife, slice the bottom off each head of roasted garlic. Then squeeze out the garlic cloves and mince if necessary. Meanwhile heat stock in a stockpot on the grill or indoors and add tortilla pieces. Add the garlic and ground chile and simmer, stirring occasionally, about 15 minutes. Taste and adjust seasonings.

To serve, divide the soup among 6 warmed ovenproof soup bowls or mugs. Add a heaping tablespoonful of cheese to the top of each serving and top with tortilla strips. Heat on grill or in oven to melt cheese and sprinkle each with caribe chile. *Makes 6 servings.*

GRILLED LAMB STEW WITH MINT & BARLEY

▼▼▼▼▼

We love this hearty soup. It freezes very well and is perfect for making the best of bones left from butterflying a leg of lamb or whenever there is a real buy on bony lamb at your market. We always serve it with the fresh mint and green onions on top.

2 pounds lamb shoulder, neck or ribs
3 cloves garlic, cut into slivers
2 carrots, cut crosswise into about 2-inch pieces
2 parsnips, cut crosswise into about 2-inch pieces
3 turnips, cut in half lengthwise
3 baking potatoes, cut in half lengthwise
1 medium fennel bulb, cut in half lengthwise
6 cups chicken broth
1/2 cup barley
1 bunch Swiss chard, washed and tough stems removed
Salt and freshly ground pepper
1/2 cup fresh mint, coarsely chopped, for garnish
3 green onions, white part only, thinly sliced, for garnish

Preheat grill to medium or 350F (175C). Trim excess fat from the lamb and cut into medium chunks. Pierce flesh with the tip of a sharp knife and insert garlic slivers into holes. Place lamb on skewers if chunks are small and place directly on the grill.

Place carrots and parsnips on a skewer. Place carrots, parsnips, turnips, potatoes and fennel on grill. Grill lamb and vegetables until lamb is browned and vegetables are lightly browned and softened, about 20 minutes.

Pour broth into a large pot and heat on the grill or on indoor stovetop. Cut lamb into bite-size pieces, removing bones. Dice carrots, parsnips, turnips and potatoes and cut fennel lengthwise into thin slices. Cut chard crosswise into 2-inch pieces. Add vegetables and lamb to simmering broth. Add barley. Simmer 1 hour or until lamb and vegetables are fork tender, then taste and adjust seasonings.

Serve in warmed bowls with a topping of the minced mint and green onions. *Makes 4 to 6 servings.*

GRILLED SHRIMP & SPINACH SOUP

▼▼▼▼▼

This soup is fast to make, and the shrimp can be grilled while the main course is just beginning to cook. If you have any leftover grilled shrimp, use them to make this soup. It makes an elegant first course.

6 cups homemade stock (page 53) or richly flavored chicken broth
1/2 medium onion, chopped
1/2 teaspoon crushed or ground pequin quebrado chile
1/2 cup small bow-tie or shell macaroni
1/2 pound shelled, deveined medium shrimp
Few drops olive oil
1 pound fresh spinach leaves, washed thoroughly and stems removed
2 teaspoons freshly squeezed lime juice
2 tablespoons sherry wine

Preheat grill to medium or 350F (175C). Pour broth into a large pot and add onion and pequin quebrado. Place pot on grill or cook indoors. Cook until onion is clear, about 10 minutes. Add macaroni and cook about 10 minutes or until almost tender.

Meanwhile, place shrimp on a skewer and lightly brush with olive oil. Cook on grill until shrimp turn pink, about 5 minutes. Then add grilled shrimp, spinach leaves and lime juice to soup. Cover and cook 2 minutes; remove from heat. Serve in warmed bowls and lace each serving with sherry. *Makes 6 servings.*

GRILLED CHICKEN STEW WITH PIÑONS & PASTA

▼▼▼▼▼

This hearty chicken stew is terrific to make ahead and have on hand. The green chile and red chile pasta (or other Southwestern-flavored pasta) make this dish quite colorful. Lots of times I double and even triple the recipe.

1 (3-lb.) chicken, quartered
4 cloves garlic, slivered
1 lemon, halved
4 carrots
1 fennel bulb, halved lengthwise
2 onions, cut in half lengthwise
4 cups chicken broth
1 cup red chile pasta or other Southwestern-flavored pasta
4 green chiles, parched (page 161), peeled and chopped or 2 (4-oz.) cans chopped
    green chiles
2 tablespoons piñon nuts, minced

Preheat grill to medium or 350F (175C). Lightly oil grill rack. Trim chicken, removing skin and fat, then pierce with a sharp knife in the fleshiest parts and insert garlic slivers. Squeeze lemon juice over chicken pieces. Place chicken on grill. Add carrots, fennel and onions to grill. Cook about 45 minutes or until chicken juices run clear when chicken is pierced with a knife and vegetables are softened. Remove from grill and cool slightly.

Pour broth into a large pot and heat on grill or indoors. Cut chicken into serving pieces, leaving on bones. Cut carrots crosswise into 1-inch pieces. Cut fennel lengthwise into 1/4-inch-wide slices and chop onions. Add to simmering broth and cook until the chicken is very tender and the vegetables are fork tender. Add pasta and green chiles and cook about 8 minutes or until pasta is tender. Serve in warmed bowls with a sprinkle of piñon nuts on top. *Makes 4 servings.*

MARGRIT'S CREAM OF GREEN CHILE CHICKEN STEW

▼▼▼▼▼

A Bavarian acquaintance I met through my Albuquerque Old Town Cooking School developed this recipe and shared it with me. We liked it so much, we adapted it to the grill. Serve with warm flour or corn tortillas. The recipe is rather large, but the leftovers freeze very well.

1-1/2 pounds boneless, skinless chicken breasts
Few drops olive oil
2 quarts chicken broth
1 cup chopped onion
2 cloves garlic, minced
1/2 cup unsalted butter
1/2 cup all-purpose flour
1 quart whole or skim milk
8 green chiles, parched (page 161), peeled and chopped or 4 (4-oz.) cans chopped
     green chiles
1 cup half-and-half or 1 (14-oz.) can evaporated skim milk
Salt and freshly ground black pepper
1 teaspoon crushed caribe chile for garnish

Preheat grill to 450F (230C). Trim chicken, removing all fat. Lightly brush with oil and place on grill. Cook chicken until golden brown on the first side; turn and brown remaining side. Remove chicken from grill and cool slightly.

Meanwhile pour broth into a large heavy pot and heat on the grill or indoors. Add onion and garlic and bring to a simmer.

Prepare the soup base: Melt butter in a medium to heavy saucepan over low heat. Stir in the flour and cook, stirring, until bubbly and light golden. Gradually stir in milk. Cook, stirring, until slightly thickened. Add broth to mixture in pot.

Cut chicken into cubes and add to soup base. Add chiles and half-and-half and cook over low heat, stirring occasionally, until hot. Season to taste with salt and black pepper. Serve in warmed bowls topped with a sprinkle of caribe chile. *Makes 14 first-course servings or 6 to 8 main-course servings.*

Bayou Gumbo with Roasted Tomatoes

▼▼▼▼▼

Gumbo is one of my favorite stews. I learned from my mother, who was raised partially in the South and always made fabulous gumbos. She swore by the fact that the freshest filé—the combination of ground sassafras and thyme—coupled with red pepper sauce, such as Tabasco, were critical to authentic flavors. However, they were not to be added to the gumbo by the cook but by the individual at the table. She always used a combination of meats and preferred it with seafood, some red meat and chicken—the more the better. Lots of okra, onion, garlic and red ripe tomatoes were absolutely necessary. Served over fluffy long-grain rice, the gumbo was the main course.

Here's a version of her delicious stew! As you will notice, it does make a generous amount; given the effort required, we always make enough to freeze for a second meal.

6 large tomatoes, roasted on the grill (page 229)
1/4 cup bacon fat or butter
1/4 cup all-purpose flour
4 large onions, chopped (about 4 cups)
8 cloves garlic, minced
2 pounds small to medium okra, sliced into 1/2-inch rounds
1-1/2 pounds beef chuck, cut into 1-inch chunks
1-1/2 pounds skinless, boneless chicken, cut into 1-inch chunks
4 cups or more chicken, beef, fish or vegetable stock
1/2 teaspoon cayenne pepper or pequin quebrado or to taste
1 pound small to medium shrimp, peeled and deveined
Salt and freshly ground black pepper

Cool tomatoes slightly, peel and coarsely chop. Heat fat in a large, heavy stockpot either over the grill or indoors. Stir in flour and cook, stirring, until lightly browned or darker. Add onions, garlic and okra and cook, stirring only occasionally, over medium-high heat until onions are clear and along with okra slightly browned on edges.

Add beef and chicken and cook, stirring only occasionally, until slightly browned. Add stock, tomatoes and cayenne. Cover and simmer over low heat about 1-3/4 hours or until meats are very tender. Add shrimp and simmer 15 minutes. Taste and season with salt and black pepper. *Makes 8 to 10 servings.*

Variation

You can grill the meat instead of browning it in the pot. Grill beef and chicken pieces on all sides, lightly brushing with oil to prevent sticking. When done, cube and add to the stockpot.

GRILLED CORN WITH GREEN CHILE SOUP

▼▼▼▼▼

Grilled corn, especially with the husk removed, is wonderfully sweet and flavorful. If any is ever left, it is wonderful in soups, salsas, salads and combined with other vegetables.

1/2 large Spanish onion, cut in half crosswise
2 teaspoons olive oil
4 large or 6 medium ears yellow sweet corn
1 red bell pepper
2 cloves garlic, grilled (page 69)
4 large green chiles, parched (page 161), peeled and chopped or 2 (4-oz.) cans
     chopped green chiles
4 cups chicken or vegetable stock
1/4 teaspoon ground cumin
Salt and freshly ground black pepper

Preheat grill to high or 475F (245C). Brush onion with some of the olive oil. Place onion, cut side down, on grill rack. Husk corn and lightly brush with olive oil; place on grill rack. Watch each vegetable carefully, rotating to evenly brown. Rinse bell pepper, pierce once with a knife and place on grill. Grill onion until soft when pierced with a fork. Grill corn until tipped with brown. Cook bell pepper, turning, until evenly blistered and browned.

When done, add bell pepper to ice water, then peel and chop. Remove corn and onion from grill and cool. Chop onion. Cut corn off the cob, scraping the cob to remove all the succulent juice and pulp. Squeeze and remove garlic cloves and mince.

Meanwhile, pour stock into a large pot and heat on the grill or stovetop. Add vegetables and cumin and simmer just a few minutes to blend flavors. Taste and season with salt and black pepper. Serve hot. *Makes 6 to 8 servings.*

VARIATION

Puree vegetables with a little of the stock, then return to pot and reheat. A cup or more of half-and-half or evaporated milk can be added for a creamier consistency.

GULF COAST GRILLED SEAFOOD CHOWDER

▼▼▼▼▼

Along the Gulf Coast, red snapper, oysters and shrimp abound, and they make wonderful chowder as well as lighter soups.

1 pound red snapper fillet
1 teaspoon plus 1 tablespoon good-quality olive oil, preferably Spanish
12 small oysters in the shell
1/2 pound small to medium shrimp, shelled and deveined
1 medium onion, diced (about 1/2 cup)
3 large potatoes, peeled and cut into 1/4-inch cubes
4 cups fish, chicken or vegetable stock
1 teaspoon crushed dried thyme
Salt and freshly ground black pepper
1/2 teaspoon pequin quebrado or to taste
Lemon Cream Topping (see below)
1 tablespoon minced fresh flat-leaf parsley or a few sprigs thyme for garnish
2 teaspoons crushed caribe chile for garnish

LEMON CREAM TOPPING

1 teaspoon minced lemon zest or to taste
1 fresh jalapeño chile, minced
1/4 cup sour cream or plain yogurt
1 tablespoon freshly squeezed lemon juice or to taste

Preheat grill to medium-hot or 400F (205C). Lightly brush fish with oil and place on the hot grill. Add oysters in the shell to grill. Place shrimp on skewers and lightly brush with oil. Place shrimp on grill. Cook fish 5 minutes and turn. Cook until beginning to flake, about 5 minutes or less. Remove oysters from grill when they pop open; discard any that remain closed. Cook shrimp until pink, about 3 minutes on each side, turning once.

Meanwhile heat 1 tablespoon olive oil in a heavy stockpot on the grill or indoor stovetop. Add onion and cook, stirring occasionally, until lightly browned. Add potatoes and stir to coat evenly with the onion-oil mixture. Add stock, thyme and black pepper. Cook until the potatoes are tender, about 20 minutes. Taste and adjust seasonings.

Cut fish into 1/2-inch cubes. Remove shrimp from skewers. Add fish, oysters with liquid from shells and shrimp to stock. Cook 5 to 10 minutes to blend flavors. Prepare Lemon Cream Topping.

To serve, ladle the chowder into warmed bowls, then top with a dollop of topping and sprinkle with minced parsley and caribe. *Makes 4 to 6 main-course servings or 8 to 12 first-course servings.*

LEMON CREAM TOPPING

Combine all ingredients in a small bowl, adjusting the amounts of ingredients to suit taste.

FISH STOCK

▼▼▼▼▼

Fish stock is perfect for seafood stews and dishes. Freezing reserved heads, tails, filleted carcasses and even shrimp shells makes a good start for the stock.

4 pounds fish parts, such as heads, tails and carcasses
1/2 cup dried shrimp
3 large onions, halved
3 large carrots
3 celery stalks with leaves
6 large sprigs flat-leaf parsley tied in a bouquet garni with 3 sprigs thyme or with 2
    teaspoons dried in a tea ball
3 bay leaves
10 white or black peppercorns
Water

Preheat grill to 350F (175C). Place all ingredients in a large stockpot or other large cooking pot. Add enough water to cover by about 1 inch. Bring to a simmer and cover, moving to a corner of the grill where it is not too hot. Remove lid and skim and stir occasionally to prevent bottom pieces from sticking.

Simmer, uncovered, about 30 minutes. Cool slightly and strain, discarding bones and seasonings. Refrigerate up to 2 days or freeze up to 1 month. *Makes 12 cups.*

GRILLED ANTELOPE STEW WITH TOMATOES, ONION & BUTTERNUT SQUASH

▼▼▼▼▼

The rich flavor of butternut squash coupled with the grilled smokiness of the tomatoes and onion make this a favorite stew for us, especially in the fall.

1 to 1-1/2 pounds antelope roast or steak, cut into 1/2- to 3/4-inch-thick pieces
2 cloves garlic, slivered
Freshly ground black pepper
1 tablespoon olive oil
1 medium butternut squash (about 4 cups when grilled and chopped)
1 medium onion, unpeeled
2 large tomatoes
Water
1/2 teaspoon ground coriander
1/2 teaspoon ground thyme
1/2 teaspoon ground cumin
1/2 teaspoon ground Mexican oregano
1/2 teaspoon ground pequin quebrado or to taste
1 cup beef stock (page 57)

Trim off any fat from meat. Using a sharp knife, make several slits in meat on both sides. Insert a sliver of garlic into each slit. Sprinkle meat with black pepper and lightly rub with oil. Halve squash lengthwise. Remove and discard seeds. Halve onion cross-wise. Rub remaining oil on cut sides of onion and over the cut sides and peel of the squash.

Preheat grill to 400F (205C). Place squash and onion on grill rack. Grill 5 minutes. Place whole tomatoes on grill. Turn vegetables when the first sides have cooked and charred a little, 10 to 15 minutes. When the second sides are somewhat charred and starting to soften, place meat on the grill and cook until browned on both sides, about 20 minutes.

Remove vegetables from grill as they are done; cool slightly. Scoop out flesh of squash and coarsely chop. Peel onion and coarsely chop. Peel, core, and chop tomatoes.

Place all vegetables in a stockpot on the grill or stovetop. Add enough water to barely cover the vegetables. Add herbs and spices. Cover and simmer about 30 minutes or until vegetables are fork tender.

Meanwhile, dice meat. Add meat and stock to a medium saucepan over medium heat. Cover and simmer about 1 hour or until very tender. Process vegetables with cooking liquid in a food processor or blender until pureed. Return vegetables to pot. Add meat with enough stock to make a good thickness and reheat. Taste and adjust seasonings. Serve hot in warmed bowls. *Makes 6 to 8 servings.*

CHICKEN STOCK

▼▼▼▼▼

Chicken stock is probably the all-round favorite stock, as most people use more chicken stock than any other. Homemade chicken stock is so much better flavored and so much more wholesome than any you can purchase.

2 (3-1/2- to 4-lb.) chickens, trimmed of excess fat and well rinsed, giblets removed
5 pounds bony chicken pieces, such as backs, wings and ribs, trimmed of excess fat
    and well rinsed
5 carrots
6 celery stalks with leaves
2 large onions, halved
6 cloves garlic, coarsely chopped
Bouquet garni of 6 sprigs flat-leaf parsley, 3 large sprigs thyme or 1 tablespoon dried
    (placed in tea ball)
2 bay leaves
10 black peppercorns
4 teaspoons salt or to taste
Water

Preheat grill to medium or 350F (175C) if not already hot. Place chickens and chicken pieces on grill rack. Grill until browned, turning as needed. Transfer chicken to a large stockpot. Add remaining ingredients and enough water to cover by about 1 inch. Bring to a simmer and cover, moving to a corner of the grill where it is not too hot. Remove lid and skim and stir occasionally to prevent bottom pieces from sticking.

Simmer on grill or stovetop about 45 minutes or until the whole chickens are tender. Remove whole chickens and cool slightly.

Remove chicken from the bones, discarding skin and bones. The chicken can be used immediately, refrigerated up to 1 day or packaged and frozen up to 3 months.

Continue simmering stock mixture, uncovered, until the stock reduces by about a fourth to make rich stock. Cool slightly and strain, discarding the bony pieces and seasonings. Refrigerate up to 2 days or freeze up to 3 months. *Makes about 24 cups, depending on size of pot and reduction of stock.*

Scott's Baked Whole Pumpkin Soup with Gruyère & Croutons

▼▼▼▼▼

Scott Sharot, a chef-consultant from New York and Miami, is now in Albuquerque teaching at our Old Town Albuquerque Cooking School. He likes to teach this soup in his Entertaining I class. I adapted it to the grill and simplified it a bit. We love this as the first course for Thanksgiving dinner. Grilling the pumpkin frees your oven for the rest of the meal.

1 celery stalk, diced
1 medium onion, diced
2 carrots, sliced crosswise into thin rounds
2 parsnips, sliced crosswise into thin rounds
1 apple, diced
2 bay leaves
5 sprigs flat-leaf parsley, minced
5 sprigs fresh marjoram or thyme or 1 teaspoon dried
1/2 teaspoon salt
Freshly ground black pepper
4 to 5 cups chicken broth
1 (about 8-inch) pumpkin
1 tablespoon vegetable oil
3 ounces (3/4 cup) shredded Gruyère cheese
1/2 cup whipping cream or evaporated skim milk
Freshly grated nutmeg
1 cup freshly made croutons, lightly baked

In a heavy stockpot, combine celery, onion, carrots, parsnips, apple, bay leaves, parsley, marjoram, salt, black pepper and broth. Cover and simmer either on the grill or stovetop until vegetables are tender, about 1 hour. Puree in a food processor or blender.

Preheat grill to medium or 350F (175C). Cut a circle off the top of the pumpkin large enough to allow your hand to go in; discard top (or bake along with the pumpkin, if desired). Scoop out seeds. Lightly oil outside of pumpkin and place on a baking sheet or heavy piece of foil. Ladle a 2-inch layer of soup into bottom of pumpkin. Add a third of the cheese and cream and a few grates of nutmeg, then more soup, another third of cheese and cream and a few grates of nutmeg and remaining soup. Add croutons, remaining cream and cheese and another grate of nutmeg.

Place baking sheet on grill rack and cover grill. If no cover is available, create a tent out of heavy foil. Cook about 1-1/2 hours, then begin testing for doneness by inserting a sharp knife at an angle into pumpkin. It should be very soft when done. Do not overcook or pumpkin will fall apart.

Ladle a bit of soup into each of 6 warmed soup bowls, then add a scoop of pumpkin flesh and repeat, serving some croutons on each serving.   *Makes 6 servings.*

BEEF STOCK

▼▼▼▼▼

Using beef stock adds flavor to any dish that you are stewing or simmering. Of course soups, stews and sauces are better when stock is used.

5 pounds beef soup bones with meat attached
2 pounds beef stew meat, cut into 2-inch chunks and skewered
4 carrots
4 celery stalks with leaves
3 large onions, halved
8 cloves garlic, chopped
3 bay leaves
12 black peppercorns
4 whole allspice (optional)
1 tablespoon salt or to taste
Water

Preheat grill to medium or 350F (175C) if not already hot. Place soup bones and beef on grill rack. Grill until browned, turning as needed. Transfer soup bones and beef to a large stockpot. Add vegetables and seasonings to beef. Add enough water to cover by about 1 inch. Bring to a simmer and cover, moving to a corner of the grill where it is not too hot or cook indoors. Remove lid and skim and stir occasionally to prevent bottom pieces from sticking. Simmer about 2 hours or until beef is tender.

Using a slotted spoon, remove beef cubes and reserve for stew.

Continue simmering stock mixture, uncovered, until the stock reduces by about a fourth to make rich stock. Cool slightly and strain, discarding bones and seasonings. Refrigerate up to 2 days or freeze up to 3 months.   *Makes about 20 cups, depending on size of pot and reduction of stock.*

VARIATION

For a richer stock, use some or all beef stock instead of water when preparing stock.

GRILLED GAZPACHO

▼▼▼▼▼

The refreshing flavor of gazpacho is more robust in this version made with grilled tomatoes, onions, chiles and garlic.

1 medium onion, unpeeled and halved crosswise
8 large tomatoes
1 small head garlic, root end removed
3 tablespoons good-quality olive oil, preferably Spanish
6 mild green chiles, parched (page 161) and peeled
2 tablespoons sherry vinegar or good-quality red wine vinegar
1 cucumber, peeled and cut into 1/4-inch pieces
Salt
Hot pepper sauce
Romaine lettuce leaves

 Preheat grill to a high heat or 400F (205C). Rub onion, tomatoes and garlic lightly with olive oil. Place tomatoes in a heavy piece of foil, foil pan or baking pan. Place tomatoes on grill rack in foil. Arrange remaining vegetables directly on grill rack. Grill vegetables until they are somewhat soft and charred, about 40 minutes for tomatoes and garlic and slightly less for onion.
 Remove vegetables from grill and cool slightly. Peel onion and tomatoes and discard skins. Finely chop onion and tomatoes. Squeeze garlic out of its skin and mince. Mince chiles. Combine grilled vegetables and chiles with vinegar, cucumber and salt in a large bowl. Refrigerate at least 1 hour or overnight. Season to taste with hot pepper sauce. Serve in lettuce-lined chilled goblets. *Makes 6 light-meal servings or 8 to 10 first-course servings*.

VEGETABLE STOCK

▼▼▼▼▼

Stocks are the essence of flavorful cooking and are critical to delicious soups and stews, to say nothing about all the other dishes improved by well-prepared stocks. Those you make yourself are much fresher and of course need not have that overdose of salt, fat or monosodium glutamate so familiar in commercial stocks.

Make use of available space on your grill to brown vegetables for stock.

8 large carrots
4 large onions
6 large celery stalks, green tops included
2 turnips or parsnips
2 mild green chiles, cut in half and seeds removed
1 teaspoon vegetable oil
4 whole allspice
4 whole cloves
4 quarts water
Salt (optional)

Preheat grill to medium or 350F (175C) if not already hot. Lightly brush vegetables with oil. Roast on the grill rack, allowing the first side to sear and brown before turning. Then brown the second side. After they begin to brown, turn frequently to uniformly brown the outside of each vegetable.

Transfer the vegetables to a stockpot. Add spices and 4 quarts water and simmer on grill or stovetop at least 1 hour or until the color is light caramel and the flavor is good, adding salt as desired. Cool slightly and strain, discarding vegetables. Refrigerate up to 2 days or freeze up to 3 months. *Makes 1 gallon (16 cups).*

Mulligatawny Soup

▼▼▼▼▼

This rather exotic soup from India takes on a whole new personality when the chicken is grilled and chiles are added.

1 (2-1/2- to 3-lb.) broiler-fryer chicken, quartered
1 tablespoon olive oil
2 carrots
2 medium onions, halved crosswise
2 celery stalks
4 green chiles, parched (page 161), peeled and chopped, or 2 (4-oz.) cans chopped
  green chiles
1 apple, unpeeled and chopped
4 cups chicken broth
1 tablespoon curry powder or to taste
2 bay leaves
2 whole cloves (optional)
Salt and freshly ground black pepper
1-1/2 cups cooked long-grain rice
1 cup plain yogurt
1 tablespoon crushed caribe chile

Preheat grill to medium or 350F (175C). Remove skin from chicken, if desired. Brush chicken with some of the oil. Place chicken on grill rack. Lightly brush carrots, onions and celery with remaining olive oil. Arrange vegetables on the grill. Grill 30 to 45 minutes, turning chicken and vegetables occasionally.

Remove chicken and vegetables from grill and cool slightly. Remove chicken from bones and chop, discarding skin and bones. Thinly slice carrots into rounds and finely chop onions and celery. Place chicken, carrots, onions, celery and chiles in a heavy stockpot. Add apple, broth, curry powder, bay leaves and cloves, if using. Cover and simmer about 30 minutes or until chicken and vegetables are tender. Taste and add salt and black pepper to taste.

To serve, scoop 1/4 cup rice into each of 6 warmed bowls, then top with soup, a dollop of yogurt and a sprinkle of caribe chile. *Makes 6 servings.*

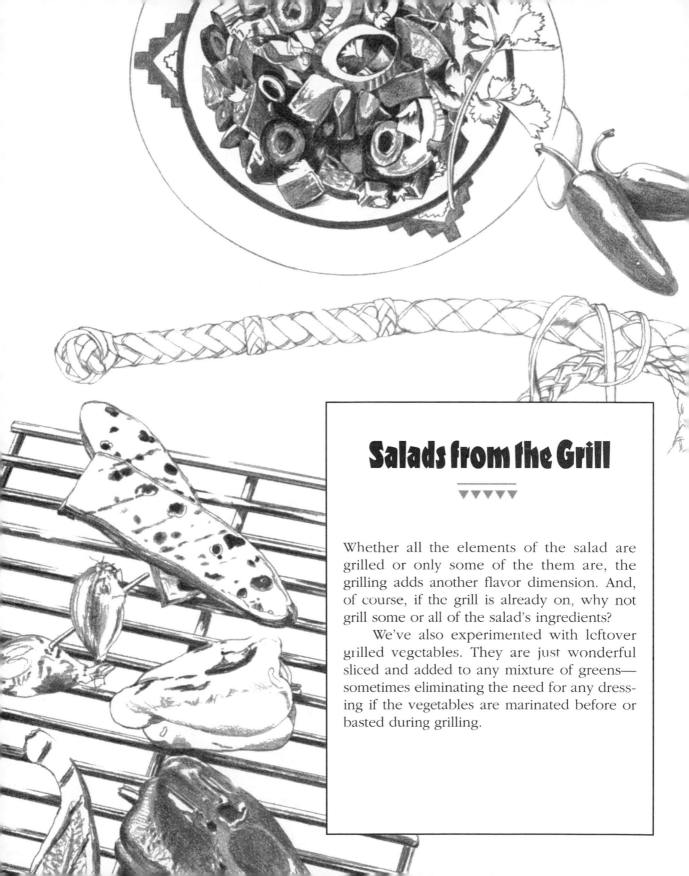

Salads from the Grill

▼▼▼▼▼

Whether all the elements of the salad are grilled or only some of the them are, the grilling adds another flavor dimension. And, of course, if the grill is already on, why not grill some or all of the salad's ingredients?

We've also experimented with leftover grilled vegetables. They are just wonderful sliced and added to any mixture of greens—sometimes eliminating the need for any dressing if the vegetables are marinated before or basted during grilling.

GRILLED SALAD ITALIANO

▼▼▼▼▼

This grilled main-dish salad is particularly flavorful: The basil, olive oil and garlic combine to create an almost pestolike flavor.

3 tablespoons good-quality olive oil, preferably Spanish
1/3 cup fresh basil leaves
4 cloves garlic, peeled
4 roma tomatoes, halved and cored
2 small eggplants, unpeeled, sliced crosswise
2 baby zucchini, thinly sliced crosswise
2 baby yellow summer squash, thinly sliced crosswise
1 green bell pepper, quartered
2 green chiles, parched (page 161), peeled and diced
1/2 cup freshly grated Romano cheese

Preheat grill to medium-high or 400F (205C) if not already hot. Process oil, basil and garlic in a food processor until thickened. Arrange tomatoes, eggplants and squash on separate skewers. Place all the vegetables on a baking sheet. Evenly brush vegetables with oil mixture. Place vegetables on grill rack and cook 5 to 7 minutes. Turn and grill other side. Vegetables are done when they brown around edges and grill marks appear. If tomatoes are done first, remove to a bowl.

Cut bell pepper into 1/2-inch-wide strips. Add all the vegetables to the bowl as they are done and toss to mix with cheese. Serve warm.   *Makes 4 servings*.

GRILLED VEGETABLE SALAD WITH WARM HERB OIL DRESSING

▼▼▼▼▼

The fresh orange juice lacing the dressing makes it a particularly nice accent for any poultry or pork main dish. Heating herbs in oil intensifies their flavor.

1 red bell pepper, rinsed and left whole
1 green bell pepper, rinsed and left whole
1 small zucchini, cut lengthwise into 1/2-inch-thick slices
1 small yellow summer squash, cut lengthwise into 1/2-inch-thick slices
1 small eggplant, cut lengthwise into 1/2-inch-thick slices
1 Vidalia or other sweet onion, cut crosswise into 1/2-inch-thick slices
1 tablespoon good-quality olive oil, preferably Spanish

WARM HERB OIL DRESSING

2 tablespoons good-quality olive oil, preferably Spanish
2 teaspoons ground cumin
1 teaspoon ground coriander
3 tablespoons freshly squeezed orange juice
1 tablespoon white wine vinegar
1/4 teaspoon salt

Preheat grill to medium-high or 400F (205C) if not already hot. Place bell peppers on grill rack. Arrange remaining vegetables on separate skewers for ease in turning. Lightly brush with oil and place on grill rack. Grill bell peppers until evenly blackened and blistered, turning often. Grill remaining vegetables 5 to 7 minutes or until charred on edges and grill marks are apparent.

Place grilled bell peppers in ice water to cool. Drain and peel, then cut into about 3/4-inch squares. Place squash, eggplant and onion on a cutting board and slice into matchsticks. Prepare dressing. To serve, place vegetables in a large bowl and toss with dressing. *Makes 4 servings.*

WARM HERB OIL DRESSING

In a small pan that will not get blackened by grill, heat oil with cumin and coriander about 1 minute, stirring frequently. Remove from heat and stir in remaining ingredients.

HEARTY GRILLED SWEET POTATO SALAD

▼▼▼▼▼

A dark beer would be a good accompaniment for the smokiness of the sausage and sweet potatoes—a perfect fall lunch.

3 large sweet potatoes, cut into 1/2-inch-thick slices
1/2 cup plus 1 tablespoon good-quality olive oil, preferably Spanish
1 (12- to 14-oz.) precooked kielbasa or Polish sausage
1 tablespoon Dijon mustard
1/2 cup cider vinegar
1/4 cup balsamic vinegar
2 teaspoons sugar
3/4 teaspoon salt
1 Spanish onion, thinly sliced crosswise and separated into rings
Freshly ground black pepper
Few sprigs flat-leaf parsley

Preheat grill to medium-high or 400F (205C) if not already hot. Brush sweet potato slices on both sides with the 1 tablespoon oil. Arrange sweet potato slices on grill rack. Grill 3 to 5 minutes or until slightly charred. Turn sweet potato slices and add whole sausage. Grill sweet potatoes until tender and sausage until charred all over on outside, about 10 minutes. Remove from grill and cut potatoes into 1-inch squares. Cut sausage into 1/4-inch-thick rounds.

In bottom of a large salad bowl, whisk together the remaining 1/2 cup olive oil, mustard, vinegars, sugar and salt until slightly thickened. Add sweet potato squares, onion, sausage slices and black pepper. Toss together. Garnish with parsley.   *Makes 6 servings*.

Smoked Potato Salad
with Salsa Dressing

Smoking potatoes creates a whole new flavor sensation! Using them in any favorite potato salad recipe will yield a salad with a wonderful smoky taste. Gordon has always preferred this mayonnaise-less potato salad; it is spicier than traditional recipes. Grilled potatoes are also good in this recipe.

4 to 6 medium smoked potatoes (page 221), unpeeled

Salsa Dressing

1/4 cup finely chopped Spanish onion or green onions
1 tablespoon crushed caribe chile
1/4 cup each diced red and green bell peppers
1/2 cup diced celery
2 hard-cooked eggs (see Note), finely chopped
2 tablespoons fresh or canned tomato-based salsa
3 tablespoons good-quality olive oil, preferably Spanish
2 tablespoons cider or white vinegar
1/2 teaspoon salt or to taste

Dice potatoes and add to a medium bowl. Add remaining ingredients and lightly toss together; do not mash potatoes. Taste and adjust seasonings.   *Makes 4 to 6 servings.*

NOTE: Hard-cooked eggs can be smoked with the potatoes for a smokier flavor. Smoke peeled eggs 25 to 30 minutes or until a light tan color.

Sarah's Best Blue Cheese–Smoked Potato Salad

▼▼▼▼▼

Hailing from Chicago, Sarah Larson, who joined our Pecos Valley Spice Company, made this for us and we loved it! Her original recipe did not use smoked potatoes; however, we like it even better with them.

4 smoked medium Russet potatoes (page 221), unpeeled
1/2 cup diced celery
2 tablespoons diced red onion
1/4 cup mayonnaise
1/4 cup regular or light sour cream
1/4 cup crumbled blue cheese
1 tablespoon chipotle-marinated vinegar (see Note)
1/4 teaspoon salt
1 teaspoon crushed caribe chile

Dice potatoes and add to a medium bowl. Add remaining ingredients except caribe chile and lightly toss together; do not mash potatoes. Taste and adjust seasonings. Garnish with caribe chile. *Makes 4 servings.*

NOTE: Soak a chipotle chile in cider vinegar for a day before using the vinegar.

Southwestern Grilled Turkey Salad

▼▼▼▼▼

Delicious and easy, this salad is somewhat reminiscent of a fajita salad but with corn and black beans. Add a favorite bread or crisped tortilla strips.

Lime Vinaigrette (see below)
1-1/2 cups cooked corn (fresh, frozen or canned)
2 cups cooked or canned black beans
2 tablespoons pickled jalapeño chiles, minced
1/2 cup diced Spanish onion
1 tablespoon each ground pure mild and hot New Mexican chile
1-1/2 teaspoons ground cumin
2 cloves garlic, minced
1/2 teaspoon salt
1 pound boneless, skinless turkey breast fillets
12 to 15 leaves red leaf lettuce
1 avocado, peeled, pitted and cut into long slivers
1 papaya or mango, peeled and cut into 1/2-inch squares

Lime Vinaigrette

1/3 cup good-quality olive oil, preferably Spanish
3 tablespoons good-quality sherry or red wine vinegar
1 tablespoon freshly squeezed lime juice
1/2 teaspoon ground Mexican oregano
1/2 teaspoon salt
1/2 teaspoon minced lime zest

Prepare vinaigrette. Toss corn, beans, jalapeño chiles and onion with half of vinaigrette in a medium bowl. Cover and refrigerate 2 hours.

Preheat grill to medium-high or 400F (205C), heating only a small part of it. Combine chile, cumin, garlic and salt in a small bowl. Rub chile mixture on turkey. Brush grill rack with oil and add seasoned turkey. Grill first side about 5 minutes; turn and grill another 5 minutes or until outside is browned and inside is no longer pink.

Dice turkey and toss with remaining vinaigrette in a medium bowl. Arrange lettuce leaves on 6 serving plates; top each with a mound of corn mixture. Arrange avocado strips around corn mixture like petals. Top with turkey and papaya. *Makes 6 servings.*

Lime Vinaigrette

Whisk together all ingredients in a small bowl.

Summer Vegetable & Quinoa Salad

▼▼▼▼▼

Quinoa is light, quick cooking and perfect for summer salads. Toss in a vinaigrette with your choice of grilled veggies, either leftovers or freshly cooked. You can even cook quinoa on the grill if you wish.

2 cups water
1/2 teaspoon salt
1 cup quinoa
Lime Vinaigrette (see below)
1 large red bell pepper
2 small zucchini
2 small yellow summer squash, cut into long 1/2-inch-thick slices
2 heads Belgian endive, halved lengthwise
2 navel oranges, peeled and sliced lengthwise into 1/2-inch-thick slices
12 green onions, including tender green tops, trimmed
2 cups fresh spinach leaves, rinsed, large stems removed and chilled
2 cups curly green leaf lettuce, rinsed, torn into pieces and chilled

Lime Vinaigrette

Grated zest of 1 lime
2 tablespoons freshly squeezed lime juice
2 teaspoons Dijon mustard
1/2 teaspoon ground cumin or to taste
1/4 cup good-quality olive oil, preferably Spanish

Preheat grill to medium-high or 400F (205C). Bring water and salt to a boil in a 5-quart pot on grill or stovetop. Place quinoa in a strainer and rinse quinoa several times, shaking strainer. Add quinoa to boiling water, stirring to make sure all of it is moistened. Place on cooler part of grill, cover and cook 20 minutes, checking every few minutes and stirring.

Meanwhile prepare vinaigrette and vegetables. Rinse bell pepper, pierce it on opposite sides with tip of a sharp knife. Place bell pepper on grill rack. Grill until blistered on all sides, turning as needed. Brush vegetables and orange slices with a little vinaigrette. Place vegetables and oranges on grill rack and grill them about 5 minutes on first side or until charred a bit around edges. Turn and grill second side about 5 minutes.

Place bell pepper in ice water to cool, then peel and cut into 1/2-inch pieces. Toss quinoa with a fork to make it fluffy; set aside uncovered to cool to room temperature.

Combine spinach and lettuce in a large bowl. Slice vegetables crosswise into strips. Toss cooled quinoa with spinach and lettuce. Then add vegetable strips. Toss with remaining vinaigrette and serve.   *Makes 6 servings.*

LIME VINAIGRETTE

Whisk all of the ingredients together until smooth.

FRESH TOMATO BASIL SALAD WITH MOZZARELLA CHEESE & GRILLED GARLIC DRESSING

▼▼▼▼▼

This particular salad conjures up very pleasant memories of the first vine-ripened tomatoes out of the garden. Home-grown tomatoes cannot be topped; they have that sweet, full flavor. Grilled or oven-roasted garlic has a mellow aspect that is perfectly wonderful.

When preheating the grill or when grilling other foods, take advantage of the "free" heat and grill oodles of garlic ahead for uses such as this wonderful dressing. You can do several heads at once and store them for later use in a sealed jar in just enough vegetable oil to barely cover.

1 small to medium head garlic
1/4 cup good-quality olive oil, preferably Spanish
2 tablespoons good-quality red wine vinegar
Freshly ground black or mixed peppercorns
1/4 cup coarsely chopped fresh basil
2 large or 4 medium vine-ripened tomatoes
8 ounces good-quality mozzarella cheese, preferably buffalo
Leaf lettuce

Preheat grill to high or 450F (230C) if not already hot. Peel papery outer coating from garlic. Lightly brush with oil and wrap in foil. Place on grill rack. Grill about 1 hour or until garlic is soft when squeezed. Remove from grill and cool.

Chill salad plates. Cut bottom end off garlic head, wasting as little garlic as possible. Using flat side of a heavy knife, such as a chef's knife, on a cutting board, force garlic out of skins by pressing toward cut end. Flesh should easily pop out. Place garlic in a small bowl. Add oil, vinegar, black pepper and basil. Whisk to combine.

Slice tomatoes about 1/2 inch thick and cheese about 1/4 inch thick. Cover chilled salad plates with lettuce, then alternate slices of tomato with cheese and drizzle with dressing.   *Makes 4 to 6 servings.*

HOT-OFF-THE-GRILL RADICCHIO SALAD

▼▼▼▼▼

The bitter, almost strong flavor of fresh radicchio is tamed somewhat by grilling. Most of those I have offered it to are amazed at the simple yet flavorful salad it yields. I only prepare this salad when I already have a hot grill.

2 medium heads radicchio
2 tablespoons good-quality olive oil, preferably Spanish
1/2 teaspoon coarse sea salt
Freshly ground black pepper
1 lime, quartered, or 1 tablespoon balsamic vinegar

Preheat grill to high or 400 to 500F (205 to 260C) if not already hot. Rinse radicchio heads and trim off stems. Then cut each head in half lengthwise through core and brush outside surfaces with a bit of oil. Arrange cut sides down on grill rack and grill 2 minutes. Turn and grill 1 to 2 minutes or until starting to brown and slightly softened. Transfer radicchio to salad plates. Immediately sprinkle with salt, black pepper and a squeeze of lime juice. Serve warm or cold.   *Makes 4 servings.*

CAREN'S CHINESE COLE SLAW, WEST VANCOUVER STYLE

▼▼▼▼▼

This is another wonderful recipe from Caren McSherry Valagos and her Vancouver Cooking School. Use your grill to toast the seeds and nuts while you're grilling an entree.

1/2 cup (3-1/2 oz.) sesame seeds
1/2 cup slivered almonds
1 (2-1/2- to 3-lb.) head green cabbage, shredded
5 green onions, including tender green tops, minced
1/2 cup vegetable oil
1/4 cup sugar
1 teaspoon freshly ground white or black pepper
1 teaspoon salt
1/3 cup rice wine vinegar
2 cups Chinese noodles

Preheat grill to medium or 350F (175C) if not already hot. Place seeds and nuts in a thin pan, such as a pie plate or skillet (without a wooden handle), and toast 5 to 8 minutes, checking frequently until toasted. Set aside.

Place shredded cabbage and onions in a large salad bowl. Whisk together oil, sugar, pepper, salt and vinegar in a small bowl and stir into cabbage mixture. Cover and refrigerate at least 1 hour or up to 3 days.

Just before serving, sprinkle with seeds, nuts and noodles and toss together. *Makes 6 to 8 servings.*

MARINATED GRILLED EGGPLANT SALAD

▼▼▼▼▼

This salad is almost minus calories, depending on how much oil you use. If you use only what I suggest, each serving should be under 50 calories. You can use this as a salad or a vegetable dish. I like it with lamb, such as Roasted Leg of Lamb with Fresh Spinach, Feta & Chipotle Stuffing (page 184) or Shashlik Shish Kabobs (page 186). Plan to cook eggplant so that it will have at least 30 minutes to marinate before serving.

1 medium eggplant, unpeeled, sliced 1/2 inch thick
3/4 teaspoon salt
3 tablespoons good-quality olive oil, preferably Spanish
3 cloves garlic, minced
2 teaspoons crushed caribe chile
1 teaspoon ground Mexican oregano
2 tablespoons red wine vinegar
1 Vidalia or other sweet onion, thinly sliced

About 1 hour before starting to grill, place several layers of paper towels on a baking sheet. Using a meat fork, score entire outside surface of eggplant. Then slice and lightly salt both sides of each slice. Cover with more paper towels. Press down and allow to stand about 1 hour.

Preheat grill to high or 400F (205C) if not already hot. Blot each slice of eggplant, pressing down hard to remove as much moisture as possible from each slice. Arrange eggplant slices on grill rack. Grill 4 to 6 minutes and turn. Grill another 4 to 6 minutes or until each slice is soft, charred around edges and shows grill marks.

Whisk together olive oil, garlic, caribe chile, oregano and vinegar in a small bowl. To marinate, place grilled eggplant slices in a single layer on a plate or platter, brush with dressing and top each slice with an onion slice. Allow to set at room temperature 30 minutes before serving.   *Makes 6 servings.*

QUICK GRILLED ROMAINE
À LA ROMANESQUE SALAD

▼▼▼▼▼

For a delicious and different quick salad, try this one! Use inner leaves of one small Romaine head for every two people. If there is no such thing as a small head at your supermarket, then remove about half of the coarser outer leaves for another salad or stew.

2 small Romaine lettuce hearts
2 tablespoons good-quality olive oil, preferably Spanish
1 tablespoon merlot wine vinegar
Freshly ground black or mixed peppercorns
1 lime, cut lengthwise into quarters

Preheat grill to high or 450F (230C) if not already hot. About 15 minutes before grilling, slice lettuce hearts in half lengthwise through the core, removing bottom of core. Leave lettuce on core for ease in turning. Place on a baking sheet. Whisk oil and wine vinegar together and drizzle over all sides of lettuce. Place lettuce on grill rack. Grill 2 minutes, turn and grill another 2 minutes or until edges turn a bit brown. Sprinkle with pepper and place each half on a salad plate along with a lime quarter. *Makes 4 servings.*

Caesar Salad with Cilantro Cream Dressing

▼▼▼▼▼

This version of Caesar salad has some but not all of the famous Tijuana original's ingredients. Missing are bountiful amounts of olive oil, anchovies and croutons. You can make part of this salad ahead whenever you're using the grill.

1 teaspoon vegetable oil
2 (6-inch) corn tortillas
1/2 cup pepitas
Cilantro Cream Dressing (see below)
2 small or 1 large head Romaine lettuce, rinsed and spun or blotted dry
2 green chiles, parched (page 161), peeled and cut into strips
1/2 cup grated dry white Mexican cheese, feta cheese or Parmesan cheese
1 tablespoon crushed caribe chile or to taste

Cilantro Cream Dressing

1 green chile, parched (page 161), peeled and coarsely chopped
3 large cloves garlic, roasted (page 69) or raw
1 teaspoon ground pure mild New Mexican chile
1/3 cup good-quality olive oil, preferably Spanish
3 tablespoons white wine vinegar
1/2 cup cilantro leaves
1/2 cup fat-free sour cream
1/4 cup plain yogurt

Preheat grill to high or 400F (205C) if not already hot. Meanwhile, lightly oil tortillas on both sides, then slice into 1/4-inch-wide strips. Place strips on a small baking sheet. Place pepitas in a shallow pie plate or skillet without a wood handle. Place baking sheet and skillet on grill rack. Cook tortillas until crisp and lightly toasted, stirring to keep them from sticking together. Toast pepitas 5 to 8 minutes or until they are darkened a bit in color and flavor is heightened. (These ingredients can be prepared up to 5 days ahead of time; store tortilla strips and pepitas in separate airtight jars.)

Divide toasted pepitas, using 1/4 cup in salad dressing. Prepare dressing. Rinse lettuce and cut into 6 wedges and then each in half again, cutting lengthwise through core and leaving core in. Or, tear lettuce into bite-size pieces. Divide torn lettuce or wedges among 6 chilled salad plates or bowls.

To assemble salad, top each lettuce serving with dressing. Crisscross 2 chile strips on top of each serving. Top with equal amounts of tortilla strips, remaining 1/4 cup toasted pepitas and cheese. Sprinkle with caribe.   *Makes 6 servings.*

CILANTRO CREAM DRESSING

Combine green chile, garlic, ground chile, oil and vinegar in a blender jar and process until smooth. Then slowly add cilantro and blend only enough to distribute leaves, not to liquefy them. Pour into a bowl and stir in sour cream and yogurt. Use immediately or cover and refrigerate up to 2 days.

TOMMIE'S TEXAS BLUE CHEESE DRESSING

▼▼▼▼▼

Tommie Kirksmith is a mother, model, horsewoman and lover of animals. A successful author, having written two books about horsemanship with more to come, she finds time in her busy days to create this dressing. Use it on any combination of grilled vegetables instead of the dressing given.

1/4 cup vegetable oil
1/4 cup plus 1 tablespoon good-quality olive oil, preferably Spanish
2 tablespoons apple cider vinegar
2 tablespoons freshly squeezed lemon juice
1/2 teaspoon Worcestershire sauce
1 clove garlic, crushed
1/2 teaspoon salt
Freshly ground black pepper
1/4 teaspoon ground Mexican oregano
1 tablespoon grated Parmesan or Romano cheese or a blend
1 ounce blue cheese, crumbled

Add all ingredients to a jar with a tight-fitting lid. Seal and shake to combine. *Makes 1 cup.*

WINE-BASED LOW-FAT VINAIGRETTE

▼▼▼▼▼

This low-calorie salad dressing is very good for those weight-watching days when eating simple grilled meats and vegetables are in order. Use on any greens or vegetable combination.

1/4 cup dry white wine
2 tablespoons low-sodium chicken broth
1 tablespoon good-quality olive oil, preferably Spanish
1 tablespoon white vinegar
1 tablespoon freshly squeezed lemon juice
1 small green onion, cut into 1-inch lengths
1 clove garlic, peeled
2 teaspoons Dijon mustard
Pinch of salt

Place all ingredients in a blender and process until smooth. This is best if made the day before and refrigerated. *Makes about 1/2 cup or enough for 4 to 6 servings.*

VARIATIONS

Pesto Vinaigrette Add 1 more clove of garlic and 1 cup torn basil leaves.
Herb Vinaigrette Use 1 tablespoon each chopped fresh dill, thyme and tarragon.
Cilantro Lime Vinaigrette Substitute lime for lemon and add 1 cup cilantro leaves.

CREAMY NO-FAT HONEY MUSTARD DRESSING

▼▼▼▼▼

By virtue of fat-free sour cream, you can now make this wonderful Old World dressing.

1/4 cup sweet white wine
1/4 cup low-sodium chicken broth
1 tablespoon red wine vinegar
1 tablespoon freshly squeezed lemon juice
1 small green onion, cut into 1-inch lengths
1 clove garlic, peeled
1 tablespoon Dijon mustard
3 tablespoons honey
Pinch of salt
Freshly ground black pepper
1/2 cup fat-free sour cream

Place all ingredients except sour cream in a blender and process until smooth. Pour into a bowl and stir in sour cream. Allow to set about 1 hour before using to develop flavors. *Makes about 1 cup or enough for 8 to 12 servings.*

Grilled Beef & Lamb

▼▼▼▼▼

Grilled meats are probably the most popular of all grilled foods. There are so many more variations that can add flavor and moisture than many cooks realize.

Marinades are made from an acid-herb mixture with oil added for juiciness. At least 2 hours are needed to marinate and really add flavor. Beef at room temperature absorbs flavors far faster than when refrigerated: In fact, 2 hours at room temperature are the same as overnight in the refrigerator. For convenience, some cuts of meat, such as beef cubes, can be frozen in the marinade.

Bastes are for adding flavor as a meat cooks and must be much thicker so that they will adhere to the outside surface. Bastes have more oil, less acidic ingredients and are loaded with herbs and spices.

GRILLED BARBECUE BURRITOS

▼▼▼▼▼

Burritos feature flour or wheat tortillas, and soft tacos feature corn tortillas. You can use either for this recipe. They make for a wonderful, informal lunch or dinner that can be varied to suit either your taste or what you have on hand!

1 (12-oz.) beef top round or sirloin, sliced 1 to 1-1/2 inches thick
2 teaspoons good-quality olive oil, preferably Spanish
2 cloves garlic, minced
1 tablespoon crushed caribe chile
1/2 teaspoon cumin
1/2 teaspoon Mexican oregano
1 large onion, cut crosswise into about 1/2-inch-thick slices
8 flour tortillas
1 recipe salsa of your choice

Wipe meat with a moist paper towel and then rub with olive oil, garlic, caribe chile, cumin and Mexican oregano. Rub sliced onion with oil. Let stand 1 to 2 hours at room temperature.

Preheat grill to medium-high or 450F (225C). Place rack 3 inches above heat. Arrange onion slices on grill rack. Grill about 6 minutes, turning as needed. Place meat on grill rack. Grill 5 to 6 minutes per side for rare and up to 9 minutes for well done. Grill onions until softened. (If cooking meat until well done, add onion and meat to grill at the same time.)

Heat tortillas briefly on grill rack; keep warm. Thinly slice meat crosswise and cut onion slices in halves. Serve in separate bowls or on platters with the salsa and have guests help themselves, wrapping beef, onion and salsa in tortillas. *Makes 4 servings*.

VARIATION

Pork, sausage (such as Spanish chorizo, Italian or Polish sausage) and chicken can be served the same way.

GORDON'S GRILLED BRISKET

▼▼▼▼▼

Gordon has a well-earned reputation as a brisket cook! He has probably cooked at least a ton of them. Cooked slowly with the rub just as he does, they are fork tender. If desired, you can serve the brisket with your favorite barbecue sauce.

1 (4- to 6-lb.) whole beef brisket
1 recipe Gordon's West Texas–New Mexico Border Rub (page 218)
4 chipotle chiles, reconstituted in an acid-water mix (page 202)
1 onion, sliced 1/4 inch thick

Trim hard fat from outside of brisket, leaving soft fat. Lightly rub entire surface with rub, taking care to coat it uniformly but not too heavily, or it could get salty and too strongly flavored.

Preheat grill to medium or 350F (175C). Place rack 5 inches above heat. If using charcoal, create two banks of coals for an indirect fire. If using electric or gas, then use the heating units at the sides only, not the middle, for best cooking. Spread out a piece of heavy-duty foil large enough to seal brisket. Cut chipotle chiles in halves and place 2 chipotle chiles well apart on foil. Top with brisket, then onion and remaining chipotle chiles, placing them in areas different from those of bottom ones. Seal foil with a druggist's wrap, which is made by folding two top sides together and rolling down. Allow a bit of an air vent on top for steam to escape. Then fold up ends. Place on grill rack and roast 2-1/2 to 3 hours, then check for doneness by unwrapping at top seal and sticking a meat fork into meat. The fork should go through the brisket easily when done. If using charcoal, be sure to replenish hot coals two or three times. Let brisket rest 20 minutes before slicing. Cut across the grain into thin slices. *Makes 10 to 12 servings.*

Grilled Pacific Rim Steaks

▼▼▼▼▼

Just the addition of Chinese five-spice powder and ginger makes this steak special. It's quick and fast too. Serve with quinoa or rice and grilled vegetables.

2 tablespoons coarsely cracked black or mixed peppercorns
1 teaspoon coarse salt
1 tablespoon five-spice powder
2 tablespoons crushed red caribe chile
1-1/2 teaspoons ground ginger
1 (1-1/2-lb.) beef sirloin steak, 2 inches thick

Mix all the spices together, making a Chinese-style rub. Rub mixture over whole surface of steak and allow to stand at room temperature 30 minutes to 1 hour.

Preheat grill to highest heat or broil setting, using hardwood charcoal if possible. Place rack about 4 inches above heat. When fire is hot, place steak on rack and grill 5 to 6 minutes per side for rare, which is preferred. Grill longer for medium or well-cooked.

Remove meat from grill and allow to rest about 20 minutes. Cut into paper-thin slices and serve immediately. *Makes 6 servings.*

Fajitas with Onion & Tricolored Peppers

▼▼▼▼▼

Fajitas are now one of the most popular restaurant entrees, not only in Southwestern restaurants but in contemporary chains as well. They are best when the beef is grilled whole and sliced afterward. If outdoor grilling is out of the question due to weather or other limitations, they can be pan broiled indoors.

3 tablespoons freshly squeezed lime juice
8 cloves garlic, minced
3 to 4 tablespoons good-quality olive oil, preferably Spanish
Freshly ground black pepper
2 pounds beef bottom round or sirloin tip steaks, 1/4 to 3/8 inch thick
1 large red onion, halved crosswise
1 each red, green and yellow bell pepper, each cut into 8 wedges
12 to 18 (6-inch) flour tortillas, warmed
1 recipe Aztec-Style Pico de Gallo with Chipotles (page 202)
1/2 cup sour cream (optional)

Combine lime juice, garlic, 2 tablespoons of the olive oil and black pepper in a shallow bowl or heavy plastic bag. Pound meat to tenderize it and then place slices in bag. Allow to marinate at room temperature at least 30 minutes or meat can be frozen or refrigerated in marinade. Meanwhile place onion and bell peppers on long skewers. Very lightly brush cut sides of onion with oil and whole surface of pepper pieces.

Preheat grill to medium-high or 450F (230C) and place rack 4 inches above heat. To cook, place onion and pepper skewers on rack and grill until charred and softened, turning as needed. When vegetables are about done, place beef strips on rack and grill 1 to 2 minutes per side.

To serve, slice beef and vegetables into strips about 1/2 inch wide. Serve in warm tortillas with Pico de Gallo and sour cream, if desired. *Makes 6 to 8 servings.*

DALLAS-STYLE GRILLED FLANK STEAK

▼▼▼▼▼

Flank steak is so easy to serve, it tends to be a pet of the barbecue bunch. Do remember some cardinal rules: Flank steak is very tough unless marinated in an acidic marinade and cooked only until medium rare at most —never well done.

1/2 cup red wine
1/4 cup finely minced onion
3 cloves garlic, minced
2 tablespoons Worcestershire sauce
1 teaspoon dry mustard
1 tablespoon freshly squeezed lime juice
2 tablespoons crushed pequin chiles or other very hot chiles
1 (1-1/2-lb.) beef flank steak
1 recipe salsa of your choice (optional)

Combine wine, onion, garlic, Worcestershire sauce, mustard, lime juice and chiles in a shallow bowl or a heavy plastic bag. Trim any excess fat or sinew from outside of steak and then place steak in marinade, turning to coat both sides. Cover and refrigerate overnight or up to 3 days. You can freeze steak in the marinade if you wish.

Preheat grill to medium-high or 450F (230C). Place rack 3 inches above heat. Lightly brush rack with oil and place steak on rack. Grill steak 3 to 5 minutes per side or until browned on outside and rare to medium rare on inside. Remove from grill and allow to stand about 20 minutes. Cut on the diagonal into thin slices. Serve with salsa, if desired. *Makes 4 servings.*

Grilled Burgers

▼▼▼▼▼

I think hardwood-grilled hamburgers, charred and crusty on the outside and juicy on the inside, are hard to beat. They're fast, versatile and fun to serve.

1 pound lean ground beef, as freshly ground as possible
Salt and freshly ground black pepper (optional)
4 hamburger buns
4 onion slices
4 tomato slices
Lettuce leaves

Preheat grill to medium-high or 450F (230C). Place rack 4 inches from heat. Mix meat with salt and pepper in a large bowl, if desired. Shape into 4 flat patties, handling meat as little as possible. Lightly brush rack with oil and place burgers on rack. Grill 5 to 6 minutes. Turn and grill 3 to 4 minutes or until browned on outside and medium inside. Grill buns, cut sides down, until toasted. Top each bun with a burger, onion, tomato and lettuce.   *Makes 4 servings.*

Variations

Hamburger Harry's North-of-the-Border Burgers
Two minutes before last side of burgers is done, top each with 1 slice Cheddar cheese and a piece of lightly grilled Canadian bacon. Grill just until cheese begins to melt.

My Pecos River Café Burger
Two minutes before burgers are done, top each with a slice of Monterey Jack cheese; 2 crisp bacon strips; 1 green chile, parched (page 161), peeled, opened and seeds removed; and a grilled medium-thick onion slice. Cook just until cheese melts.

New Mexican Burgers
Before toasting buns, lightly spread cut sides with soft unsalted butter, then sprinkle with dried or fresh tarragon and basil. About 3 to 4 minutes before burgers are done, place buns on grill to toast. If desired, top burgers with Jack, Cheddar or Swiss cheese. Serve with Sunny Salsa (page 205).

GRILLED TENDERLOIN À LA HOUSTON JET SET

▼▼▼▼▼

Very tender and flavorful, tenderloin is a wonderful entree. The bacon keeps the outside edges from getting too dry. The grilled mushrooms make a perfect garnish. All you need is your favorite grilled vegetables and perhaps a crisp green tartly dressed salad and some freshly baked crusty bread for a memorable special dinner.

1 (4- to 5-lb.) whole beef tenderloin
1 cup dry red wine
1/2 cup minced onion
2 bay leaves
1/4 cup plus 1 teaspoon good-quality olive oil, preferably Spanish
3 cloves garlic, minced
1 tablespoon hot grated horseradish
1 teaspoon crushed pequin chiles or to taste
1 tablespoon Worcestershire sauce
About 6 thick slices bacon
8 to 10 large shiitake or other meaty mushrooms, stems removed

Combine wine, onion, bay leaves, 1/4 cup olive oil, garlic, horseradish, pequin chiles and Worcestershire sauce in a shallow bowl or a heavy plastic bag. Trim any excess fat from outside of steak and then place steak in marinade, turning to coat both sides. Cover and refrigerate overnight.

Preheat grill to high or broil, or 550F (270C). While grill is heating, using wooden picks to secure ends, wrap bacon around beef, allowing about 1 inch or more between pieces of bacon. Place steak on rack. Grill about 5 minutes per side or until browned on outside and rare to medium on inside.

Brush mushrooms with remaining olive oil and place on rack when steak is turned. If bacon becomes too browned, place foil over it or discard bacon if not desired. Grill mushrooms until softened and keep warm. Remove steak from grill and allow to stand about 20 minutes. Cut on the diagonal into thin slices and serve with mushrooms on the side. *Makes 8 to 10 servings.*

Jane's Special Lamb Chops

▼▼▼▼▼

Very easy and oh so delicious! We have these when we want a satisfying quick dinner.

4 to 6 lamb chops, either rib or loin, cut at least 1 inch thick
4 cloves garlic, minced
2 teaspoons good-quality olive oil, preferably Spanish
1 tablespoon fresh minced rosemary leaves, or 1-1/2 teaspoons dried rosemary
1 tablespoon crushed caribe chile
Jalapeño jelly, preferably homemade

Trim any hard fat from around the edge of each chop. Combine garlic, olive oil, rosemary and caribe chile in a small bowl. Spread garlic mixture thinly over surface of each chop. Allow to stand about 30 minutes.

Preheat grill to high or broil, or 550F (270C). Place rack 3 to 4 inches above heat. Place chops on rack. Grill about 4 minutes per side or until browned on outside and rare to medium on inside.   *Makes 2 to 3 servings.*

Grilled Leg of Lamb à la Grecque

▼▼▼▼▼

I've long loved leg of lamb. Served with grilled fennel, carrots and potatoes, it's marvelous and often frequents our Easter table.

1 (4- to 5-lb.) whole leg of lamb, butterflied and trimmed of hard fat and parchment-like covering
8 cloves garlic, minced
3 tablespoons freshly squeezed lemon juice
3 to 4 tablespoons virgin olive oil, preferably Greek
2 tablespoons fresh mint leaves or 2 teaspoons dried mint
2 tablespoons fresh oregano or 2 teaspoons dried oregano
Freshly ground black pepper
2 heads fennel, quartered
8 to 10 carrots, halved
10 medium new potatoes, halved lengthwise

Have butcher debone leg, telling him not to tie it. Combine garlic, lemon juice and 2 tablespoons of the olive oil in a small bowl. Spread half of mixture over inside surface of lamb, reserving remainder for outside. Place mint and oregano leaves inside lamb, roll and tie together with kitchen twine. Then, apply remaining garlic mixture. Season with black pepper. Allow to stand 2 hours at room temperature or overnight in the refrigerator.

Preheat grill to medium-high or 450F (230C). If using charcoal, create two banks of coals for an indirect fire. If using electric or gas, then use the heating units at the sides only, not the middle, for best cooking. Place rack about 6 inches above heat. Roast 1 hour.

Lightly brush vegetables with remaining olive oil and place on rack, covering grill if possible. Cook lamb until it reaches desired doneness or about 1-1/2 hours total cooking time for medium-rare, turning after 45 minutes. Grill vegetables until fork tender, turning as they cook. If using charcoal, replenish hot coals after 1 hour. Allow roast to stand about 20 minutes before carving. *Makes 8 to 10 servings.*

GRILLED NEW YORK STRIPS WITH PEPPERCORN-ROASTED GARLIC BASTE

▼▼▼▼▼

To make preparation of these steaks super simple, plan ahead and have a supply of roasted garlic already done and holding in the refrigerator.

4 (8- to 10-oz.) beef top loin steaks (New York strip), about 1-1/2 inches thick
1 garlic head, roasted (page 69)
1 teaspoon each freshly cracked rose, green, and white peppercorns
1 tablespoon good-quality olive oil, preferably Spanish

Trim any excess fat from edges of steaks. To prepare baste, slice root end off garlic and using flat side of a heavy knife, force garlic cloves out of head by pressing toward cut end. Combine garlic, pepper and oil in a small bowl. Spread garlic mixture evenly over both sides of steaks. Let stand about 30 minutes.

Preheat grill to high or 400 (205C). Place rack 3 to 4 inches above heat. Place steaks on rack. Grill 8 to 10 minutes per side for medium rare. *Makes 4 servings.*

MYSTERY MARINATED CHUCK ROAST

▼▼▼▼▼

This rather complex marinating mixture really soaks into chuck and almost gives it a German flavor. Amazingly, lowly chuck takes on an uncharacteristic elegance.

1/2 cup finely minced onion
1 teaspoon dry mustard
1 teaspoon salt
Freshly ground black pepper
1 teaspoon sugar
1/4 cup soy sauce
1/4 cup good-quality olive oil, preferably Spanish
1/4 cup red wine vinegar
2 tablespoons chutney, any kind
4 cloves garlic, chopped
1 (4- to 4-1/2-lb.) boneless beef chuck roast, trimmed of excess fat

Combine all ingredients except roast in a shallow bowl large enough to hold roast or in a heavy plastic bag. Place roast in marinade and coat whole surface. Cover and refrigerate 3 days, turning twice a day.

Preheat grill to medium-high or 400F (205C). If using charcoal, create two banks of coals for an indirect fire. If using electric or gas, then use the heating units at the sides only, not the middle, for best cooking. Place rack 4 to 6 inches above heat. Place beef on rack, cover, and roast 1-1/4 hours for medium-rare, when it will be the most tender, turning once. If using charcoal, replenish hot coals after 1 hour. Allow roast to stand about 20 minutes before carving. *Makes 8 servings*.

GORDON'S SPECIAL NEW YORK STEAK WITH GRILLED ONIONS, LEEKS & MUSHROOMS

▼▼▼▼▼

This fast and easy steak is wonderful! Of course you can vary the vegetables, but leeks are so delicious, it's no wonder they're the national veggie of Wales.

4 (8- to 10-oz.) beef top loin steaks (New York strip), about 1-1/2 inches thick
1 tablespoon good-quality olive oil, preferably Spanish
Few drops Worcestershire sauce
2 tablespoons freshly cracked green or black peppercorns
1 large Spanish onion, cut into 1/2-inch-thick slices
3 or 4 leeks, trimmed and rinsed (page 228)
6 to 8 medium mushrooms
1 tablespoon sesame oil

Trim any excess fat from steaks and pat dry. Lightly rub each side with olive oil and Worcestershire sauce, then sprinkle with pepper. Let set at least 30 minutes. Arrange each vegetable on a separate skewer, then sprinkle with sesame oil.

Preheat grill to very high or broil, or 550F (275C). Place grill rack 3 to 4 inches above heat. Place onion and leeks on rack and grill about 5 minutes. Add mushrooms. Add steaks and grill about 10 minutes for rare or to desired doneness, turning steaks and mushrooms after 5 minutes. Continue grilling until onions and leeks are tender, steak reaches desired doneness and mushrooms are tender. Serve steak with onions, leeks and mushrooms arranged over the steak. *Makes 2 servings.*

Grilled Porterhouse Steak, Corpus Christi Style

▼▼▼▼▼

Really good aged porterhouse steak is difficult to come by, but when you do, nothing could be better. Hailing from South Texas, where my mother was born, chipotle marinade is a favorite of those who like spicy heat with smoky overtones.

2 (12- to 16-oz.) porterhouse steaks, cut at least 1-1/2 inches thick or thicker
2 tablespoons reconstituted dried chipotles (page 202)
1 tablespoon freshly squeezed lime juice
4 cloves garlic, minced

Trim any excess hard fat from edges of steaks. Mince chipotles and combine with remaining ingredients in a small bowl. Stir into a thick paste. Rub paste evenly over both sides of steaks. Let stand about 30 minutes.

Preheat grill to very high or broil, or 550F (275C). Place rack about 3 inches above heat. Place steaks on rack and grill 5 to 6 minutes per side for rare or to desired doneness. *Makes 2 to 4 servings.*

Roast on the Rocks

▼▼▼▼▼

This method of roasting is a great one to know, especially if you are camping or cooking out and have very limited facilities. It tastes great, too.

1/4 cup bourbon or orange juice
1 (3- to 3-1/2-lb.) beef sirloin tip roast
1 teaspoon dry mustard
2 tablespoons freshly cracked black or mixed peppercorns

Drizzle bourbon evenly over surface of roast. Combine mustard and pepper and rub over roast. Let stand, covered, at least 1 hour.

Build a good-size fire with charcoal briquettes or hardwood. When fire is well established and coals are covered with a white ash, arrange them in a mound slightly larger than roast. Place meat directly on briquettes and roast about 30 minutes. Turn meat and roast 30 minutes more. Rotate meat to another side and roast another 30 minutes. Check for doneness with a meat thermometer: 140F (60C) for rare and 160F (70C) for medium. If no thermometer is available, insert a sharp knife into roast until it reaches the middle and check for doneness. This roast is best served rare to medium. Allow to stand about 20 minutes before carving.   *Makes 8 to 10 servings.*

GRILLED SHORT RIBS, NEW MEXICO STYLE

▼▼▼▼▼

The marinade helps tenderize the short ribs and also adds a spicy flavor.

1-1/2 cups dry red wine
2 tablespoons good-quality olive oil, preferably Spanish
1/2 cup finely chopped Spanish onion
4 cloves garlic, minced
1 teaspoon salt
Freshly ground black pepper
2 bay leaves
3 tablespoons ground pure New Mexico chile
1/2 teaspoon ground cumin
1/2 teaspoon ground Mexican oregano
6 to 7 pounds meaty short ribs, trimmed

Combine all ingredients except ribs in a shallow bowl or heavy plastic bag large enough to hold ribs. Stir to mix well. Add ribs and stir to coat evenly. Cover and marinate 2 hours or overnight.

Preheat grill to medium or 350F (175C). If using charcoal, create two banks of coals for an indirect fire. If using electric or gas, then use the heating units at the sides only, not the middle, for best cooking. Place rack 6 to 8 inches above heat. Drain ribs, reserving marinade. Arrange ribs in center of grill, cover and cook about 20 minutes, then turn ribs and keep turning about every 10 minutes, basting with reserved marinade. Cook about 1 hour total or until ribs are browned on outside and slightly pink on inside. If you want them well done, reduce heat to low [220 to 225F (110C)] and continue cooking.   *Makes 8 to 10 servings.*

SOUTHWEST STACK & RACK

▼▼▼▼▼

This winning recipe was developed by Walter Weaver for a barbecue contest conducted by my former employer, Public Service Company of New Mexico. He won first place in 1976. The recipe is a good one to cook for an early evening or Sunday afternoon barbecue, as it takes 40 minutes of cooking time. Because of its heartiness and appetite-building aroma, it is great for serving at athletic events—tailgate parties, hunting brunches, Super Bowl Sunday, etc.

2 pounds extra-lean ground beef
1 pound lean pork sausage
1 teaspoon salt
1 teaspoon freshly ground black pepper
1 tablespoon Worcestershire sauce
1 pound green chiles, parched (page 161), peeled and cut into 1-inch strips or 4
    (4-oz.) cans whole green chiles, drained and cut into 1-inch strips
3 cups thinly sliced onions (3 to 4 large onions)
2 pounds thinly sliced bacon

Preheat grill to medium-high or about 450F (225C). Place grill rack 6 to 8 inches above heat. Mix together beef, sausage, salt, pepper and Worcestershire sauce in a medium bowl. On a waxed paper square on a cutting board, pat meat mixture into a 9-inch square, about 3/4 inch thick.

On top side of meat, arrange a layer of green chiles, onion slices and bacon, using half of each. Then place a wire rack on top of bacon and turn over, firmly grasping rack, meat and board. Evenly cover other side of meat with remaining chiles, onion slices and bacon. Place another wire rack on top and secure the two racks together in several places with thin wire, tucking in the ends of the bacon.

Place meat on grill rack and grill about 20 minutes or until browned. Turn meat and cover grill. Cook about 20 minutes or until browned and juices run clear when a knife is inserted in center. To serve, remove wire racks, cut into serving pieces and serve as desired. *Makes 8 to 12 servings.*

Grilled Pork

▼▼▼▼▼

The most popular grilled pork dish—barbecued spareribs—is also one of America's favorite dishes. Ribs have long been popular with barbecue sauce, of which there are so many variations—somewhat sweet, somewhat tart, maybe smoky or hot, with lots of mustard, runny to thick, and on and on. Pit masters and amateur cooks alike boast of their prowess with barbecue and fiercely defend their recipes and techniques. So much so that there are a number of annual barbecue rib burnoffs, or competitions, at various times and cities across the United States.

When grilling lean pork, such as the loin, always marinate and/or baste and use moist or quick-cooking techniques to ensure that the pork will not be overly dry and flavorless.

MESQUITE-GRILLED LEMON RUBBED RIBS

▼▼▼▼▼

These ribs are great served without barbecue sauce; however, if you prefer, serve with your favorite homemade or commercial sauce. I like to serve these with either baked sweet potatoes or white potatoes and cole slaw. A potato salad is also good.

4 pounds pork spareribs, well trimmed and cut into 2- to 4-rib portions
1/2 Fresh Lemon Zest Chile-Herb Rub (page 216)
2 lemons, thinly sliced and seeds removed
2 medium onions, peeled and thinly sliced

Rub ribs with rub, being careful to distribute rub evenly. Let stand at least 30 minutes or refrigerate overnight.

Preheat grill to high or broil, or 500F (260C). Place rack 4 to 5 inches above heat. Place ribs on rack. Grill 2 minutes on each side. Reduce heat to medium or 350F (175C). Place half of lemon and onion slices on top side of ribs. Grill 12 to 15 minutes. Just before turning, remove lemon and onion slices and place on a pan or plate and keep warm on side of grill or in an oven. Turn ribs and top with remaining lemon and onion slices. Grill 12 to 15 minutes more or until a knife inserted in meatiest portion reveals firm, white not soft, pink meat or internal temperature is 170F (75C). Serve garnished with the lemon and onion slices. If using sauce, serve with warm sauce. *Makes 4 to 6 servings.*

VARIATION

Rio Rancho Ribs with Barbecue Sauce
Decrease rub by half. Omit onions and lemons. Baste with your favorite sauce 3 to 5 minutes before ribs are done.

JAMAICAN JERK–RUBBED GRILLED PORK RIBS

▼▼▼▼▼

The heavily spiced jerk seasoning blend that has become so popular lately was developed by runaway slaves in the Caribbean. They found that the spicy blend kept pork fresh for several days, whereas otherwise it would not keep.

1/3 cup water
2 tablespoons rum
2 tablespoons ground allspice
1-1/2 teaspoons ground cinnamon
1 tablespoon ground coriander
3/4 teaspoon ground nutmeg
2 teaspoons ground turmeric
6 green onions, thinly sliced
3 cloves garlic, minced
1 fresh habanero (Scotch Bonnet) chile, minced or 1/2 to 1 teaspoon dried habanero
    chile, or, for milder heat, 1 teaspoon crushed pequin quebrado chile
1 teaspoon salt
3 pounds meaty country-style pork ribs

Combine all the ingredients except the ribs in a blender in the order given. Process until blended, scraping down sides of bowl as necessary. Trim ribs of excess fat. Place ribs in a large, flat glass baking dish and, using a rubber scraper and tongs or rubber gloves, carefully coat both sides of ribs. Once covered with paste, refrigerate several hours or overnight or freeze up to 1 month in a heavy plastic bag or freezer container.

Preheat grill to very high or broil, or 550F (270C). Place rack 4 inches above heat. Arrange ribs on rack. Grill 15 to 20 minutes per side or until a knife inserted in meatiest portion reveals firm, white not soft, pink meat or internal temperature is 170F (75C). *Makes 6 to 8 servings.*

GRILLED CAJUN-STYLE RIBS

▼▼▼▼▼

These blackened ribs get their fire from the Cajun rub. With the spicier rub, most do not serve these with barbecue sauce, but you may.

4 to 5 pounds pork spareribs
1 recipe Cajun Rub (page 216)

Trim excess fat from ribs, then cut into serving portions of 1 to 2 ribs each. Rub ribs with rub, being careful to distribute rub evenly. Let stand 30 minutes.

Preheat grill to high or 500F (260C). Place rack 4 or 5 inches above heat. If using charcoal, create two banks of coals for an indirect fire. If using electric or gas, then use the heating units at the sides only, not the middle, for best cooking. Place ribs on rack over coals. Grill 2 minutes on each side. Reduce heat to medium or 350F (175C). If cooking with charcoal, raise rack to reduce heat. Move ribs to center of rack and grill 20 minutes. Turn and grill another 20 minutes or until a knife inserted in meatiest portion reveals firm, white not soft, pink meat or internal temperature is 170F (75C). *Makes 6 to 8 servings.*

GRILLED PORK CHOPS WITH CARAMELIZED ONIONS & ORANGE SALSA

▼▼▼▼▼

Onions and oranges are traditional complements to pork. Here their flavors are accented with the richness of sherry.

4 (1/2-inch-thick) pork chops
1 teaspoon vegetable oil
4 sprigs fresh sage or 1-1/2 teaspoons rubbed sage
Freshly ground black or green pepper
1 large yellow or white onion, unpeeled and halved
1/4 cup sherry
2 seedless oranges
3 cloves garlic, roasted (page 69)
2 tablespoons crushed caribe chile
1/2 teaspoon salt or to taste

Trim excess fat from edges of chops, leaving at least a 1/4-inch layer around sides. Lightly oil both sides of each pork chop. Then crush sage between your palms and rub over each side. Season with pepper.

Preheat grill to medium or 350F (175C). Place rack 4 inches above heat. Lightly oil cut sides of onion and place on rack, cut sides down. Add pork chops to rack. Grill onions and chops 5 minutes. Turn onion and chops and grill 5 minutes or until onion is softened and chops are browned and centers are light pink or 160F (70C). Remove onion and set aside to cool. Place chops in a baking pan and drizzle with sherry. Cover and set on side of grill to keep warm.

Meanwhile, zest 1 orange to yield 2 teaspoons zest; set zest aside. Peel both oranges, making certain that no white pith remains. Cut oranges into sections, cutting between membranes. Cut each section into halves or thirds to make 1/2-inch pieces. Peel and chop onion into 1/2-inch pieces. Slice tip off each garlic clove. Squeeze flesh out of its casing and mince. Combine oranges, grilled onion, garlic, orange zest, chile and salt in a medium bowl. Taste and adjust seasonings. Arrange pork chops on warmed plate and top with orange salsa.   *Makes 2 to 4 servings.*

GRILLED SALSA-MARINATED PORK CHOPS

▼▼▼▼▼

This super-quick and easy recipe combines the flavors of the Southwest with a touch of Spain in the orange marmalade. Any favorite rice dish, a fruit and green salad with a tart dressing and a bread or dessert will make for a very satisfying yet easy dinner.

2/3 cup salsa, preferably a thick homemade one, such as Sunny Salsa (page 205) or a thick commercial one with a tomato base
2 tablespoons orange marmalade
4 (1/2-inch-thick) loin pork chops, trimmed of excess fat

Combine 1/3 cup of the salsa with marmalade in a shallow glass or stainless steel bowl. Place chops in bowl, pressing chops into the marinade and turning and pressing again. Let stand at room temperature at least 1 hour or cover and refrigerate overnight.

Preheat grill to medium-high or 450F (230C). Place rack 4 inches above heat. Remove chops from marinade, reserving marinade. Place chops on rack and spoon half of marinade over chops; reserve remaining marinade. Grill about 4 minutes. Turn and spoon remaining marinade over chops. Grill 4 minutes or until browned and centers are light pink or 160F (70C). Serve with remaining salsa.   *Makes 2 to 4 servings.*

GRILLED PORK STEAK WITH APPLES & ONIONS

▼▼▼▼▼

My mother always loved this combination. She thought pork deserved apples one way or another and felt that sage and onion were great additions. One of the sweet potato recipes (pages 222 and 223) could complete the meal.

4 (1/2- to 3/4-inch-thick) pork shoulder steaks, trimmed of excess fat
4 sprigs fresh sage, minced, or 1 teaspoon ground dried sage
1 teaspoon vegetable oil
1 large onion, cut crosswise into 1/2-inch-thick rounds
4 cooking apples, peeled, cored and cut into 1/2-inch-thick slices
1/2 cup sherry or applejack
Freshly ground nutmeg
Salt and freshly ground black pepper

Preheat grill to medium or 350F (175C). Place rack 4 inches above heat. Season steaks with sage. Lightly brush onion and apples with oil.

Arrange steaks and onion on rack; grill 12 to 15 minutes. Turn steaks and onion. Add apples to a vegetable holder or skewers and place on rack. Grill 12 to 15 minutes or until onion and apples are tender and steaks are browned and centers are light pink or 160F (70C).

As foods are done, place in a large skillet that can be used on the grill. When everything is done and in the skillet, pour sherry over contents, cover and steam 5 to 7 minutes over low heat of grill. Serve steaks smothered with onion and apple slices. *Makes 4 servings.*

GRILLED LOIN OF PORK WITH CHIPOTLE MARINADE

▼▼▼▼▼

The smoky blend of chipotle and grilled or roasted garlic of this heavenly loin makes your mouth water. Garden fresh basil and red ripe tomatoes provide a wonderful finish for sauce.

1 large head garlic, roasted (page 69) and minced
3 large dried chipotle chiles, reconstituted with 1/2 cup water and 2 tablespoons
    balsamic vinegar (page 202)
2 cups peeled and chopped tomatoes
1/4 cup coarsely chopped fresh basil
1 (2-1/2-lb.) pork loin roast

Grill garlic and reconstitute chiles. When chipotles are soft, chop finely, reserving juice. Measure 3 tablespoons chiles and 1/4 cup of juice; combine in a medium bowl. Add garlic, tomatoes and basil to chiles. Place roast in a glass baking dish. Pour marinade over roast and turn to coat evenly. Marinate 1 hour.

Preheat grill to medium-high or 400F (260C). Place rack 5 inches above heat. If using charcoal, create two banks of coals for an indirect fire. If using electric or gas, then use the heating units at the sides only, not the middle, for best cooking. Place roast on rack over coals. Grill 3 minutes on each side. Reduce heat to medium or 300F (150C). If cooking with charcoal, raise rack to reduce heat. Move roast to center of rack and roast 35 minutes. Turn and roast another 20 minutes or until meat reaches an internal temperature of 160F (70C) or is firm and juicy not soft and pink when pierced with a knife. Simmer marinade until reduced by half and serve over slices of roast. *Makes 8 to 10 servings.*

NOTE: Because the roast is relatively small, you can use the rest of the grill space for grilling vegetables, bread or even a dessert like Low-Fat Banana Zucchini Cake (page 254).

GRILLED PORK PINWHEELS WITH FENNEL SALSA

▼▼▼▼▼

These are very pretty and low in fat and calories. What more could you ask of so easy a dish?

1 tablespoon plus 2 teaspoons good-quality olive oil, preferably Spanish
1 bulb fennel, tops removed and base chopped into 1/2-inch pieces
1 large sweet red bell pepper, parched (page 161), peeled and cut into 1/2-inch squares
3 cloves garlic, minced
1 medium onion, cut into 1/2-inch pieces
1 cup cooked black beans, drained
2 fresh jalapeño chiles, seeds and veins removed and finely chopped
3/4 teaspoon salt or to taste
2 (about 1-lb.) pork tenderloins, trimmed
1 teaspoon lemon zest
1 sprig fresh thyme, minced, or 1 teaspoon dried thyme
Freshly ground black or white pepper

Heat 2 tablespoons of the olive oil in a heavy skillet over medium heat. Add fennel and cook, stirring occasionally, until slightly soft, 3 to 5 minutes. Add bell pepper, garlic and onion and cook about 3 minutes or until they begin to soften. Remove skillet from heat and stir in beans and chiles. Add salt if desired.

Using a sharp knife, slice each tenderloin in half lengthwise, cutting almost to the opposite side. Flatten out between 2 sheets of plastic wrap and pound with a mallet or rolling pin until each becomes uniformly thin, about 1/4 inch thick.

Preheat grill to medium or 350F (175C). Place rack 4 inches above heat. Divide fennel mixture between the tenderloins, spreading it to within 1 inch of edges of each. Roll each and tie with kitchen twine.

Brush each rolled tenderloin lightly with remaining oil. Sprinkle each with lemon zest, thyme and black pepper. Place on rack and sear each side, turning after about 10 minutes. Cover grill and cook about 10 minutes or until pork reaches an internal temperature of 160F (70C) or until meat in center is white, firm and juicy, not pink and soft. Let stand at least 5 minutes for juices to settle, then slice and serve. *Makes 6 to 8 servings.*

LEMON-BASTED PORK TENDERLOIN ROUNDS WITH WILTED SPINACH & PECANS

▼▼▼▼▼

This is both pretty and delicious. The toasted pecans add a nice crunch.

2 teaspoons olive oil
1 (1-lb.) pork tenderloin, trimmed and cut crosswise into 8 pieces
1 teaspoon lemon zest
2 tablespoons freshly squeezed lemon juice
1 teaspoon crushed pequin quebrado chile
2 tablespoons chopped pecans
4 green onions, 2 sliced into thin rounds and 2 cut into thin slices for garnish
1 pound fresh spinach, thoroughly rinsed and stems discarded
8 lemon slice twists

Preheat grill to medium or 350F (175C). Place rack 4 inches above heat. Rub 1 teaspoon of the olive oil over both sides of each slice of pork. Heat remaining olive oil in a large, heavy skillet on grill or stovetop. Add lemon zest, juice, pequin quebrado and pecans and cook 3 to 5 minutes or until pecans begin to toast. Remove pecans to a small dish. Add chopped green onions and spinach to skillet. Place pork rounds on rack. Grill 3 to 5 minutes per side or until it reaches an internal temperature of 160F (70C). Cook spinach, stirring occasionally, and remove when well wilted.

To serve, place a bed of spinach on each of 4 plates. Top each serving with 2 slices of pork, green onion slices and 2 lemon twists. Sprinkle with pecans and serve. *Makes 4 servings.*

SAKE-MARINATED GRILLED PORK TENDERLOIN WITH MUSHROOMS

▼▼▼▼▼

This oriental-inspired marinade and sauce is definitely influenced by fusion cooking—a style incorporating ideas from several of the world's cuisines—and has become ever more popular in the Southwest. The sauce is good spooned over any starchy side dish such as rice, grilled potatoes or pasta.

2 tablespoons soy sauce
1-1/2 teaspoons Dijon mustard
1 (2-1/2-lb.) pork loin roast, trimmed
3/4 cup sliced mushrooms, preferably shiitake or brown mushrooms
1/3 cup sake
2 green onions, thinly sliced (using only tender part of beginning of green tops)
1 teaspoon crushed caribe chile

Combine soy sauce with mustard in a small bowl. Rub over surface of roast and let stand in a plate or shallow bowl about 1 hour at room temperature.

Preheat grill to medium or 350F (175C). Place rack 5 inches above heat. If using charcoal, create two banks of coals for an indirect fire. If using electric or gas, then use the heating units at the sides only, not the middle, for best cooking. Place roast in center of rack. Cover grill and roast about 1 hour, turning every 20 minutes. The roast is done when browned on outside, only slightly pink in center and firm to the touch or when center reaches a temperature of 160F (70C).

Meanwhile, using a shallow skillet on the grill or on stovetop, heat reserved marinade and add mushrooms, sake, green onions and chile. Heat until mushrooms and onions are soft, about 5 minutes. Let roast stand 20 minutes. Cut into thin slices and serve with sauce.   *Makes 8 to 10 servings.*

Grilled Poultry

▼▼▼▼▼

Poultry takes to the grill quite well. With low fat content and quick cooking as frequent goals, chicken parts, such as boneless, skinless breasts or thighs, are good choices because of their adaptability to many cooking methods. Turkey tenders or breast can be substituted for chicken in any of the following recipes. Grilled vegetables are always great with the chicken or duck. Pasta is a perfect partner and can even be cooked on the grill, particularly if you have a side burner.

SAGE & LEMON CHILE CHICKEN

▼▼▼▼▼

This delicious and flavorful chicken is fast and easy to do. For the best flavor, do not skimp on fresh ingredients!

2 tablespoons good-quality olive oil, preferably Spanish
4 cloves garlic, peeled
1/4 cup fresh sage, minced
1/4 cup freshly squeezed lemon juice
1 red or green (or half of each) jalapeño chile
1 (3-lb.) chicken, trimmed of excess fat and pin feathers

Using a mini food processor or a blender, puree olive oil, garlic, sage, lemon juice and chile until thick. Rinse chicken and cut into quarters. Place in a glass baking dish. Spoon puree over whole surface of each piece; let stand 30 minutes. Turn chicken and spoon any excess mixture over flesh side of each piece.

Preheat grill to medium or 350F (175C). Place rack 4 inches above heat. Arrange chicken on grill, skin side down. Grill until browned, 15 to 18 minutes. Turn and brown other side, basting with any drippings remaining in baking dish. Reduce heat to low or 250F (120C) and grill until drumsticks move easily, a knife inserted in thickest part of flesh yields clear juice and a meat thermometer inserted in fleshiest portion registers 185F (85C). Total cooking time is 45 to 60 minutes. *Makes 2 to 4 servings.*

GRILLED ROSEMARY GARLIC CHICKEN BREASTS

▼▼▼▼▼

These are favorites to serve with pasta. I like to prepare them on evenings when I want a fast meal that is on the lighter side. If serving with pasta, heat water about the time you light the grill. Start pasta cooking before you start grilling the chicken.

4 boneless, skinless chicken breasts, well trimmed
2 tablespoons good-quality olive oil, preferably Spanish

6 cloves garlic, minced
1 tablespoon rosemary leaves, minced
1 teaspoon crushed caribe chile

Rinse chicken and pat dry. Using a mini food processor or a blender, puree olive oil, garlic, rosemary and caribe chile until thick. Place chicken in a glass baking dish. Rub both sides of each breast with puree and allow to marinate 30 minutes.

Preheat grill to medium or 350F (175C). Place rack 4 inches from heat. Place chicken on rack; grill 4 to 6 minutes on first side. Turn and grill 3 to 5 minutes on second side or until chicken is firm when pressed and internal temperature registers 185F (85C). *Makes 4 servings.*

VARIATION

If desired, you could serve this with freshly grated Parmesan or Romano cheese. If serving with pasta, arrange pasta on a platter, indenting center. Place chicken in center of pasta.

GRILLED CHICKEN ADOBO
▼▼▼▼▼

Adobado sauce is a favorite Northern New Mexico chile marinade. Generally reserved for pork, it is excellent on chicken breast or thighs, or even on shrimp or red snapper. Serve as a main course or place in a tortilla along with black beans and rice to make burritos.

2 pounds boneless, skinless chicken breasts or thighs
1 cup or 1/2 recipe Adobo Sauce (page 202)

Trim visible fat and connective tissue from chicken pieces. Place chicken in a glass baking dish or shallow bowl. Add sauce and stir to coat well. Marinate at least 1 hour at room temperature or cover and refrigerate overnight.

Preheat grill to medium-high or 400F (205C). Place rack 4 inches above heat. Remove chicken from sauce, reserving sauce, and, if chicken pieces are small, skewer chicken. Place chicken on rack; grill about 4 minutes on first side. Turn, spoon remaining sauce on grilled side of chicken and grill about 5 minutes or until almost all pink color is gone. *Makes 4 to 6 servings.*

GRILLED CHICKEN LEGS WITH TROPICAL FRUIT SALSA & DIPPING SAUCE

▼▼▼▼▼

This very attractive dish is a good example of fusion cooking, a style blending ideas from nearly all points of the globe. If you are rushed for time or want to keep calories at a bare minimum, do not make Dipping Sauce.

Tropical Fruit Salsa (see below)
Dipping Sauce (see below)
1/4 cup sugar
1-1/2 teaspoons salt
2 teaspoons ground sage
2 teaspoons ground cumin
1 teaspoon ground Mexican oregano
1 teaspoon crushed pequin quebrado chile
8 chicken legs with thigh attached

TROPICAL FRUIT SALSA

1 mango or peach, peeled, pitted and cut into 1/2-inch cubes
2 cups fresh or canned pineapple, cut into 1/2-inch dice
1/2 cup diced sweet onion
1 small firm banana, cut into 1/4-inch cubes
1 jalapeño chile or to taste, minced
2 tablespoons freshly squeezed lemon juice

DIPPING SAUCE

1 teaspoon peanut or vegetable oil
2 green onions, thinly sliced
3/4 cup smooth peanut butter
2 tablespoons freshly squeezed lemon juice
2 tablespoons light soy sauce
1-1/2 teaspoons crushed pequin quebrado chile
2 tablespoons flaked coconut, finely chopped
1 cup water
2 tablespoons sugar
1/4 cup coarsely chopped cilantro leaves (optional)

Prepare salsa and sauce and set aside. Combine sugar, salt, sage, cumin, oregano and crushed chile in a small bowl to make a rub. Coat chicken evenly with rub.

Preheat grill to medium-high or 400F (205C). Place rack 4 inches above heat. Place chicken on rack. Grill about 15 minutes on first side, then turn and grill 15 minutes or until joints move easily and centers register 185F (85C). Serve napped with salsa and with sauce on side. *Makes 8 servings.*

TROPICAL FRUIT SALSA

Combine all the ingredients and set aside for about 30 minutes while grilling chicken.

DIPPING SAUCE

Heat oil in a small saucepan over medium heat. Add onions and cook until clear. Add remaining ingredients except cilantro and simmer 8 to 10 minutes or until slightly thickened. Stir in cilantro, if using.

CHICKEN BREASTS WITH LEMON-MUSTARD TARRAGON BASTE

▼▼▼▼▼

This is a quick and easy favorite for grilling when weather permits or for pan-broiling when it doesn't. I like to serve it in summer, when my tarragon is abundant. I serve it with mashed or grilled squash with minced hot green chiles and a fresh tomato and basil salad.

1/4 cup good-quality olive oil, preferably Spanish
3 tablespoons freshly squeezed lemon juice
1 fresh red or green jalapeño, minced
1 tablespoon Dijon mustard
2 tablespoons minced fresh tarragon, or 2 teaspoons dried tarragon
4 boneless, skinless chicken breast halves, well trimmed

Whisk together all ingredients except chicken in a small bowl. Place chicken breasts on a plate and pour marinade over them, turning to coat. Marinate 30 minutes.

Preheat grill to medium-high or 400F (205C). Place rack 4 inches above heat. Remove chicken from marinade and place on rack; grill about 5 minutes on first side. Turn and grill another 5 minutes or until chicken is no longer pink and centers register 185F (85C). *Makes 4 servings.*

GRILLED MARINATED CHICKEN & PASTA SALAD WITH GARBANZOS

▼▼▼▼▼

This spicy Southwestern-flavored chicken is wonderful with the nutlike taste of garbanzos and red or green chile-flavored pasta—a specialty of New Mexico. You can of course substitute plain or another flavored pasta.

1 whole boneless, skinless chicken breast
Juice of 1 lemon
5 cloves garlic, minced
8 ounces red or green chile fusilli pasta
10 cherry tomatoes, quartered
6 green onions, with dark green tops discarded, thinly sliced
1 green bell pepper, chopped
1 cup chard leaves or spinach, washed thoroughly, stems removed and sliced crosswise
    into 1-inch strips
1 (12-oz.) can garbanzos, drained
6 slices pickled jalapeño chile, minced
1/3 cup good-quality olive oil, preferably Spanish
1/4 cup balsamic vinegar
1/4 cup coarsely sliced cilantro leaves

Trim chicken breast and place on a plate. Combine lemon juice with 3 cloves garlic in a small bowl. Pour lemon-garlic mixture over chicken, turning to coat. Set aside to marinate.

Cook pasta in boiling salted water according to package directions. Drain. In a large salad bowl, combine vegetables, pasta and remaining garlic. Whisk together olive oil with vinegar and stir in cilantro. Pour over pasta mixture and toss to combine; cover and refrigerate.

Preheat grill to medium-high or 400F (205C), adding your favorite wood chips. Place rack 4 inches above heat. Remove chicken from marinade and place on rack. Grill about 5 minutes on first side. Turn and grill another 5 minutes or until chicken is no longer pink and centers register a temperature of 185F (85C).

To serve, divide pasta mixture among plates. Cut chicken into strips and top each salad serving with chicken. *Makes 3 to 4 servings.*

GRILLED CHICKEN BREAST WITH SUN-DRIED TOMATO VINAIGRETTE OVER FUSILLI

▼▼▼▼▼

Sun-dried tomatoes, dried at their peak, bring a touch of summer to any season. Use the blue corn pasta, if available, as it is just right with this salad, but plain fusilli will also work.

1 large skinless, boneless chicken breast
Juice of 1 lime
2 cloves garlic, minced
1/4 cup good-quality olive oil, preferably Spanish
8 ounces blue corn fusilli pasta
1/2 cup sun-dried tomatoes, reconstituted according to package directions and diced
1/3 cup fresh salsa (pages 202 to 209) or commercial salsa
2 tablespoons red wine vinegar

Trim chicken breast and place on a plate. Combine lime juice with garlic and 2 teaspoons of the olive oil in a small bowl. Pour lime-garlic mixture over chicken, turning to coat. Set aside to marinate.

Cook pasta in boiling salted water according to package directions. Drain. In a medium salad bowl, combine pasta and sun-dried tomatoes. Whisk together remaining olive oil with salsa and vinegar. Pour over pasta mixture and toss to combine; cover and refrigerate.

Preheat grill to medium-high or 400F (205C), adding your favorite wood chips. Place rack 4 inches above heat. Remove chicken from marinade and place on rack. Grill about 5 minutes on first side. Turn and grill another 5 minutes or until chicken is no longer pink and centers register 185F (85C). To serve, divide pasta mixture among plates. Cut chicken into about 1-inch squares and top each salad serving with chicken. *Makes 3 to 4 servings.*

GRILLED CHICKEN WITH MINT & ROSEMARY LEMON BASTE & SUNNY SALSA

▼▼▼▼▼

1 (3-lb.) chicken, quartered
Juice of 1 lemon
2 tablespoons good-quality olive oil, preferably Spanish
2 tablespoons fresh mint leaves
1 tablespoon fresh rosemary
Sunny Salsa (page 205)

Rinse chicken and trim off excess fat, then pat dry. Place chicken in a glass baking dish. Combine lemon juice, olive oil, mint and rosemary in a blender and puree. Spread over whole surface of chicken and marinate 30 minutes.

Meanwhile, preheat grill to medium or 350F (175C). Place rack 5 inches above heat. Place chicken on rack; grill chicken 15 to 20 minutes. Turn and grill another 20 to 30 minutes or until juices run clear when pierced with a knife and interior is 185F (85C). If wings and legs brown too quickly, cover with foil. Serve with salsa. *Makes 4 servings*.

GRILLED MARINATED CHICKEN WITH HARVEST VEGETABLES

▼▼▼▼▼

The finish of orange flavor is so fresh tasting with these hearty harvest vegetables! You don't need to spend much time readying this good-enough-for-company dinner either!

2 (2-1/2- to 3-lb.) chickens
1-1/3 cups freshly squeezed orange juice
Zest of 1 orange
1/3 cup balsamic vinegar
2 tablespoons good-quality olive oil, preferably Spanish
1 tablespoon crushed caribe chile or to taste
1 teaspoon fresh Mexican oregano, minced, or 1/2 teaspoon ground dried oregano
1 teaspoon ground cumin
2 cloves garlic, minced
2 fresh bay leaves
1 acorn or butternut squash, cut crosswise into 3/4-inch-thick slices
2 Spanish onions, halved crosswise
4 carrots
4 turnips, cut into 3/4-inch-thick slices
2 teaspoons vegetable oil
1 tablespoon honey
Salt and freshly ground pepper
Freshly grated nutmeg

Rinse chicken and remove excess fat and any pin feathers. Trim off tail and tips of wings if desired. Cut chicken into halves. Combine orange juice, zest, vinegar, olive oil, caribe chile, oregano, cumin, garlic and bay leaves in a large, shallow glass or stainless steel bowl. Place chicken in marinade, turning to coat. Cover and marinate 30 minutes at room temperature or longer in the refrigerator.

Preheat grill to medium or 350F (175C). Place rack 5 inches above heat. Drain chicken, reserving marinade. Rub cut surfaces of vegetables with vegtable oil. Drizzle honey over squash. Season with salt, pepper and nutmeg. Arrange vegetables on rack and grill about 15 minutes, then add chicken, skin side down. Grill 15 minutes, then turn everything. Grill chicken, basting with marinade, and vegetables another 15 minutes and check for doneness. Vegetables usually take 45 to 60 minutes and chicken 30 to 45 minutes. Vegetables should be tender; chicken is done when joints move easily, juices run clear when pierced with a knife and interior is 185F (85C). Serve immediately. *Makes 4 servings.*

GRILLED CHICKEN WITH LEMON-PECAN BUTTER

▼▼▼▼▼

Pecans grow all over the Southwest. Due to the popularity of the nuts, more and more retirees plant pecan orchards to supplement their retirement income. The richness of pecans tinged with tart lemon and tarragon is delicious. This dish can be served with grilled vegetables.

Lemon-Pecan Butter (see below)
6 boneless, skinless chicken breast halves, trimmed
3 tablespoons freshly squeezed lemon juice
2 tablespoons unsalted butter, melted
Salt and freshly ground white or black pepper
6 sprigs flat-leaf parsley or tarragon

LEMON-PECAN BUTTER

1/4 cup pecans
1 stick (1/2 cup) unsalted butter, softened
Zest of 1 lemon, minced
2 teaspoons fresh tarragon or 1 teaspoon dried tarragon
1 tablespoon freshly squeezed lemon juice

Prepare Lemon-Pecan Butter and refrigerate. Brush chicken with lemon juice and butter, and season lightly with salt and pepper.

Preheat grill to medium or 350F (175C). Place rack 4 inches above heat. Arrange chicken on rack; grill 6 minutes. Turn and grill 5 to 6 minutes or until juices run clear when chicken is pierced with a knife and interior is 185F (85C). To serve, place 1 breast half on a plate and top with 2 thin slices Lemon-Pecan Butter. Garnish with parsley. *Makes 6 servings.*

Lemon-Pecan Butter

Finely grind pecans in a blender or food processor. Add butter, lemon zest, tarragon and lemon juice and process until combined. Place on plastic wrap or waxed paper, forming into a log about 1 inch in diameter. Refrigerate until firm. *Makes 6 servings.*

Variation

If serving potatoes, cut into 1/2-inch-thick slices and start potatoes first. When they have cooked about 15 minutes, turn them and place chicken on grill.

Southwestern Herb-Rubbed Chicken Drumsticks

▼▼▼▼▼

These drumsticks are wonderful served with your favorite hot 'n' spicy salsa or a spicy sauce or dip.

3 cloves garlic
1-1/2 teaspoons salt
1 teaspoon sugar
1/2 teaspoon ground cumin
1 dried bay leaf
1/2 to 1 teaspoon crushed pequin quebrado chile
1 thin slice of onion
12 drumsticks, rinsed and checked for pin feathers

Using a blender or mini processor combine all ingredients except chicken and process well. Rub mixture over chicken legs and allow to stand at least 2 hours or overnight, or they can be frozen with rub on them.

Preheat grill to medium-high or 400F (205C). Place rack 4 inches above heat. Arrange chicken on rack; grill 15 minutes. Turn and grill another 15 minutes or until juices run clear when chicken is pierced with a knife and interior is 185F (85C). *Makes 4 to 6 servings.*

FRESH SAGE & CIDER VINEGAR–MARINATED TURKEY BREAST

▼▼▼▼▼

Turkey breast grills beautifully! Try to select one of uniform thickness. It is definitely better to use fresh sage here, if possible. The better the quality of the cider vinegar, the fresher the flavor too. I was lucky enough to use some homemade apple cider vinegar made by my Albuquerque friend Charlotte Pugh. Serve this dish with grilled vegetables, such as Grilled Sweet Potato Rounds with Honey Butter (page 223). The Ginger Pear Salsa (page 206) or any favorite fruit-based salsa is an excellent accompaniment.

2 pounds (1/2- to 3/4-inch-thick) boneless, skinless turkey breast slices or tenders
1/3 cup good-quality olive oil, preferably Spanish
1/4 cup apple cider vinegar
3 tablespoons minced fresh sage or 1-1/2 tablespoons dried leaf sage

Place turkey in a glass baking dish. Whisk together olive oil, vinegar and sage. Spoon mixture over turkey and marinate 30 minutes.

Preheat grill to medium-high or 400F (205C). Place rack 4 inches above heat. Remove turkey from marinade and place on rack; grill 4 to 5 minutes. Turn and grill 4 to 5 minutes or until juices run clear when turkey is pierced with a knife and interior is 185F (85C). *Makes 6 to 8 servings.*

GRILLED MOLE-MARINATED TURKEY TENDERS

▼▼▼▼▼

The spicy, pungent flavor of mole is a classic with turkey. Served either in corn or flour tortillas as soft tacos or burritos or over fluffy rice, this turkey is fabulous. We like a tart citrus dressing, such as a tangy lemon vinaigrette, over baby greens to complement this dish.

1 cup chicken broth
2 tablespoons pure ground hot chile or to taste
2 corn tortillas, torn into 1-inch pieces
1 ounce unsweetened chocolate
2 tablespoons ground almonds
2 tablespoons raisins
2 garlic cloves
1/2 teaspoon ground cumin or to taste
1/2 teaspoon ground cinnamon
2 pounds turkey tenders, cut into uniform pieces
1 teaspoon vegetable oil

Early in the day, or the evening before, combine all ingredients except turkey and oil in a blender or food processor and process until pureed. Pour into a heavy saucepan and simmer, stirring occasionally, until chocolate is melted and flavors are blended, about 15 minutes. Taste and adjust seasonings. Let cool.

Rinse turkey and pat dry with paper towels. Place cooled mole in a large plastic bag. Add turkey, seal and marinate 1 hour at room temperature or refrigerate overnight.

Preheat grill to medium or 350F (175C). Place rack 4 inches above heat. Brush grill with oil. Remove turkey from marinade and place on rack; grill 5 minutes. Turn and grill 4 to 5 minutes or until juices run clear when turkey is pierced with a knife and interior is 185F (85C). *Makes 6 to 8 servings.*

LIME-CILANTRO TURKEY

▼▼▼▼▼

Turkey thighs, breast or tenders are all tasty when treated to this tangy, herbed rub. It is quick and easy and oh so gentle on the waistline. You can serve the turkey as a simple entree or cut it into strips and place over a hearty assortment of greens and vegetables for a luncheon or light dinner salad. Or toss into pasta! A spicy salsa, such as Hot Orange (page 204), is wonderful with turkey too.

1 pound skinless, boneless turkey breast, rinsed and patted dry
Juice of 1 lime
1-1/2 teaspoons salt
1-1/2 teaspoons sugar
1 teaspoon pure ground hot chile or crushed pequin quebrado chile
1 teaspoon grated lime zest
2 tablespoons coarsely chopped cilantro leaves
1 recipe Hot Orange Salsa (page 204) (optional)

Trim any connective tissue or fat from turkey. Place in a glass baking dish. Squeeze lime juice over whole surface of turkey. Combine salt, sugar, hot chile, lime zest and cilantro in a small bowl. Evenly sprinkle over surface of turkey. Let stand 30 minutes.

Preheat grill to medium-high or 400F (205C). Place rack 4 inches above heat. Remove turkey from marinade and place on rack; grill 4 to 5 minutes. Turn and grill 4 to 5 minutes or until juices run clear when turkey is pierced with a knife and interior is 185F (85C). *Makes 3 or 4 servings.*

HERB-BASTED DUCK WITH SEARED TURNIPS

▼▼▼▼▼

Grilled duck loses much of its fat, because the hot direct heat melts the fat right out of the duck, especially when the skin is pricked several times with the tines of a sharp meat fork. The herbs you use can be more pungent than those normally used for other poultry such as chicken. This dish is wonderful with fresh crusty bread such as Coffee-Can Mushroom Bread (page 236).

2 (4- to 5-lb.) ducks
1/4 cup plus 1 tablespoon good-quality olive oil, preferably Spanish
2 bay leaves, halved
1 tablespoon fresh rosemary or 1-1/2 teaspoons dried rosemary
1 tablespoon fresh lavender or 1-1/2 teaspoons dried lavender
1-1/2 teaspoons fennel seeds
1 tablespoon chopped flat-leaf parsley
Zest of 1 orange, minced
1/4 cup freshly squeezed orange juice
12 medium turnips, rinsed and unpeeled
1 orange, sliced, for garnish

Rinse duck and remove pin feathers and excess fat. Cut each duck in half, then prick breast several times with tines of a sharp meat fork. Combine 1/4 cup oil with bay leaves, rosemary, lavender, fennel seeds, parsley, orange zest and orange juice in a small bowl. Divide among duck cavities and outside surface and rub in. Let stand 1 hour or cover and refrigerate overnight.

Preheat grill to medium-high or 400F (205C). Place rack 5 inches above heat. Cut turnips in half crosswise and rub cut surfaces with remaining oil. Arrange turnips and ducks, skin side down, on rack; grill about 20 minutes. Turn and grill about 20 minutes and check for doneness. Some people like duck rather rare. It should feel fairly firm to the touch. To check doneness, insert a sharp knife at fleshiest portion of breast; if juices are too pink, continue grilling. Let stand 20 minutes before carving.

Cut each turnip into 1/4-inch-thick slices and brush with remaining 1 tablespoon olive oil. Place on grill as soon as ducks are removed. Grill until grill marks appear on first side, then turn and grill until fork tender. To serve, encircle each duck half with grilled turnip slices and a twisted circle of orange, made by cutting once into each slice and pulling apart so as to twist each slice. *Makes 4 servings.*

GRILLED SHERRIED SESAME DUCK
À LA BRATEL

▼▼▼▼▼

A food editor friend of mine, Barbara Bratel Collier of *The Cleveland Press,* gave me some of her favorite barbecue recipes. This somewhat Polynesian-influenced marinade is a good foil for the richness of duck. I added caribe chile to the marinade as we like the "punch" it gives.

2 (4- to 5-lb.) ducks
1 cup sherry
1/3 cup honey
2 tablespoons soy sauce
1 tablespoon crushed caribe chile
1 teaspoon freshly grated gingerroot
1 teaspoon dry mustard
2 tablespoons sesame seeds, toasted (see Note)

Rinse duck and remove pin feathers and excess fat. Cut each duck in half, then prick breast several times with tines of a sharp meat fork. Combine all remaining ingredients except sesame seeds in a large shallow glass baking dish. Add ducks to marinade, spooning marinade over ducks to coat. Cover and refrigerate 8 hours or overnight.

Preheat grill to medium-high or 400F (205C). Place rack 5 inches above heat. Arrange ducks on rack, skin side down; grill about 20 minutes. Turn and grill about another 20 minutes and check for doneness. Some people like duck rather rare. It should feel rather firm to touch. To check doneness, insert a sharp knife at fleshiest portion of breast; if juices are too pink, continue grilling. Let stand 20 minutes before carving.

To serve, slice breast meat, fanning out the slices on each plate. Cut back quarter off each carcass, placing it against breast meat. Sprinkle with sesame seeds. *Makes 4 servings.*

NOTE: To toast sesame seeds, place in a heavy skillet over medium heat and cook, stirring occasionally, until golden, 3 to 5 minutes.

Grilled Seafood

▼▼▼▼▼

Seafood is a natural for the grill. The direct heat, particularly if it is laced with aromatic fruitwood or hardwood chips, such as hickory or alder, is wonderful for locking in the delicate flavors of the sea.

The grill is also good for opening the muscles of shellfish. The heat cooks and softens the muscle while steaming the clams or oysters, making them easy to open and wonderful to eat as is with your favorite topping or just a bit of lemon.

When cooking side dishes with seafood, always start them first as they almost always take longer. Most seafood cooks in just a few minutes.

GRILLED LAS CRUCES–STYLE TROUT WITH GREEN CHILE & PECAN STUFFING

▼▼▼▼▼

Amazingly, all the ingredients for this dish are grown in New Mexico. The flavors blend well and complement grilled trout.

4 (8- to 12-oz.) fresh trout, ready to cook
1/4 cup pecans, toasted, finely chopped (see Note)
2 tablespoons good-quality olive oil, preferably Spanish
4 garlic cloves, minced
2 tablespoons parched (page 161), peeled and chopped green chile
2 tablespoons coarsely chopped fresh cilantro leaves (optional)
1 lime
1 teaspoon vegetable oil

Preheat grill to medium-high or 400F (205C). Position rack 3 inches above heat. Rinse trout and pat dry. Combine pecans, olive oil, garlic, green chile and cilantro, if using, in a small bowl. Cut lime in half crosswise and squeeze juice over pecan mixture. Slice remaining lime half into 4 rounds and set aside. Stuff cavity of each fish with pecan mixture, securing stuffing with wooden picks or small metal skewers.

Using vegetable oil, lightly oil fish and place on grill rack. Grill about 6 minutes or until trout becomes lightly browned. Turn gently, keeping trout whole, and grill other side about 5 minutes or until fish begins to flake. Garnish with lime.   *Makes 4 servings.*

NOTE: Pecans can be toasted in a heavy skillet on the grill or indoors over medium heat for about 5 minutes, stirring occasionally.

RED SNAPPER WITH CARIBE MARINADE

▼▼▼▼▼

Red snapper really takes to this sauce of Northern New Mexico. Made with caribe chiles, which came to New Mexico with the Spanish and were given to them by Caribe Indians in the Caribbean, this sauce was originally used for marinating pork. Then I discovered how wonderful it is on chicken breast as well as on red snapper and shrimp.

1-1/2 pounds red snapper fillet
1 cup (1/2 recipe) Adobo Sauce (page 202)

Rinse fish and pat dry. Spoon a third of the sauce into a glass baking dish. Add fish and spoon remaining sauce over fish. Cover and marinate about 1 hour.

Preheat grill to medium or 350F (175C). Place rack 3 inches above heat. Remove fish from sauce, reserving sauce. Place fish on rack. Grill about 5 minutes. Turn and grill another 5 minutes or until fish flakes when checked with a fork.

Meanwhile, heat reserved sauce in a small saucepan over high heat until slightly thickened. Drizzle sauce over each serving.   *Makes 4 to 6 servings.*

VARIATION

Substitute 1-1/2 pounds shelled, deveined medium shrimp for red snapper. Skewer shrimp and grill about 3 minutes per side.

MARGARITA-MARINATED GRILLED RED SNAPPER

▼▼▼▼▼

The flavors that create a margarita are surprisingly compatible with seafood. We particularly like it on red snapper, but other firm-fleshed fish, such as catfish, are good with this marinade.

1-1/2 pounds red snapper fillet
1/2 cup freshly squeezed lime juice
1/3 cup tequila, preferably white or silver
2 tablespoons triple sec
1 teaspoon minced lime zest
1 recipe Aztec-Style Pico de Gallo with Chipotles (page 202)

Rinse fish and pat dry. Combine lime juice, tequila, triple sec and zest in a glass baking dish. Add fish to marinade, turning to coat. Cover and marinate about 1 hour at room temperature.

Preheat grill to medium or 350F (175C). Place rack 3 inches above heat. Remove fish from marinade, reserving marinade. Place fish on rack. Grill about 5 minutes. Turn, brush with marinade and grill 5 minutes or until fish flakes when checked with a knife.

Serve napped with pico de gallo.   *Makes 4 to 6 servings.*

HICKORY-GRILLED SALMON WITH LEMON VERMOUTH BUTTER

▼▼▼▼▼

I adapted this delicious recipe for salmon after being treated to a fresh grilled salmon in Seattle, where they put all the seasonings in a butter mixture and simply basted the fish. I think a simple rub applied first and allowed to set about 30 minutes yields a richer, fuller flavor.

1-1/2 teaspoons salt
1-1/2 teaspoons freshly ground pepper
1-1/2 teaspoons sugar
1 teaspoon ground pure hot chile
2 cloves garlic, minced
4 (about 8-oz.) salmon steaks or small whole salmon, ready to cook
2 tablespoons unsalted butter, melted
2 tablespoons freshly squeezed lemon juice
1 teaspoon minced lemon zest
2 tablespoons dry vermouth
1 lemon, scored lengthwise and sliced thinly

Combine salt, pepper, sugar, chile and garlic in a small bowl. Rinse fish and pat dry. Evenly sprinkle rub over fish and pat it in well. If using whole fish, also place some in cavity. Set aside.

Preheat grill to medium or 350F (175C). Place rack 3 inches above heat. Combine butter, lemon juice, zest and vermouth in a small bowl. Place fish on rack and drizzle with half of butter mixture; grill about 5 minutes. Turn, drizzle with remaining butter mixture and grill another 5 minutes or until fish flakes when checked with a knife. Serve immediately, garnished with lemon slices.   *Makes 4 servings.*

WHISKEY-MARINATED GRILLED SALMON

▼▼▼▼▼

This somewhat Hawaiian-inspired marinade is wonderful on other firm-fleshed fish, such as tuna, bluefish or shark. Fresh vegetables such as squash and jicama can be cooked along with the fish.

4 (8-oz.) whole salmon, ready to cook
2 tablespoons vegetable oil
1/4 cup light soy sauce
1/2 cup whiskey
2 cloves garlic, minced
1/4 cup freshly squeezed orange juice
1 recipe fruit salsa (pages 203 to 208)

Rinse fish and pat dry. Combine oil, soy sauce, whiskey, garlic and orange juice in a glass baking dish. Place fish in marinade and turn to coat, spooning marinade into each center cavity. Cover and marinate about 1 hour at room temperature or all day in refrigerator, turning 2 or 3 times and continuing to spoon marinade into cavities.

Preheat grill to medium or 350F (175C). Place rack 4 inches above heat. Remove fish from marinade, reserving marinade. Place fish on rack; grill about 5 minutes. Turn, brush with marinade and grill another 5 minutes or until fish flakes when checked with a knife. When turning fish, be very careful to use a large, heavy spatula as near to the size of the fish as possible and gently slide it under fish as you lift to turn. If skin comes off, place fish right back down where skin from first side is. Place fish on plates and serve salsa over center of each fish. *Makes 4 servings.*

Hot Tuna Teriyaki with Sushi Rice

▼▼▼▼▼

The teriyaki taste is hard to beat. I like this basic marinade on other firm-fleshed fish such as snapper, salmon, or monkfish. It's also great on chicken, turkey and beef. Tropical Salsa (page 205) is a good accompaniment.

4 (6-oz.) tuna fillets, about 1 inch thick
1/3 cup soy sauce, preferably light
2 tablespoons sherry
2 cloves garlic, minced
1 (2-inch) piece gingerroot, peeled and grated or finely minced
2 tablespoons sugar

Sushi Rice

2 cups water
1 teaspoon salt
1 cup long-grain white rice
1 tablespoon white vinegar or to taste
2 tablespoons sugar

Rinse fish and pat dry. Combine soy sauce, sherry, garlic, gingerroot and sugar in a glass or stainless steel shallow bowl. Add fish and turn to coat. Cover and marinate 1 hour at room temperature, turning once or twice, or refrigerate overnight.

Preheat grill to medium or 350F (175C). Place rack 4 inches above heat. While grill is heating, bring water and salt to a boil in a heavy saucepan with a tight-fitting cover. Add rice, stir and cover. Reduce heat to just maintain a simmer and cook 15 minutes. Remove cover and stir in vinegar and sugar. Taste and adjust seasonings. Replace cover and keep warm.

Remove fish from marinade, reserving marinade. Place fish on rack; grill about 5 minutes. Turn and grill another 5 minutes or until fish is still medium in center when checked with a knife.

While fish cooks, bring marinade to a boil in a small saucepan, stirring occasionally. Serve fish with a mound of rice, topped with a bit of heated sauce. *Makes 4 servings.*

SCROD MEXICANA WITH ORANGE, LEMON & SMOKED PINEAPPLE SALSA

▼▼▼▼▼

The fresh clear taste of citrus always complements seafood. The combination of orange and lemon in this marinade is light and tasty, especially when paired with salsa garnish for serving. This entire meal is nothing but light and healthy—and yet so fabulously flavorful!

4 (4- to 6-oz.) scrod fillets or other firm-fleshed mild fish
2 tablespoons good-quality olive oil, preferably Spanish
Zest of 1 orange and 1 lemon, minced
1/3 cup freshly squeezed orange juice
2 tablespoons freshly squeezed lemon juice
2 tablespoons coarsely chopped cilantro leaves or flat-leaf parsley
1 teaspoon ground cumin
4 cloves garlic, minced
Grilled Fennel (page 224)
Grilled Spaghetti Squash (page 230)
1/2 teaspoon crushed caribe chile
Orange, Lemon & Smoked Pineapple Salsa (page 203)

Rinse fish and pat dry. Combine olive oil, zests, juices, cilantro, cumin and garlic in a glass or stainless steel shallow bowl. Add fish and turn to coat. Cover and marinate 1 hour at room temperature, turning once or twice, or refrigerate 6 to 8 hours.

Preheat grill to medium or 350F (175C). Place rack 4 inches above heat. Add fennel and squash, turning as needed.

When fennel and squash are almost tender, remove fish from marinade, reserving marinade. Place fish on rack; grill about 4 minutes. Turn, spoon marinade over fish and grill another 3 minutes or until fish begins to flake when checked with a knife.

Meanwhile, divide vegetables among 4 warmed plates, scooping spaghetti squash out of shell. Garnish squash with caribe chile. Place cooked fillets on plates and top each with salsa. *Makes 4 servings.*

Monkfish with Hot Orange Salsa

▼▼▼▼▼

The firm-fleshed monkfish, which tastes almost like lobster, is complemented by the butter in the marinade. The spicy orange-based salsa is wonderful on fish.

4 (5- to 7-oz.) monkfish fillets
Zest of 1 orange, minced
2/3 cup freshly squeezed orange juice
3 tablespoons butter, melted
3 tablespoons chipotle chile juice, from reconstituting dried chiles (page 202)
1 teaspoon ground coriander
Hot Orange Salsa (page 204)

Rinse fish and pat dry. If fillets are odd shaped or thick in center, making it difficult to cook evenly, then cut into 1-inch cubes and skewer. Combine orange zest, orange juice, butter and chile juice in a glass or stainless steel shallow bowl. Add fish and turn to coat. Cover and marinate 30 minutes at room temperature.

Preheat grill to medium or 350F (175C). Place rack 4 inches above heat. Remove fish from marinade, reserving marinade. Place fish on rack and drizzle with some of marinade. Grill 7 to 8 minutes. Turn, drizzle with remaining marinade and grill another 7 to 8 minutes or until fish begins to flake when checked with a knife. Spoon salsa in pools on plates and place fish on salsa. *Makes 4 servings.*

Grilled Lobster, New Mexico Style

▼▼▼▼▼

Grilling makes a lobster much more succulent and flavorful than steaming or boiling, especially if fruitwood or other hardwood chips are added to the fire.

1/4 cup good-quality olive oil, preferably Spanish
1 tablespoon orange zest, minced
Juice of 1 orange
4 cloves garlic, minced
4 (1-1/2- to 2-pound) lobsters
Hot Orange Salsa (page 204) or Aztec-Style Pico de Gallo with Chipotles (page 202)

Preheat grill to medium or 350F (175C); add wood chips if desired. Place rack 3 inches above heat. Combine olive oil, orange zest, orange juice and garlic in a small bowl.

To kill the lobsters, plunge the tip of a sharp knife into each lobster at the point where the tail and body join. Place each lobster on a cutting board, upside down. Using a heavy chef's knife, quickly cut in two from top to tail dissecting thorax and leaving one claw on each side. Place lobsters, shell sides down, on grill. Drizzle cut sides with juice mixture, repeating every few minutes. Turn lobster after 4 to 5 minutes or when shell is red and somewhat blackened around edges. The lobster is done when it is uniformly red all over. Center a pool of salsa on each of 4 plates and top each with 2 lobster halves. *Makes 4 servings.*

GRILLED LOBSTER CHILI

▼▼▼▼▼

Grilled lobster is wonderful, especially if you manage to impart a subtle smokiness from fruitwood chips or other aromatic wood such as hickory or pecan. I have also used this recipe with leftover grilled lobster.

1 teaspoon vegetable oil
2 large onions, cut crosswise into 1/2-inch slices
3 or 4 green chiles
2 (14-oz.) cans cooked white beans, navy or cannellini, drained
2 cups chopped grilled lobster meat [2 (1-lb.) lobsters or 1 (2-lb.) lobster] (page 126)
2 cups fish stock or chicken broth (pages 53 and 55)
1/2 teaspoon ground pequin quebrado chile
2 teaspoons cumin
1/2 teaspoon salt or to taste
Sunny Salsa (page 205) or salsa of your choice

Preheat grill to medium or 350F (175C). Place rack 4 inches above heat. Lightly oil onion slices and place on grill rack. Place chiles on grill, piercing each once with tip of a sharp knife. When onion slices are lightly blackened and somewhat soft, turn them over. Grill chiles, rotating them to uniformly blister. When chiles are uniformly blistered, place in ice water.

Chop onions. Peel chiles and coarsely chop. Combine onions, chiles and remaining ingredients except salsa in a large, heavy pot. Simmer 15 to 20 minutes on grill or indoors over medium heat. Serve in warm shallow bowls with a topping of salsa. *Makes 4 servings.*

SOUTHWESTERN MUSSELS VINAIGRETTE

▼▼▼▼▼

I have always loved mussels. They must be super fresh to be sweet and juicy. Succulent mussels really take to garlic and the flavors of the Southwest. They make a wonderful light meal outdoors with grilled slices of fresh crusty bread and a grilled vegetable salad. Just dip grilled vegetables into the same salsa vinaigrette that you are using for the mussels.

4 pounds fresh mussels
6 cloves garlic, minced
1/2 cup white wine
Salsa Dressing (page 65)

Preheat grill to medium-high or 400F (205C). Place rack 3 inches above heat. Clean mussels, debearding them and scrubbing shells. Using a heavy pot such as a cast-iron skillet with a lid or a Dutch oven, place half of the mussels in the pot, then sprinkle with half of the garlic. Place remaining mussels on top and sprinkle with remaining garlic. Add wine, cover and place on grill rack. Cook 6 to 10 minutes or until steam starts to escape from around lid, then shake pot to move mussels about. Check every few minutes to see if shells have opened, shaking once or twice more. The mussels should take no more than 15 minutes. Discard any mussels that do not open. When done, serve with bowls of dressing.   *Makes 4 servings.*

NOTE: If grilling vegetables, check for suggested cooking times. Often vegetables take longer than mussels and should be started first.

CARIBBEAN GRILLED PRAWNS WITH SALSA

▼▼▼▼▼

The spiciness of shrimp combines well with this hearty salsa. For a real Caribbean night, serve the remaining cream of coconut in piña coladas. Steamed rice or linguine makes a wonderful bed for serving the shrimp with their juices and salsa.

1 tablespoon vegetable oil
1/2 cup chopped fresh onion
2 cloves garlic, minced
1 tablespoon gingerroot, grated or minced
1/2 teaspoon ground allspice
1/2 teaspoon turmeric
2 tablespoons freshly squeezed lime juice
1/3 cup cream of coconut
1-1/2 pounds medium shrimp, shelled and deveined
12 ounces to 1 pound steamed rice or cooked linguine
Black Bean & Corn Salsa (page 206), using papaya variation

Combine oil, onion, garlic, gingerroot, allspice, turmeric, lime juice and cream of coconut in a medium bowl; allow to set while you shell and devein shrimp. Add shrimp and allow to marinate for at least 30 minutes.

Heat grill to medium or 350F (175C). Place rack 3 inches from heat. Place shrimp on skewers and grill, basting with marinade as you turn them, for about 2 minutes a side or until they have just turned pink. Serve over rice or linguine and napped with salsa. *Makes 4 to 6 servings.*

Raspberry Vinegar–Marinated Scallop Kabobs

▼▼▼▼▼

The fruity flavors of raspberry vinegar combined with fresh fruits in the kabob make a delicious light entree for lunch or dinner. Serve over a bed of fluffy steamed rice, quinoa or orzo.

1-1/2 pounds fresh sea scallops
2 navel oranges
1/3 cup raspberry vinegar
2 tablespoons vegetable oil
1 tablespoon chopped chives
1 tablespoon ground pure hot chile
1 red Delicious apple
1/4 fresh pineapple
1/3 cup raspberry jelly, melted

Rinse scallops, discarding shell remnants, and pat dry. Remove zest from 1 orange and juice. Combine raspberry vinegar, oil, chives, chile and 1/4 cup of the orange juice in a shallow glass or stainless steel bowl. Add scallops to juice mixture.

Preheat grill to medium or 350F (175C). Place rack 3 inches above heat. Meanwhile, cut unpeeled orange and apple into at least 8 wedges. Cut pineapple into at least 12 chunks. Remove scallops from marinade, reserving marinade. Alternate scallops with fruit on skewers. Place skewers on grill rack. Brush fruit with raspberry jelly and drizzle scallops with marinade as they cook. The kabobs should cook 3 to 5 minutes or until seared slightly on first side. Rotate and cook other side, drizzling with remaining marinade. Scallops are done when white in center. Do not overcook. *Makes 6 to 8 servings.*

Smoked Meats

▼▼▼▼▼

Smoking imbues meats with a special personality and creates a whole new flavor sensation. Properly done, it is rather difficult to beat a well-smoked roast—be it beef, pork or lamb. Do remember one cardinal rule: never turn meats as they smoke.

Generally, it is the larger cuts that are smoked, as the long, slow cooking moisturizes and tenderizes them. The smoked meats from each of these recipes freeze very well. Most of the recipes yield several servings, so freezing is a very convenient way to stock up for later meals.

HICKORY-SMOKED FRESH HAM WITH CHIPOTLE SAUCE

▼▼▼▼▼

Fresh ham takes on quite a different and delicious flavor when freshly smoked—a process very different from that used for the commercial hams one can buy. This roast can take up to 12 hours, so you may wish to smoke it one day and serve it the next. Chiles, especially chipotles, are fabulous with the mild flavor of pork.

1 (8- to 10-lb.) fresh ham, skinned and excess fat removed
8 cloves garlic, slivered
1 recipe Chipotle Rub (page 218)

CHIPOTLE SAUCE

6 to 8 dried smoked chipotle chiles (about 1/4 cup after cooking and mincing) (page 202)
1 each red and yellow bell peppers
1/2 cup honey
2/3 cup balsamic vinegar
1/3 cup fresh cilantro leaves, coarsely chopped

Eight to 12 hours (durations vary because of size and fat content of ham—fattier ones cook faster, and bigger hams take longer) before you wish to serve, begin to heat your smoker, following manufacturer's instructions. If using charcoal, build a double-layer fire of charcoal briquettes. After charcoal briquettes begin to catch fire, fill water pan with hot water, so it can heat as charcoal begins to burn hotter. When surface of coals is coated with gray ash, add 6 to 8 green or soaked hickory chunks. Or, turn on gas or electric smoker as manufacturer suggests for a large pork roast or fresh ham. Add a small handful of soaked hickory or other hardwood chips.

Using a sharp knife, make 1-inch or deeper slits spaced over outside edge of ham. Insert garlic slivers in slits. Last, spread rub over entire surface.

Smoke ham, placing it on rack closest to bottom. Check on smokiness of wood chunks about once every hour. About every 4 hours or as needed, add more charcoal briquettes. You will need to light more charcoal 30 to 45 minutes before needed.

While ham is smoking, prepare sauce. Cook and mince chipotle as directed. Roast bell peppers under a broiler or on a burner until blistered and blackened. Place in iced water to chill, remove peel, then chop and place in a nonreactive bowl. Add chipotles, honey, vinegar and cilantro. Stir together, cover and let set at room temperature.

Continue to smoke ham, checking for doneness after about 10 hours of smoking. To check, insert a meat thermometer in fleshiest portion. It should register 160F (70C). If you do not have a thermometer, cut a deep slit with a sharp slicing knife to center of fleshiest portion. The juices should be clear and flesh should be only slightly pink.

Allow to stand about 20 minutes after removing from smoker. Cut into 1/2-inch slices and place either on a platter or individual plates. Serve with sauce. *Makes 12 to 16 servings.*

CHERRY-SMOKED PORK CHOPS WITH DRIED CHERRY SALSA

▼▼▼▼▼

The cuttings from cherry trees are best for this dish. If you must substitute, preferably use another fruitwood. These chops are excellent with a hearty side dish such as wild rice, whole-wheat pasta or buckwheat groats and your favorite green vegetable.

4 (1-1/2-inch-thick) pork loin chops
2 tablespoons good-quality olive oil, preferably Spanish
2 tablespoons minced fresh sage, or 2 teaspoons dried sage
2 tablespoons minced fresh thyme, or 2 teaspoons dried thyme
3 tablespoons minced chives
2 tablespoons chopped green chile
1 recipe Dried Cherry Salsa (page 208)

About 3 hours before you wish to serve, begin to heat your smoker, following manufacturer's instructions. If using charcoal, build a single-layer fire of charcoal briquettes. After charcoal briquettes begin to catch fire, fill water pan with hot water, so it can heat as charcoal begins to burn hotter. When coals are coated with gray ash, add 2 to 4 green or soaked chunks of cherry or other fruitwood. Or, turn on gas or electric smoker as manufacturer suggests for pork chops. Add a small handful of soaked fruitwood chips.

Trim any excess fat from chops and pat dry. Using a small sharp knife, cut a pocket for stuffing. Combine olive oil, sage, thyme and chives in a mini processor or blender and process until pureed. Stir in chopped green chile, then spoon herb blend into pocket of each chop. Rub remaining herb mixture over surface of each chop.

Place pork chops on bottom rack. Check on smokiness of wood chunks about once every hour. Chops should be done in about 2-1/2 hours. When done, a thermometer inserted in center will register 160F (70C) or when cut with a sharp knife, meat will be light pink and juice clear. Serve each chop napped with cherry salsa. *Makes 4 servings.*

JUST PEACHY SMOKED PORK LOIN

▼▼▼▼▼

Gingered peaches are wonderful anytime; in fact they are reminiscent of mangos, which can be substituted. Pork takes kindly to sweet fruity sauces, and this recipe is a good example. Smoking allows these flavors to really penetrate. Serve with your preference of smoked sweet or white potatoes and stir-fried chard.

1 (3-lb.) pork loin, well trimmed
4 fresh peaches, peeled and pitted
1 tablespoon molasses or to taste
2-inch piece gingerroot, peeled and coarsely chopped
1 tablespoon light soy sauce
2 teaspoons crushed pequin quebrado chile
2 tablespoons dry white wine or white wine vinegar
1 tablespoon good-quality olive oil, preferably Spanish

Place pork in a self-sealing plastic bag. In a blender, combine all remaining ingredients; process until blended. Pour marinade over pork, turning to coat. Refrigerate overnight or at least 3 hours.

About 4 hours before you wish to serve, begin to heat your smoker, following manufacturer's instructions. If using charcoal, build a double-layer fire of charcoal briquettes. After charcoal briquettes begin to catch fire, fill water pan with hot water, so it can heat as charcoal begins to burn hotter. When surface of coals is coated with gray ash, add 4 to 6 green or soaked fruitwood chunks. Or, turn on gas or electric smoker as manufacturer suggests for a pork roast. Add a small handful of soaked fruitwood chips.

Drain pork, reserving marinade. Place pork on bottom rack. Pour remaining marinade into a small pan and simmer until thickened slightly; taste and adjust seasonings if needed. Check on smokiness of wood chunks about once every hour. It should be done in 4 to 5 hours. When done, a thermometer inserted in center will register 160F (70C) or when fleshiest portion is cut with a sharp knife, meat will be light pink and juice clear. Slice and serve in a pool of reduced marinade, allowing 3 to 4 slices per serving.   *Makes 6 to 8 servings.*

SMOKED SPARERIBS

▼▼▼▼▼

Ribs are generally grilled or broiled, sometimes boiled or baked—but rarely smoked. Smoking creates juicier, more tender ribs with an overtone of whatever wood smoke was used. They are so good with just a rub that we often enjoy them without barbecue sauce.

3 to 4 pounds lean or meaty country-style pork ribs, well trimmed
Fresh Lemon Zest Chile-Herb Rub (page 216) or rub of your choice
Barbecue sauce (optional)

About 6 hours before you wish to serve, begin to heat your smoker, following manufacturer's instructions. If using charcoal, build a single-layer fire of charcoal briquettes. After charcoal briquettes begin to catch fire, fill water pan with hot water, so it can heat as charcoal begins to burn hotter. When coals are coated with gray ash, add 4 to 6 green or soaked mesquite or other hardwood chunks. Or, turn on gas or electric smoker as manufacturer suggests for country-style pork ribs. Add a small handful of soaked mesquite chips.

Spoon rub over ribs, lightly rubbing over entire surface. Let stand at least 30 minutes. Place ribs on bottom rack. Check on smokiness of wood chunks about once every hour. Ribs should be done in 4 to 5 hours. They are done when meat becomes tender and starts to pull away from the bones. Serve hot with warm barbecue sauce, if desired. *Makes 4 servings.*

OUR FAVORITE MESQUITE-SMOKED SIRLOIN TIP

▼▼▼▼▼

Heavenly smokiness might be the best way to start describing the flavor of this roast. It is so juicy, and the interaction of orange juice, bourbon and other marinade ingredients creates a beautiful brown crust and gives an almost rosy cast to the meat inside. We love to smoke potatoes alongside and make Sarah's Best Blue Cheese–Smoked Potato Salad (page 66). We think buttered fresh beets, and steamed spinach or beet greens served with a vinaigrette make a wonderful and memorable dinner.

1/4 cup good-quality olive oil, preferably Spanish
1/2 cup bourbon
2 bay leaves, crushed
4 cloves garlic
1/4 cup freshly squeezed orange juice
3 tablespoons Worcestershire sauce
3 tablespoons ground pure hot chile
1 (3- to 4-lb.) beef sirloin tip or rump roast
Salsa or other sauce (see Sauces, Salsas, Marinades, Bastes & Rubs, page 201)

Combine olive oil, bourbon, bay leaves and garlic in a shallow nonreactive dish in which roast can fit. Add roast, and turn to coat with marinade. Cover and marinate at room temperature at least 2 hours or overnight in refrigerator, turning occasionally.

About 6 hours before you wish to serve, begin to heat your smoker, following manufacturer's instructions. If using charcoal, build a double-layer fire of charcoal briquettes. After charcoal briquettes begin to catch fire, fill water pan with hot water, so it can heat as charcoal begins to burn hotter. When coals are coated with gray ash, add 4 to 6 soaked or green mesquite wood chunks. Or, turn on gas or electric smoker as manufacturer suggests for a 3- to 4-pound beef roast. Add a small handful of soaked mesquite chips.

Remove roast from marinade, pat dry and place on bottom rack of smoker. Check on smokiness of wood chunks about once every hour. Add charcoal after 4 hours if needed. You will need to light more charcoal 30 to 45 minutes before needed. Smoke 5 hours for medium rare or until desired doneness.

Serve roast sliced with your favorite salsa or cream sauce and with potato salad and vegetables alongside. *Makes 8 to 10 servings.*

VARIATION

If doing potatoes for the salad, cook potatoes on second rack about 2 hours.

FAMILY-STYLE SMOKED ARM ROAST

▼▼▼▼▼

This simple-to-prepare roast is perfect for lazy days, when all you feel like doing is periodically tending a fire. If you desire, carrots, onions and potatoes can be smoked halfway through the smoking process.

1 (3- to 4-lb.) beef chuck arm roast, at least 2 inches thick
1-1/2 teaspoons salt
1-1/2 teaspoons freshly cracked black pepper
1 teaspoon ground pure hot New Mexican chile

About 7 hours before you wish to serve, begin to heat your smoker, following manufacturer's instructions. If using charcoal, build a double-layer fire of charcoal briquettes. After charcoal briquettes begin to catch fire, fill water pan with hot water, so it can heat as charcoal begins to burn hotter. When coals are coated with gray ash, add 4 to 6 green or soaked hardwood chunks. Or, turn on gas or electric smoker as manufacturer suggests for a 3- to 4-pound beef roast. Add a small handful of soaked hardwood chips.

Trim excess fat from roast. Combine remaining ingredients in a small bowl, then spoon onto surfaces of roast, rubbing it in. Set aside for about 30 minutes while fire gets hot.

Place roast on bottom rack. Check on smokiness of wood chunks about once every hour. About every 4 hours or as needed, add more charcoal briquettes. You will need to light more charcoal 30 to 45 minutes before needed. Smoke roast 6 hours or until a thermometer inserted in center registers 170F (75C) or well done.   *Makes 8 to 10 servings.*

GORDON'S FAVORITE
FOURTH OF JULY BRISKET

▼▼▼▼▼

Fourth of July demands this brisket. Somehow the aroma of mesquite combined with the aroma of smoking brisket stirs many memories. This is a great party dish as it almost prepares itself and serves lots! Do smoke potatoes and make a smoked potato salad to serve alongside.

1 (5- to 6-lb.) beef brisket
Chipotle Rub (page 218)
Barbecue sauce (optional) (pages 211 to 214)

About 8 hours before you wish to serve, begin to heat your smoker following manufacturer's instructions. If using charcoal, build a double-layer fire of charcoal briquettes. After charcoal briquettes begin to catch fire, fill water pan with hot water, so it can heat as charcoal begins to burn hotter. When coals are coated with gray ash, add 6 to 8 green or soaked mesquite chunks. Or, turn on gas or electric smoker as manufacturer suggests for a 5- to 6-pound beef brisket. Add a small handful of hardwood chips.

Trim excess fat and connective tissue from both sides of beef. Apply rub, being careful to spoon rub onto roast and then lightly rub it over entire surface.

When fire is hot, place roast on bottom rack. Check on smokiness of wood chunks about once every hour. About every 4 hours or as needed, add more charcoal briquettes. You will need to light more charcoal 30 to 45 minutes before needed. Smoke 6 to 7 hours. Brisket will be fork tender and well done when ready to serve. Cool at least 30 minutes before slicing thinly across grain. Serve warm with or without barbecue sauce. *Makes 15 to 20 servings.*

SMOKED PRIME RIB ROAST WITH HORSERADISH DILL CREAM

▼▼▼▼▼

Smoked prime rib roast is about as wonderful as life ever gets! If you are not a horseradish fancier, prepare a red wine–beef broth mushroom sauce or serve the roast as is. The side dishes are up to you. With the smoky flavor of the beef, I like the contrast of au gratin potatoes and a simple vegetable or two. Creamed spinach is also very good with this.

1 (5- to 6-lb.) beef prime rib roast
1 recipe Mesquite Prime Rib Rub (page 218)
1 recipe Horseradish Dill Cream (page 210) (optional)

About 7 hours before you wish to serve, begin to heat your smoker, following manufacturer's instructions. If using charcoal, build a double-layer fire of charcoal briquettes. After charcoal briquettes begin to catch fire, fill water pan with hot water, so it can heat as charcoal begins to burn hotter. When coals are coated with gray ash, add 6 to 8 green or soaked hardwood chunks. Or, turn on gas or electric smoker as manufacturer suggests for a 5- to 6-pound beef roast. Add a small handful of soaked hardwood chips.

While fire is heating, trim excess fat from roast, then apply rub, being careful to spoon rub onto roast and then lightly rub it over entire surface.

When fire is hot, place roast on bottom rack. Check on smokiness of wood chunks about once every hour. About every 4 hours or as needed, add more charcoal briquettes. You will need to light more charcoal 30 to 45 minutes before needed. Smoke to desired doneness. Start checking for doneness with a thermometer after about 5 hours of smoking for medium rare. When done, remove from smoker and let stand 30 minutes before carving. Serve sliced with sauce on side. *Makes 6 to 8 servings.*

Prime Rib Beef Bones

▼▼▼▼▼

The bones from beef are much larger than pork ribs. They are much better smoked than grilled, as slow, moist heat enhances their flavor. Beef ribs are often on sale, due to seemingly little demand.

3 to 4 pounds prime rib beef bones
Mesquite Prime Rib Rub (page 218)
Barbecue sauce (pages 211–214)

About 5 hours before you wish to serve, begin to heat your smoker, following manufacturer's instructions. If using charcoal, build a single-layer fire of charcoal briquettes. After charcoal briquettes begin to catch fire, fill water pan with hot water, so it can heat as charcoal begins to burn hotter. When coals are coated with gray ash, add 4 to 6 green or soaked mesquite or other hardwood chunks. Or, turn on gas or electric smoker as manufacturer suggests for 3 to 4 pounds of beef ribs. Add a small handful of soaked hardwood chips.

While fire is heating, trim excess fat from ribs, then spoon rub on each, lightly rubbing over entire surface. This can be done ahead of time. The ribs are best if allowed to set at least 30 minutes.

When fire is hot, place ribs on bottom rack and smoke, checking smokiness of wood chunks every hour or so. Smoke about 4 hours. Ribs are done when meat starts to pull away from bones. Serve hot with warm barbecue sauce of your choice. *Makes 4 servings.*

SMOKED HERBED LEG OF LAMB

▼▼▼▼▼

Lamb, perhaps even more than pork or beef, takes on a whole new personality when smoked. The crush of herbs and chiles makes this lamb flavorful, juicy and succulent! Try smoking vegetables for side dishes. We like fennel and turnips with this roast.

1 (4- to 5-lb.) leg of lamb
1/4 cup good-quality olive oil, preferably Spanish
1/4 cup freshly squeezed lemon juice
1/2 Spanish onion, cut into chunks
6 cloves garlic, peeled
1 tablespoon fresh rosemary leaves or 1-1/2 teaspoons dried rosemary
1/2 cup fresh mint leaves or 1/4 cup dried mint
2 teaspoons crushed pequin quebrado chile
Grilled Fennel & Fresh Mint Salsa (page 207) (optional), using smoked instead of grilled fennel

Trim excess fat and remove parchmentlike covering from lamb. Place lamb in a large baking dish. Combine olive oil, lemon juice, onion, garlic, rosemary, mint and chile in a blender and process until pureed. Pour mixture over lamb, coating surface with mixture, and allow to set 2 hours at room temperature.

About 7 hours before you wish to serve, begin to heat your smoker, following manufacturer's instructions. If using charcoal, build a double-layer fire of charcoal briquettes. After charcoal briquettes begin to catch fire, fill water pan with hot water, so it can heat as charcoal begins to burn hotter. When coals are coated with gray ash, add 4 to 6 green or soaked hardwood chunks. Or, turn on gas or electric smoker as manufacturer suggests for a 4- to 5-pound leg of lamb. Add a small handful of soaked hardwood chips.

When fire is hot, place roast on bottom rack. Check on smokiness of wood chunks about once every hour. About every 4 hours or as needed, add more charcoal briquettes. You will need to light more charcoal 30 to 45 minutes before needed. Smoke to desired doneness. Start checking for doneness with a thermometer after 5 to 6 hours of smoking. (If making salsa, smoke fennel on top rack about 1 hour or until softened.) When done, remove lamb from smoker and let stand 30 minutes before carving into slices about 1/4 inch thick. Serve hot with salsa.   *Makes 4 to 6 servings.*

SMOKED VENISON, ANTELOPE OR ELK

▼▼▼▼▼

Smoking is best for game; it offsets the gaminess of the meat and also tenderizes it.

1 (3- to 4-lb.) venison, antelope or elk roast
1-1/2 cups dry red wine
1-1/2 teaspoons ground ginger
1 teaspoon salt
1 teaspoon freshly ground black pepper
1 tablespoon crushed pequin quebrado chile
4 cloves garlic, minced
1/2 cup finely minced onion
6 bacon slices

Trim fat and membranes from roast. Combine wine, ginger, salt, black pepper, chile, garlic and onion in a shallow nonreactive bowl or dish. Add roast and turn to coat with wine mixture. Cover and marinate at room temperature 2 hours or refrigerate overnight. Rotate roast three to four times while it is marinating.

About 30 minutes before you wish to begin smoking, prepare the fire. While it is heating, place bacon slices on top of roast, securing with wooden picks.

About 6 hours before you wish to serve, begin to heat your smoker, following manufacturer's instructions. If using charcoal, build a double-layer fire of charcoal briquettes. After charcoal briquettes begin to catch fire, fill water pan with hot water, so it can heat as charcoal begins to burn hotter. When coals are coated with gray ash, add 6 to 8 green or soaked mesquite or hardwood chunks. Or, turn on gas or electric smoker as manufacturer suggests for a 4- to 5-pound leg of lamb. Add a small handful of soaked hardwood chips.

When fire is hot, drain roast and pat dry. Place roast on bottom rack, and smoke, checking smokiness of wood chunks every hour or so. After 4 hours or as needed, add more charcoal briquettes. You will need to light more charcoal 30 to 45 minutes before needed. Smoke 4 or 5 hours or until roast is firm to the touch or has an internal temperature of 170F (75C) or well done. Let stand 20 minutes before carving. Serve sliced with any desired sauce. *Makes 6 to 8 servings*.

VARIATIONS

Rabbit or any small game may be prepared this same way but smoked for a shorter time. Strong-flavored game can be marinated overnight in the refrigerator in enough milk or buttermilk to cover.

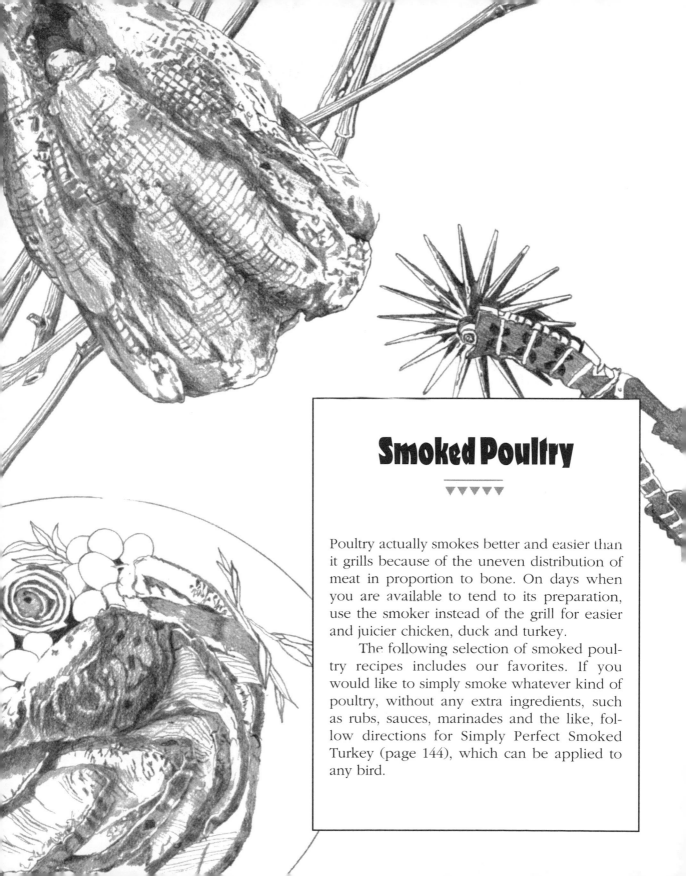

Smoked Poultry

▼▼▼▼▼

Poultry actually smokes better and easier than it grills because of the uneven distribution of meat in proportion to bone. On days when you are available to tend to its preparation, use the smoker instead of the grill for easier and juicier chicken, duck and turkey.

The following selection of smoked poultry recipes includes our favorites. If you would like to simply smoke whatever kind of poultry, without any extra ingredients, such as rubs, sauces, marinades and the like, follow directions for Simply Perfect Smoked Turkey (page 144), which can be applied to any bird.

SIMPLY PERFECT SMOKED TURKEY

▼▼▼▼▼

Smoking imparts a fuller flavor to turkey or to any poultry for that matter. Personally, I prefer to use a rub or some embellishment for flavoring the flesh. But if you prefer a simpler taste, you can always embellish it later with sauces and incorporate the turkey in pasta sauces, salads, sandwiches, pizzas and whatever else you might like.

1 (8- to 12-lb.) turkey
1 to 1-1/2 tablespoons salt
2 to 4 tablespoons unsalted butter, olive oil, vegetable oil or rendered poultry fat
Herbs such as thyme, sage, marjoram, chives or chervil, allowing 1 tablespoon total of
    dried or 2 tablespoons minced fresh herbs (optional)

Rinse turkey inside and out, trimming excess fat and removing pin feathers. Measure salt, allowing 1 tablespoon for each 7 pounds, and rub into interior cavities.

About 8 hours before you wish to serve, begin to heat your smoker, following manufacturer's instructions. If using charcoal, build a double-layer fire of charcoal briquettes. After charcoal briquettes begin to catch fire, fill water pan with hot water, so it can heat as charcoal begins to burn hotter. When coals are coated with gray ash, add 6 to 8 green or soaked hickory chunks or other hardwood. Or, turn on gas or electric smoker as manufacturer suggests for turkey. Add a small handful of soaked hickory or other hardwood chips.

Place turkey on lowest rack. Check on smokiness of wood chunks about once every hour. About every 4 hours or as needed, add more charcoal briquettes. You will need to light more charcoal 30 to 45 minutes before needed.

Continue to smoke turkey, checking for doneness after about 7 hours of smoking. To check, insert a meat thermometer in thigh, not touching bone. It should register 185F (85C). If you do not have a thermometer, cut a deep slit with a sharp slicing knife; juices should be clear, joints should move easily and skin should be browned. Let stand about 30 minutes before carving. *Makes 10 to 12 servings.*

Applewood-Smoked Turkey with Honey Glaze

▼▼▼▼▼

Try to get applewood chunks, as they really do impart a wonderful, sweet flavor. We like this turkey cold as well as hot.

1 (8- to 12-lb.) turkey
1 to 1-1/2 tablespoons salt
2/3 cup honey
2 tablespoons Dijon mustard
1 medium onion, coarsely chopped
1 apple, cut into chunks

About 6 to 8 hours before you wish to serve, begin to heat your smoker, following manufacturer's instructions. If using charcoal, build a double-layer fire of charcoal briquettes. After charcoal briquettes begin to catch fire, fill water pan with hot water, so it can heat as charcoal begins to burn hotter. When coals are coated with gray ash, add 6 to 8 green or soaked applewood or other hardwood chunks. Or, turn on gas or electric smoker as manufacturer suggests for turkey. Add a small handful of soaked hardwood chips.

Rinse turkey inside and out, trimming excess fat and skin, and removing pin feathers. Rub salt over inside of turkey, making sure to also rub inside neck cavity. Mix together honey and mustard and set aside. Place onion and apple inside turkey cavity. Spread honey mixture over entire skin surface.

Place turkey on lowest rack. Check on smokiness of wood chunks about once every hour. About every 4 hours or as needed, add more charcoal briquettes. You will need to light more charcoal 30 to 45 minutes before needed.

Continue to smoke turkey, checking for doneness after about 7 hours of smoking. To check, insert a meat thermometer in thigh, not touching bone. It should register 185F (85C). If you do not have a thermometer, cut a deep slit in thigh with a sharp slicing knife; juices should be clear, joints should move easily and skin should be brown. Let stand about 30 minutes before carving. Discard apple and onion. *Makes 10 to 12 servings.*

HICKORY-SMOKED TURKEY WITH PORT WINE MUSHROOM SAUCE

▼▼▼▼▼

Small turkeys work best for smoking whole. However, Gordon has smoked many, many large ones with our big Smokearoma® commercial-style smoker and even took orders for them when he had a restaurant in Hilton Head. One year he gave a smoked turkey to his minister, who in turn thanked him from the pulpit for his fabulously delicious "heavenly" turkey!

1 (8- to 12-lb.) turkey
1 recipe Fresh Lemon Zest Chile-Herb Rub (page 216)
Port Wine Mushroom Sauce (see below)

PORT WINE MUSHROOM SAUCE

2 tablespoons unsalted butter
1/4 cup finely diced onions
1 cup thinly sliced mushrooms
3 tablespoons all-purpose flour
2 cups chicken broth
2 tablespoons Port wine or to taste

About 6 to 8 hours before you wish to serve, begin to heat your smoker, following manufacturer's instructions. If using charcoal, build a double-layer fire of charcoal briquettes. After charcoal briquettes begin to catch fire, fill water pan with hot water, so it can heat as charcoal begins to burn hotter. When coals are coated with gray ash, add 6 to 8 green or soaked hickory or other hardwood chunks. Or, turn on gas or electric smoker as manufacturer suggests for turkey. Add a small handful of soaked hardwood chips.

While smoker is heating, rinse turkey inside and out, trimming excess fat and removing pin feathers. Prepare rub, then spoon mixture lightly over outside and inside of turkey, making sure to also rub inside neck cavity. Pat lightly to make sure rub is evenly applied and sticking to turkey. Place turkey on lowest rack. Check on smokiness of wood chunks about once every hour. About every 4 hours or as needed, add more charcoal briquettes. You will need to light more charcoal 30 to 45 minutes before needed.

Continue to smoke turkey, checking for doneness after about 7 hours of smoking. To check, insert a meat thermometer in thigh, not touching bone. It should register 185F (85C). If you do not have a thermometer, cut a deep slit in thigh with a sharp slicing knife; juices should be clear; joints should move easily and skin should be brown. Let stand about 30 minutes before carving. Prepare sauce and serve warm with turkey. *Makes 10 to 12 servings.*

PORT WINE MUSHROOM SAUCE

Melt butter in a heavy saucepan or skillet over medium heat. Add onion and mushrooms and cook, stirring constantly, until golden. Stir in flour and cook, stirring constantly, until lightly browned. Slowly add stock, stirring to make a thick sauce. Add Port and taste and adjust seasonings.

MESQUITE-SMOKED TEXAS-SIZED TURKEY LEGS

▼▼▼▼▼

These are quite popular in the Southwest at state fairs and smokehouses and are even sold by the side of the road. We like them with Smoked Potato Salad (page 65) and warm bread.

4 turkey legs
Gordon's West Texas–New Mexico Border Rub (page 218) or Mexican Oregano &
    Garlic Rub (page 217)
Barbecue sauce (optional)

Rinse turkey legs, then spoon rub on each leg and lightly pat it over entire surface.
About 4 hours before you wish to serve, begin to heat your smoker, following manufacturer's instructions. If using charcoal, build a double-layer fire of charcoal briquettes. After charcoal briquettes begin to catch fire, fill water pan with hot water, so it can heat as charcoal begins to burn hotter. When coals are coated with gray ash, add 2 to 4 green or soaked hardwood chunks. Or, turn on gas or electric smoker as manufacturer suggests for turkey. Add a small handful of soaked hardwood chips.
Place legs on rack just above hot water with larger skin side up.
Check on smokiness of wood chunks about once an hour, until flesh of the legs squeezes easily, skin is dark brown and internal temperature is 185F (85C) or about 3 hours. *Makes 4 servings.*

Fruitwood-Smoked Chicken with Smoked Apple Chipotle Salsa

▼▼▼▼▼

All who were lucky enough to sample this smoked chicken on a balmy February Sunday in Albuquerque can still recall woodsy yet mellow flavors of chicken with salsa. Needless to say we loved it! And, the best part is, once you set up your smoker with the rubbed chicken and vegetables, you basically can forget about it; you need only to check about once an hour to make sure the fire is still hot and smoking away. This chicken is absolutely fabulous cold, so you may want extras.

2 whole chickens, halved or quartered
1 recipe Fresh Lemon Zest Chile-Herb Rub (page 216)
3 to 4 large baking potatoes, cut in half lengthwise and cut sides dusted with rub

Smoked Apple Chipotle Salsa

3 apples, halved, cored and dusted with rub
1 large Spanish white or yellow onion, halved crosswise, peeled and cut sides dusted
    with rub
1 head garlic, sliced to remove bottom root portion
2 dried chipotle chiles, stewed in water to cover with 1 teaspoon cider vinegar added
    (1/3 cup minced chipotle and 1/3 cup chipotle liquid)
1/4 cup coarsely chopped flat-leaf parsley

About 5 hours before you wish to serve, begin to heat your smoker, following manufacturer's instructions. If using charcoal, build a double-layer fire of charcoal briquettes. After charcoal briquettes begin to catch fire, fill water pan with hot water, so it can heat as charcoal begins to burn hotter. When coals are coated with gray ash, add 2 to 4 green or soaked fruitwood or other hardwood chunks. Or, turn on gas or electric smoker as manufacturer suggests for chicken. Add a small handful of soaked hardwood chips. (For more information on smoking in general, see introduction to smoking, pages 15–21.)

Meanwhile, while fire is heating, rinse chickens, trimming excess fat, picking pin feathers and removing giblets. Then lightly sprinkle surface of each chicken with rub and inside body and neck cavities, patting it in lightly. Prepare fruit and vegetables and set aside.

Place chickens, cut side down, on rack closest to fire. Place potatoes, apples, onion and garlic on top rack. Check on smokiness of wood chunks about once every hour. Smoke vegetables and apples until softened. Continue to smoke chicken, checking for doneness after 4 to 5 hours of smoking. To check, insert a meat thermometer in thigh, not touching bone. It should register 185F (85C). If you do not have a thermometer, cut a deep slit in thigh with a sharp slicing knife; juices should be clear, joints should move easily and skin should be brown. Let stand about 30 minutes before carving. Prepare salsa. Serve chicken with potatoes and salsa. *Makes 4 to 8 servings, depending on side dishes.*

Smoked Apple Chipotle Salsa

Cut apples and onion into 1/2-inch pieces. Squeeze out smoked garlic using the flat side of a large knife, mincing if necessary. Combine apples, onion and garlic in a medium bowl. Add minced chipotle, chipotle liquid and parsley, and stir to combine.

Smoked Chicken Legs with Cabernet Cream

▼▼▼▼▼

If I have a lot of chicken legs on hand, I often smoke them all, as they are wonderful to have available in the freezer for quick meals. Once thawed in the refrigerator, they can be served cold or used in numerous ways, such as in pasta. Of course they can be served with barbecue sauce, too.

8 to 12 chicken legs
Mexican Oregano & Garlic Rub (page 217)
Cabernet Cream (page 25)

About 4 hours before you wish to serve, begin to heat your smoker, following manufacturer's instructions. If using charcoal, build a double-layer fire of charcoal briquettes. After charcoal briquettes begin to catch fire, fill water pan with hot water, so it can heat as charcoal begins to burn hotter. When coals are coated with gray ash, add 2 to 4 green or soaked hardwood chunks such as mesquite. Or, turn on gas or electric smoker as manufacturer suggests for chicken quarters. Add a small handful of soaked hardwood chips.

Rinse chicken legs, then while they are still moist, spoon rub lightly onto skin and gently rub in, making sure not to add too much.

Place legs on rack closest to fire with large skin side up. Check on smokiness of wood chunks about once every hour. Smoke 3 to 4 hours or until joints move easily, skin is dark brown and internal temperature is 185F (85C).

To serve, prepare Chipotle Cabernet Cream and serve 1 or 2 legs in a pool of sauce. If serving 2 legs per person, interlace 2 legs together to make a vertical teepee effect—it is rather striking. *Makes 4 to 12 servings.*

Smoked Chicken in Tomato Herb Sauce with Sun-Dried Tomatoes & Ripe Olives over Penne

▼▼▼▼▼

This is one of our favorite pasta toppings. You can serve it with or without grated cheese. With your favorite green salad and perhaps some bread sticks or freshly baked bread you have a quick meal.

1 tablespoon good-quality olive oil, preferably Spanish
1-1/2 cups coarsely chopped Spanish onion
4 cloves garlic, minced
7 cups chopped fresh tomatoes or Winter's Pleasure Grilled Tomatoes (page 229)
1 tablespoon chopped fresh Italian oregano or 1 teaspoon dried oregano
1 tablespoon chopped fresh basil or 1 teaspoon dried basil
2 bay leaves
1/2 cup sun-dried tomatoes, reconstituted and chopped
1 teaspoon crushed caribe chile
2 cups chopped smoked chicken or turkey
1/2 cup oil-cured ripe olives, pitted and coarsely chopped or to taste
Salt and freshly ground black pepper
1 pound penne pasta
1/4 cup coarsely chopped flat-leaf parsley (optional)
1/2 cup freshly grated Parmesan or Romano cheese or a blend of the two

Heat oil in a large skillet over medium heat. Add onion and garlic and cook until soft. Add tomatoes, oregano, basil, bay leaves, sun-dried tomatoes and caribe chile. Bring to a boil, reduce heat and simmer about 30 minutes. Add chicken and olives and heat until hot. Taste and add salt and black pepper to taste.

Cook pasta in boiling salted water according to package directions until just tender. Drain and divide pasta among individual plates. Spoon sauce over hot pasta, top with parsley, if desired, and cheese. *Makes 4 to 6 servings.*

Variations

If desired, 8 to 12 ounces of lean ground pork can be cooked with the onion and garlic. Drain off fat and continue with preparation of sauce. Omit all meat for a vegetarian sauce.

Mesquite-Smoked Chicken Breast in Red Chile Sauce

▼▼▼▼▼

The sauce for this chicken breast is inspired by Adobo Sauce (page 202), which I keep in my freezer for occasions when I want a quick entree. For faster preparation, the chicken can be grilled.

2 cups water
1/4 cup crushed caribe chiles
2 tablespoons ground hot chile
2 tablespoons ground mild chile
2 garlic cloves, peeled
1 tablespoon ground cumin
1 teaspoon ground Mexican oregano
1 teaspoon salt
4 whole boneless, skinless chicken breasts

Combine all the ingredients except chicken in a blender and puree. Pour about 1/4 of sauce into a shallow glass dish. Add chicken and turn to coat. Cover and refrigerate chicken and extra sauce.

About 3 hours before you wish to serve, begin to heat your smoker, following manufacturer's instructions. If using charcoal, build a single-layer fire of charcoal briquettes. After charcoal briquettes begin to catch fire, fill water pan with hot water, so it can heat as charcoal begins to burn hotter. When coals are coated with gray ash, add 2 to 4 chunks green or soaked hardwood chunks. Or, turn on gas or electric smoker as manufacturer suggests for chicken breast. Add a small handful of soaked hardwood chips.

When fire is well started and hot, remove chicken from marinade and refrigerate marinade. Place chicken on lowest rack, spooning a little marinade over each piece. Check on smokiness of wood chunks about once every hour. (Be careful—too much will put out the fire.) Smoke 2 to 3 hours or until chicken is firm when pressed with your hand or until a meat thermometer registers 185F (85C). Bring reserved marinade to a boil in a small saucepan, reduce heat and simmer 5 minutes. Serve with chicken. *Makes 4 to 8 servings.*

Smoked Caribbean "Jerk"-Style Chicken

▼▼▼▼▼

This jerk marinade can be used interchangeably with beef, pork or lamb—even rabbit. Originating in Jamaica, where runaway slaves developed this chile- and spice-laden marinade to keep meat without refrigeration, it is almost inedible to all but the most seasoned fire eaters if made with habanero or Scotch Bonnet chiles. Therefore, I suggest you might prefer pequin quebrado, jalapeño or another hot substitute that's lower on the chile Richter scale.

1 tablespoon good-quality olive oil, preferably Spanish
1 cup finely chopped Spanish onion
6 cloves garlic, minced
1 to 3 teaspoons very finely pureed or ground habanero, pequin or jalapeño chile
3 bay leaves, preferably fresh
1 teaspoon ground dried thyme
3/4 teaspoon ground allspice
1/2 teaspoon ground turmeric (optional)
1 teaspoon salt
1/4 cup light rum
1/4 cup freshly squeezed lime juice
1 (3-lb.) chicken, quartered

First prepare jerk marinade, by heating oil in a heavy saucepan over medium heat. Add onion and garlic and cook until light golden. Add chile, bay leaves, thyme, allspice, turmeric, if using, and salt and cook until onion becomes quite soft, about 5 minutes. Add rum and lime juice and cook about 5 minutes or until sauce thickens slightly and becomes richly colored. Taste and adjust seasonings. Set aside to cool.

Rinse chicken and pat dry. Remove excess fat and remove skin, if desired. Place chicken pieces in a large glass baking pan and rub jerk mixture over entire surface of chicken; cover and refrigerate at least 4 hours or overnight.

About 4 hours before you wish to serve, begin to heat your smoker, following manufacturer's instructions. If using charcoal, build a single-layer fire of charcoal briquettes. After charcoal briquettes begin to catch fire, fill water pan with hot water, so it can heat as charcoal begins to burn hotter. When coals are coated with gray ash, add 2 to 4 green or soaked hardwood chunks. Or, turn on gas or electric smoker as manufacturer suggests for chicken breast. Add a small handful of soaked hardwood chips.

Place chicken on rack, skin side up if skin is left on. Check on smokiness of wood chunks about once every hour. Smoke 3 to 4 hours or until chicken joints move easily, color has darkened and internal temperature is 185F (85C).   *Makes 2 to 4 servings.*

SMOKED BARBECUED CHICKEN

▼▼▼▼▼

What could be easier to prepare and a surer bet for a crowd? Gordon says he has literally smoked hundreds, if not thousands, for fund-raisers and for his restaurants. With or without a barbecue sauce of choice, you're sure to love this classic.

2 (3-lb.) chickens, halved or quartered
1 recipe Fresh Lemon Zest Chile-Herb Rub (page 216) or Gordon's West Texas–New
    Mexico Border Rub (page 218)
1 recipe barbecue sauce (pages 211 to 214)

Rinse chickens and pat dry. Remove excess fat. Lightly spoon rub over chickens, patting it in slightly.

About 4 hours before you wish to serve, begin to heat your smoker, following manufacturer's instructions. If using charcoal, build a single-layer fire of charcoal briquettes. After charcoal briquettes begin to catch fire, fill water pan with hot water, so it can heat as charcoal begins to burn hotter. When coals are coated with gray ash, add 2 to 4 green or soaked hardwood chunks, such as mesquite. Or, turn on gas or electric smoker as manufacturer suggests for chicken halves or quarters. Add a small handful of soaked hardwood chips.

Place chickens, cut side down, on rack closest to fire. Check on smokiness of wood chunks about once every hour. Smoke 3 to 4 hours or until chicken joints move easily, color has darkened and internal temperature is 185F (85C).   *Makes 4 to 8 servings, depending on side dishes.*

CILANTRO CHICKEN PATTIES

▼▼▼▼▼

If you have leftover smoked chicken or turkey and cooked rice, you may wish to try this fast and easy entree. For appetizers, just make the patties smaller.

1/3 cup skim milk
1 tablespoon all-purpose flour
1/4 teaspoon salt
1 teaspoon crushed caribe chile or pequin quebrado
1 teaspoon freshly squeezed lime juice
1/4 cup egg substitute or 1 egg, beaten
1-1/2 cups cubed smoked chicken
1/2 cup coarsely chopped onion
1/4 cup coarsely chopped cilantro
1 cup cooked rice
2 teaspoons vegetable oil
1 cup soft bread crumbs
Wedges of fresh lime dusted with mild chile
Salsa (optional)

In a small, heavy saucepan combine milk, flour, salt, chile, lime juice and egg substitute. Cook, stirring constantly, over medium to low heat until bubbly. Set aside. Combine chicken, onion, cilantro and rice in a food processor and pulse until chopped. Add chicken mixture to thickened sauce and combine well.

Heat oil in a large nonstick skillet over medium heat. Form chicken mixture into 12 patties. Coat lightly with crumbs and fry on each side until golden, about 5 minutes per side. Serve with wedges of lime and salsa, if desired. *Makes 4 servings.*

Mesquite-Smoked Duckling with Chile Honey Glaze & Ginger Pear Salsa

▼▼▼▼▼

I created this dish because I love to eat duck. Smoking makes it even more juicy and flavorful than roasting. I like to serve it with Ginger Pear Salsa, a hearty wild rice casserole and a simply dressed green salad. Do think about cooking more than one duck at a time to have leftovers.

1 (5-lb.) duck
1 lemon
1-1/2 teaspoons salt
7 cloves garlic
2 tablespoons ground hot chile
3 tablespoons honey
Ginger Pear Salsa (page 206)

About 6 hours before you wish to serve, begin to heat your smoker, following manufacturer's instructions. If using charcoal, build a double-layer fire of charcoal briquettes. After charcoal briquettes begin to catch fire, fill water pan with hot water, so it can heat as charcoal begins to burn hotter. When coals are coated with gray ash, add 3 to 4 green or soaked mesquite chunks. Or, turn on gas or electric smoker as manufacturer suggests for chicken halves or quarters. Add a small handful of soaked hardwood chips.

Meanwhile, rinse duck and pat dry. Remove excess fat and any pin feathers. Cut lemon in half and squeeze half of it into duck's cavities, both neck and body. Cut remaining half into 4 pieces and place 3 in body cavity, 1 in neck cavity. Sprinkle neck and body cavities with salt. Peel and mince 3 cloves garlic and sprinkle over inside cavities. Using a very sharp meat fork, pierce skin on breast cavity and sides of duck. Peel remaining garlic and cut into slivers. Poke a sliver of garlic into each pierced hole, holding up skin so that garlic sliver will go all the way in. Combine chile and honey in a small bowl and spoon over outside surface of duck.

Place duck, breast side up, on rack. Check on smokiness of wood chunks about once every hour. After about 4 hours or as needed, add more charcoal briquettes. You will need to light more charcoal 30 to 45 minutes before needed.

Smoke duck 5 to 6 hours or until legs or wings move easily at joints, skin is deep brown and internal temperature is 185F (85C). *Makes 2 to 3 servings.*

NOTE: If you do prepare more than one duck or have leftovers, they can be successfully frozen for up to 3 months.

Asian Smoked Duck Breast Salad

▼▼▼▼▼

This salad is a delicious way to use any leftover smoked duck. Of course you could smoke duck just for this purpose. You can vary ingredients to suit your own taste and what you have on hand. For example, fresh fruit of most any kind or most nuts can be used.

8 ounces rice noodles or fine spaghetti
Sesame Dressing (see below)
1-1/2 cups boneless, skinless smoked duck breast, cut into thin strips (about 12 oz.)
4 thinly sliced green onions
1/2 cup 1/2-inch jicama squares or 1 (4-oz.) can water chestnuts, drained
6 ounces fresh snow peas, string removed and cut into 1/2-inch slices
1 cup thinly sliced red radishes
2 cups greens or 1 pound fresh spinach leaves or Romaine lettuce torn in pieces

Sesame Dressing

2 tablespoons vegetable oil
2 tablespoons sesame oil
2 tablespoons rice wine vinegar or 1 tablespoon each white wine vinegar and dry sherry
1 tablespoon prepared mustard
2 teaspoons peeled and grated gingerroot
2 cloves garlic, minced
1 tablespoon light soy sauce
1 teaspoon crushed caribe chile

Cook noodles in salted boiling water according to package directions. Drain, rinse with cold water and refrigerate. Prepare dressing and set aside.

Combine duck, green onions, jicama, snow peas and radishes in a large bowl. Combine duck mixture with noodles and greens. Drizzle dressing over salad and toss to combine.   *Makes 4 servings.*

Sesame Dressing

Combine all of the dressing ingredients in a small bowl and whisk or beat with a fork until blended.

Note: Garnish with onion drumettes, if desired. Cut tops off green onions at beginning of dark green top, leaving some of top attached. Slice off roots, removing firm portion attached to root. Then using a sharp knife, thinly slice both ends of each green onion about 1 inch deep into each end. Chill in ice water at least 1 hour before serving to allow for curling. Each will curl where cut.

Smoked Seafood

▼▼▼▼▼

Smoking produces seafood that is moist and delicious! And the best part is that so much flavor is gained through the smoking process that you can keep the seasonings and sauces quite simple. For just the right accent, salsas are the perfect accompaniment.

In all the recipes, you can substitute other types of fish. Always select a firm-fleshed fish, not a delicate fish such as sole or flounder, which would be overwhelmed by the smoking process. For example, any firm-fleshed fish that is sturdy enough to cut steaks from, such as tuna, halibut, sea bass or haddock, can be substituted for the suggested fish. Most any knowledgeable fish or seafood dealer should be able to help you with substitutions.

Shellfish are also very flavorful and moist when smoked. You can create some of the world delicacies, such as smoked mussels, oysters and the like, right in your own smoker.

GARY'S SMOKED SACRAMENTO
PESTO SALMON

▼▼▼▼▼

I met Gary Rominger at the world's largest Balloon Fiesta in Albuquerque. After talking a while, he told me about his favorite grilled salmon recipe and then sent it to me. We tried it and found it to be terrific. To quote Gary, "This is my all-time favorite way to serve salmon to guests."

6 (6- to 8-oz.) salmon fillets, with skin attached
1 cup good-quality olive oil, preferably Spanish
2 cups tightly packed coarsely chopped basil leaves
1 teaspoon salt or to taste
1/2 teaspoon freshly ground black pepper
3 cloves garlic, peeled
2 tablespoons piñon nuts
Crushed caribe chile
1 lime

About 2 hours before you wish to serve, begin to heat your smoker following manufacturer's instructions. If using charcoal, build a single-layer fire of charcoal briquettes. After charcoal briquettes begin to catch fire, fill water pan with hot water, so it can heat as charcoal begins to burn hotter. When coals are coated with gray ash, add 2 to 4 hardwood chunks, green or soaked, preferably alder or applewood. Or, turn on gas or electric smoker as manufacturer suggests for fish. Add a small handful of soaked alder or applewood chips.

Rinse salmon, pulling out any bones, and pat dry. In a blender, combine oil, basil, salt, pepper, garlic and piñons, and process until finely pureed.

Temperature inside smoker should be at least 200 to 250F (95 to 120C). Place fish, skin side down, on rack. Smoke about 10 minutes. Open and quickly look at salmon. If top of flesh is slightly darkened and fat globules have formed, quickly spoon equal amounts of pesto over tops of salmon and smoke another 15 to 20 minutes. Using a fork, gently pierce center of fleshiest piece. If fish flakes, it is done.

To serve, use a large, long-handled spatula to gently lift each fillet to a warm plate. Do not worry if skin sticks, just be sure to get salmon and pesto out in one piece. Sprinkle with caribe. Cut lime into 6 wedges and place a wedge on each serving. *Makes 6 servings.*

APPLEWOOD-SMOKED SALMON STEAKS

▼▼▼▼▼

Ever since I first tasted applewood-smoked salmon appetizers in Seattle many years ago, I vowed to make some myself. This recipe is slightly embellished, as it is an entree, not an appetizer. If desired, when smoking these steaks, smoke some plain salmon strips (that have just been salted, peppered and lightly brushed with a bit of vegetable oil) very slowly as steaks are cooking and leave in after steaks are done to gain a smoky almost leathery quality. These salmon strips are super as appetizers or canapés.

4 (4- to 6-oz.) 1-inch-thick salmon steaks
2 tablespoons plus 1 teaspoon olive oil
3 tablespoons red wine vinegar
2 tablespoons balsamic vinegar
1/2 teaspoon crushed pequin quebrado chile or to taste
Freshly ground black pepper
Orange, Lemon & Smoked Pineapple Salsa (page 203)

Begin preparation of this salmon at least a half day ahead or the evening before you wish to serve it. Rinse salmon, pulling out any bones. Combine olive oil, vinegars, chile and black pepper in a glass or stainless steel shallow bowl. Add salmon and turn to coat. Cover and refrigerate at least 2 hours or overnight.

Follow manufacturer's instructions for your smoker. If using charcoal, build a single-layer fire of charcoal briquettes. After charcoal briquettes begin to catch fire, fill water pan with hot water, so it can heat as charcoal begins to burn hotter. When coals are coated with gray ash, add 2 to 4 green or soaked applewood chunks. Or, turn on gas or electric smoker as manufacturer suggests for fish. Add a small handful of soaked applewood chips. (Chips are used instead of chunks in electric or gas smokers.)

Place salmon steaks on rack. Smoke 30 minutes, then check for doneness with a fork: salmon should flake easily. If not, continue smoking, checking every 10 minutes or so until steaks are done. Serve steaks with salsa. *Makes 4 servings.*

NOTE: Ingredients for salsa can be smoked at the same time as fish.

MESQUITE-SMOKED TROUT WITH CILANTRO SALSA

▼▼▼▼▼

Smoking trout makes it so succulent—juicier than when quickly grilled. The crisp clean taste of Cilantro Salsa is a great accompaniment. We also serve the salsa with warm bread or double the recipe and serve it over pasta.

Cilantro Salsa (see below)
1 (1-1/2- to 2-lb.) whole trout, ready to cook, rinsed
1 fresh lime
Salt and freshly ground black pepper

CILANTRO SALSA

1 cup packed cilantro leaves
1/2 cup finely chopped onion
1 red bell pepper, parched, peeled and chopped (see Note)
1/4 cup green chiles, parched, peeled and chopped (see Note)
4 cloves garlic, minced
2 tablespoons good-quality olive oil, preferably Spanish
2 tablespoons freshly squeezed lime juice

Prepare salsa. About 2 hours before you wish to serve, begin to heat your smoker, following manufacturer's instructions. If using charcoal, build a single-layer fire of charcoal briquettes. After charcoal briquettes begin to catch fire, fill water pan with hot water, so it can heat as charcoal begins to burn hotter. When coals are coated with gray ash, add 2 to 4 green or soaked mesquite chunks. Or, turn on gas or electric smoker as manufacturer suggests for fish. Add a small handful of soaked mesquite chips. (Chips are used instead of chunks in electric or gas smokers.) Lightly oil rack.

Halve lime and squeeze juice of 1 half over outside and inside of fish. Lightly sprinkle inside cavity and outside surface with salt and pepper. Spoon 1/4 cup salsa into cavity of fish. Reserve remaining salsa to serve with fish.

Place fish on rack. Smoke about 1-1/2 hours or until flesh flakes when pierced with a fork. Place fish on a platter. Cut remaining lime half into wedges and place over fish. Spoon remaining salsa around fish and serve.   *Makes 4 servings.*

Cilantro Salsa

Combine all the salsa ingredients in a medium bowl.

NOTE: Both bell peppers and chiles are parched by placing them over a hot grill or burner or under a broiler and rotating them until they are uniformly blistered. Then chill in ice water and peel or store in refrigerator or freezer for later use.

Grape-Smoked Trout Fillets with Triple Zest

▼▼▼▼▼

These are light and very fresh tasting. Some call this combination of white grapes and chicken or fish *veronique*. This recipe reminds me of spring—of the first fishing trip of the season. For a delicious lunch or dinner, serve the trout with a favorite rice or risotto and a salad.

4 (8- to 10-oz.) fresh trout, ready to cook
1/2 cup white seedless grapes, rinsed and halved
1-1/2 teaspoons each minced lime, lemon and orange zest
1 tablespoon freshly squeezed lime juice
2 tablespoons freshly squeezed lemon juice
3 tablespoons freshly squeezed orange juice
1 tablespoon crushed caribe red chile plus a bit more for garnish
3 tablespoons good-quality olive oil, preferably Spanish

About 2 hours before you wish to serve, begin to heat your smoker, following manufacturer's instructions. If using charcoal, build a single-layer fire of charcoal briquettes. After charcoal briquettes begin to catch fire, fill water pan with hot water, so it can heat as charcoal begins to burn hotter. When coals are coated with gray ash, add a large handful of grape cuttings. Or, turn on gas or electric smoker as manufacturer suggests for fish. Add a small handful of grape cuttings. Lightly oil rack.

Rinse trout and place grapes in each cavity, securing with a wooden pick or skewer. Combine remaining ingredients in a large glass or stainless steel bowl and place fish in marinade. After a few minutes, turn trout in marinade. Let set about 30 minutes.

Place fish on rack. Smoke about 1-1/2 hours or until flesh flakes when pierced with a fork. *Makes 4 servings.*

MESQUITE-SMOKED MUSSELS

▼▼▼▼▼

Remember those canned smoked mussels? If you liked them, you'll absolutely love these. Serve them tossed with a primavera medley over pasta or salad greens or eat them as is as an appetizer. For a light meal, enjoy them with crisp-crusted French-style bread to dip in the wine-garlic sauce.

To clean the mussels, place them all in a sink full of water. Sprinkle with some cornmeal. After about an hour, scrub and remove beards.

1 cup white wine
2 pounds mussels, scrubbed and debearded
6 cloves garlic, coarsely chopped

About 2 hours before you wish to serve, begin to heat your smoker, following manufacturer's instructions. If using charcoal, build a single-layer fire of charcoal briquettes. After charcoal briquettes begin to catch fire, fill water pan with hot water, so it can heat as charcoal begins to burn hotter. When coals are coated with gray ash, add 2 to 4 chunks green or soaked fruitwood or alder chunks. Or, turn on gas or electric smoker as manufacturer suggests for seafood. Add a small handful of soaked fruitwood chips. (Chips are used instead of chunks in electric or gas smokers.)

Place wine and mussels in a foil pan or a pan that will not get hurt by smoke, layering them with garlic. Place pan on rack closest to heat. Mussels are done when they open. This should take about 2 hours. Discard any mussels that do not open. *Makes 4 servings.*

VARIATION

You can also smoke mussels directly on the rack, placing hinge side of shells down. You will need a good pair of long-handled tongs to place and remove mussels.

SMOKED OYSTERS ON THE HALF SHELL WITH HORSERADISH DILL CREAM

▼▼▼▼▼

What is better than fresh oysters—freshly smoked! These can be served as a main course or as appetizers.

24 oysters, shucked, with oyster still on half shell
1 recipe Horseradish Dill Cream (page 210)

About 1-1/2 hours before you wish to serve, begin to heat your smoker, following manufacturer's instructions. If using charcoal, build a single-layer fire of charcoal briquettes. After charcoal briquettes begin to catch fire, fill water pan with hot water, so it can heat as charcoal begins to burn hotter. When coals are coated with gray ash, add 2 to 4 green or soaked fruitwood or alder chunks. Or, turn on gas or electric smoker as manufacturer suggests for seafood. Add a small handful of soaked fruitwood chips. (Chips are used instead of chunks in electric or gas smokers.)

Place oysters, shell side down, right on rack or, for ease in handling, place them in shallow pans that fit inside smoker. Smoke about 30 minutes or until oysters have turned white and edges have begun to curl. If not done, check every 5 minutes. Serve with sauce. *Makes 4 main-dish servings or 6 appetizer servings.*

SMOKED SCALLOPS WITH
FRESH LIME-GINGER CREAM

▼▼▼▼▼

The sweet succulence of scallops is enhanced by fruitwood smoke. These are wonderful served alone or over a salad of mixed greens, using the sauce as a dressing.

1-1/2 pounds fresh sea scallops
1/2 lime, plus 2 tablespoons juice
1 tablespoon good-quality olive oil, preferably Spanish
Salt and freshly ground black pepper

FRESH LIME-GINGER CREAM

1/2 cup regular or light sour cream
1/2 cup yogurt
2 teaspoons minced gingerroot
1 teaspoon minced lime zest
1 tablespoon honey

About 1-1/2 hours before you wish to serve, begin to heat your smoker, following manufacturer's instructions. If using charcoal, build a single-layer fire of charcoal briquettes. After charcoal briquettes begin to catch fire, fill water pan with hot water, so it can heat as charcoal begins to burn hotter. When coals are coated with gray ash, add 2 to 4 soaked or green fruitwood chunks. Or, turn on gas or electric smoker as manufacturer suggests for seafood. Add a small handful of soaked fruitwood chips. (Chips are used instead of chunks in electric or gas smokers.)

Place scallops horizontally on skewers, spacing them so they do not touch. Squeeze lime half evenly over scallops, then brush with oil and lightly sprinkle with salt and pepper. Place on rack closest to smoke. Smoke about 1 hour or until scallops are smoky and firm. While scallops are smoking, prepare sauce. Serve scallops on a bed of sauce or over salad greens. *Makes 4 servings.*

FRESH LIME-GINGER CREAM

Mix all the ingredients together in a small bowl. Taste and adjust seasonings, if desired.

MESQUITE-SMOKED SHRIMP WITH PASTA

▼▼▼▼▼

Shrimp takes rather reluctantly to a real smokiness, making mesquite a good wood for smoking it. In addition to serving this shrimp over linguine, you could serve it fajita-style with a feisty pico de gallo (page 202) or over greens.

1/4 cup dry white wine, such as chardonnay
1 fresh jalapeño chile, minced
4 cloves garlic, minced
2 tablespoons good-quality olive oil, preferably Spanish
1 pound medium shrimp, shelled and deveined
3 roma tomatoes
12 ounces red or green chile pasta such as linguini
1/3 cup Mediterranean olives, pitted and slivered
1/3 cup fresh basil leaves, chopped
1/4 cup coarsely grated Romano or Parmesan cheese

Combine wine, chile, garlic and olive oil in a shallow glass or stainless steel baking pan. Skewer shrimp and place in pan, spooning liquid over shrimp. Cover and marinate at least 30 minutes.

About 1-1/2 hours before you wish to serve, begin to heat your smoker, following manufacturer's instructions. If using charcoal, build a single-layer fire of charcoal briquettes. After charcoal briquettes begin to catch fire, fill water pan with hot water, so it can heat as charcoal begins to burn hotter. When coals are coated with gray ash, add 2 to 4 chunks soaked or green mesquite chunks. Or, turn on gas or electric smoker as manufacturer suggests for seafood. Add a small handful of soaked wood chips. (Chips are used instead of chunks in electric or gas smokers.)

Remove shrimp from marinade. Place skewered shrimp and tomatoes on rack closest to smoke. Smoke about 30 minutes, then check for doneness. Shrimp should be pink and firm; tomatoes should be shriveled and soft. If not, continue checking every 10 to 15 minutes until done; it should definitely not take over 1 hour.

Just before removing shrimp and tomatoes from smoker, cook pasta. Peel and coarsely chop tomatoes and combine tomatoes and shrimp with remaining ingredients except cheese. Pour mixture over pasta and toss to combine. Divide pasta among warm plates and add cheese to taste. *Makes 4 servings.*

NOTE: If desired, tomatoes can be used as is without smoking. The smoking adds a richer flavor.

Smoked Whole Snapper with Mushrooms & Chiles

▼▼▼▼▼

A whole red snapper is so elegant to serve unless you just find fish with their heads on disgusting! In that case, fillets can be used and the cooking time shortened. (The flavors won't be as subtle though.) Placing thinly sliced lemons and limes inside the fish and on top along with onion, herbs and chiles imparts a wonderful flavor. Mushrooms and chiles that are smoked simultaneously are then used to flavor steamed rice.

1 (3-lb.) whole red snapper (with head on)
2 fresh lemons
2 fresh limes
1 small red onion, thinly sliced and separated into rings
1 teaspoon ground coriander
1 teaspoon ground Mexican oregano
3/4 teaspoon salt
1 tablespoon caribe, Northern New Mexican crushed red chile
2 cups whole mushrooms, such as porcini, shiitake or button mushrooms
3 fresh New Mexico green chiles
Steamed rice
Salsa, such as Hot Orange Salsa (page 204)

About 4 hours before you wish to serve, begin to heat your smoker, following manufacturer's instructions. If using charcoal, build a single-layer fire of charcoal briquettes. After charcoal briquettes begin to catch fire, fill water pan with hot water, so it can heat as charcoal begins to burn hotter. When coals are coated with gray ash, add wood chunks. Or, turn on gas or electric smoker as manufacturer suggests for seafood. Add a small handful of soaked fruitwood chips. (Chips are used instead of chunks in electric or gas smokers.)

Prepare fish. Rinse and remove any remaining excess body tissue, then scale with a knife to remove any remaining scales. Zest both lemons and limes. Then thinly slice each. Inside, place one-half of both zests, 1 sliced lemon, and 1 sliced lime, about half the onion, and half the seasonings—down through caribe. Place remaining half of zests and sliced lemon, lime, onion and seasonings on top of snapper and place fish on bottom grate of smoker. Then skewer mushrooms and chiles and place on top grate. Smoke 1-1/2 hours, then check to see if mushrooms and chiles are smoky and soft. If they are, remove. Check to see if heat is still moderately hot and fish is still smoking. Add more coals and wood if needed. Continue to smoke 1-1/2 to 2 more hours or until fish flakes.

Meanwhile, chop smoked mushrooms, peel and chop smoked chiles and stir into steamed rice.

Remove smoked snapper from bones and serve fillets with salsa or plain with just a garnish of lime and lemon slices, accompanied by rice. *Makes 4 servings.*

MESQUITE-SMOKED RUBBED CATFISH FILLETS WITH BLACK BEAN SALSA

▼▼▼▼▼

Although catfish is somewhat mild and tender, its succulent flesh really takes to Fresh Lemon Zest Chile-Herb Rub and rallies to Black Bean Salsa. When you use a rub, there's no marinating time to wait and you can just build a fire in the smoker big enough to handle the entire smoking period of the fish. You'll really enjoy the ease of preparing this for your family or guests!

Fresh Lemon Zest Chile-Herb Rub (page 216)
1-1/2 pounds catfish fillets
Black Bean & Corn Salsa (page 206)

Prepare rub if necessary, or use rub that was previously made and frozen. Rinse fillets and pat dry; lightly smear with rub.

About 1-1/2 hours before you wish to serve, begin to heat your smoker, following manufacturer's instructions. If using charcoal, build a single-layer fire of charcoal briquettes. After charcoal briquettes begin to catch fire, fill water pan with hot water, so it can heat as charcoal begins to burn hotter. When coals are coated with gray ash, add 2 to 4 soaked or green mesquite chunks. Or, turn on gas or electric smoker as manufacturer suggests for seafood. Add a small handful of soaked fruitwood chips. (Chips are used instead of chunks in electric or gas smokers.)

Place fillets on grate just above smoke and smoke about 30 minutes, checking to see if fillets flake and are firm and well smoked. If not, continue checking every 10 to 15 minutes until done; it should definitely not take over 1 hour. Serve with salsa napped over fillets or in a bed underneath, depending on side dishes you are serving. *Makes 4 servings.*

SMOKED LOBSTER TAIL

▼▼▼▼▼

Smoking makes lobster meat sweet and juicy. I am particularly fond of using a fruit-wood to smoke a lobster. You can also smoke whole lobsters if you wish—just slice the live crustaceans down the center before placing them on the grate of the smoker. Hot lime-scented olive oil is a wonderful alternative to the usual lemon butter.

4 (8-oz.) lobster tails
1 to 2 teaspoons vegetable oil
Juice of 1 lime
3 tablespoons good-quality olive oil, preferably Spanish
2 teaspoons pequin quebrado or hot crushed pure chile of your choice
Fresh salsa, such as Orange, Lemon & Smoked Pineapple (optional) (page 203)

About 1-1/2 hours before you wish to serve, begin to heat your smoker, following manufacturer's instructions. If using charcoal, build a single-layer fire of charcoal briquettes. After charcoal briquettes begin to catch fire, fill water pan with hot water, so it can heat as charcoal begins to burn hotter. When coals are coated with gray ash, add 2 to 4 green or soaked fruitwood chunks, such as cherry or apple. Or, turn on gas or electric smoker as manufacturer suggests for seafood. Add a small handful of soaked fruitwood chips. (Chips are used instead of chunks in electric or gas smokers.)

Prepare lobster tail, cutting membrane on belly with a utility shears. Then sharply bend each tail back to break shell and to make it lie flat. Rinse each and pat dry; lightly rub each with vegetable oil. Place lobster tails on grate and smoke about 1 hour, checking to see if lobster is firm and well smoked.

Meanwhile, prepare hot lime-scented oil by combining lime juice, olive oil and chile. Divide mixture among 4 small bowls. Prepare salsa if desired. Serve lobster with dipping sauce and salsa. *Makes 4 servings.*

Quick Smoking

▼▼▼▼▼

Tender, moist meats—the ones that you would ordinarily grill or sauté—can be quickly smoked for a change of taste and pace. This method is much quicker than hardwood smoking in a smoker and the entire process is done indoors. So when wind, rain or snow is blowing and the weather or your available time is not good for outdoor grilling or smoking, this method is an ideal answer. If you have a covered grill, you can use it for quick smoking.

Benefits of quick smoking are that you do not add any fat when cooking, the cooked foods are quite moist and the entire process is fast. A variety of smoking materials may be used. Pair the appropriate smoking material with the food you are smoking. An example is that milder foods, such as most fish, seafood or chicken, are wonderful smoked with tea. More aromatic wood chips, such as mesquite, hickory or fruitwoods, might be more flavorful with beef, pork, lamb, veal or even vegetables.

Spices such as allspice or cloves can be used for flavoring. Herbs are too mild and do not yield their same essence when burned.

TECHNIQUES

- Select a heavy pan with a close-fitting cover. The diameter of the pan should allow the meat or fish being cooked to lie flat on a rack. Do not use a pan with a nonstick finish; it can delaminate from exposure to the high heat involved.
- Use a trivet to hold the food to be smoked above the smoking material. If you do not have one, you can always use a steamer such as the one you use to hold vegetables. Always select a trivet made of metal—not plastic or wood, as these can be burned.
- Preheat the oven before starting the pot to smoke on the surface unit or burner.
- When placing food on the trivet, drain it thoroughly and pat dry, so it will be as dry as possible. If food is very dry and somewhat sticky, lightly oil the trivet to prevent sticking.
- To assure juicy, flavorful foods, check for doneness after the minimum time for smoking listed for recipe.
- Use plain black or green tea. Do not use flavored teas. If you do not have loose tea, open a tea bag and use the leaves. One regular tea bag contains about 1-1/2 teaspoons of loose tea.
- If you have a smoke alarm in your kitchen, disarm it before you begin smoking. Don't forget to rearm it after you finish cooking.

Quick-Smoked Sea Scallops with Chilied Lime-Cilantro Cream

▼▼▼▼▼

Fresh succulent scallops are wonderful when prepared using this simple method. They can be served singly as an appetizer—on top of a bed of interesting greens or with pasta dressed with Chilied Lime-Cilantro Cream—or they can be served as a dinner entree.

1 pound sea scallops
Juice of 1 lime
1 teaspoon fresh lime zest, minced
1 teaspoon ground pure hot chile
3/4 teaspoon salt
2 tablespoons tea leaves
8 long strips lime zest for a garnish

Chilied Lime-Cilantro Cream

1 cup plain yogurt or light sour cream
1 large green chile, parched (page 161), peeled and chopped, or 2 tablespoons canned
    chopped chiles, drained
1/4 cup coarsely chopped cilantro
1 tablespoon freshly squeezed lime juice
1 teaspoon minced lime zest

Rinse scallops and pat dry. Pour lime juice into a shallow bowl. Add scallops, let stand 10 minutes, then turn and let stand another 10 minutes. Combine lime zest, hot chile and salt in a small bowl. Remove scallops from marinade and place on a draining rack. Dust top and bottom of each with half of the zest mixture and pat in.

Place tea leaves in bottom of a nonstick Dutch oven large enough to hold scallops on a trivet. Add trivet and place pan over medium-high heat. Preheat oven to 425F (220C). When tea leaves begin to smoke, add seasoned scallops, carefully placing each, flat side down, on rack; cover pan. Place pan in oven and smoke scallops 5 minutes. When done, scallops will be opaque, not translucent. Prepare sauce. Serve with sauce and garnish with lime zest strips intertwined on top of scallops. *Makes 4 servings.*

Chilied Lime-Cilantro Cream

Combine all ingredients in a small bowl.

Tea & Chipotle–Smoked Red Snapper

▼▼▼▼▼

The dried chipotle chiles add a spicy subtlety to this marinated red snapper. Serve it with calabacitas, a medley of zucchini, tomatoes, corn and onions. Rice is an ideal accompaniment with reduced marinade served on top.

1 (1-lb.) skinless red snapper fillet
1/2 cup freshly squeezed orange juice (1 orange)
2 teaspoons coarsely chopped orange zest
4 dried chipotle chiles, cooked in 2 teaspoons vinegar and 1/2 cup water
4 cloves garlic, minced
1/2 teaspoon ground Mexican oregano
2 tablespoons tea leaves
4 additional dried chipotle chiles (optional), broken

Rinse fish and remove any bones; pat dry. In a nonreactive bowl, combine orange juice, zest, cooked chipotles with liquid, garlic and Mexican oregano. Add fish to marinade, cover and let marinate about 1 hour.

Place tea leaves and dry chipotle chiles, if using, in bottom of a nonstick Dutch oven large enough to hold fish flat on a trivet. Add trivet and place pan over medium-high heat. Preheat oven to 425F (220C). When tea leaves and chipotles begin to smoke, remove fish from marinade, reserving marinade, and pat dry. Place fish on trivet and cover. Place pan in oven and smoke fish 5 minutes.

Meanwhile, place remaining marinade in a small saucepan and simmer to reduce for a sauce. When done, fish should flake and flesh should be opaque, not clear. Serve with sauce as desired. *Makes 4 servings.*

Spicy Quick-Smoked Chicken

▼▼▼▼▼

You can smoke either boneless, skinless chicken breasts or thighs using this method. It is best to choose one or the other—breasts are quickest but not as juicy as boneless, skinless thighs. Amazingly, the flavor and moist, wonderful texture belie the ease with which these chicken parts can be smoked. They are great served over a big tossed salad or pasta, either dressed with a vinaigrette. Or, serve them with or without barbecue sauce and your favorite style of potatoes and salad. Smoked chicken is also great chunked and placed in flour tortillas alongside freshly made salsa in burritos.

2 whole chicken breasts, skinned and boned
About 1 tablespoon Mexican Oregano & Garlic Rub (page 217)
2 tablespoons tea leaves

Rinse chicken breast and cut each in half, trimming off any bits of fat or cartilage; pat dry. Place on a plate and lightly dust each side of each breast with about 1/4 teaspoon of rub; gently and evenly rub into surface.

Place tea leaves in bottom of a nonstick Dutch oven large enough to hold chicken on a trivet. Add trivet and place pan over medium-high heat. Preheat oven to 425F (220C). When tea leaves begin to smoke, add chicken; cover pan. Place pan in oven and smoke chicken 7 minutes or until chicken is firm to the touch and juices are clear when cut in thickest part. Serve as desired.   *Makes 4 servings.*

SOUTHWESTERN RUBBED PORK STEAKS

▼▼▼▼▼

Buy boneless, lean pork steaks, or trim out bone from 1/2-inch-thick pork chops. The bone makes smoking slower and less even. These steaks are excellent served with a spicy barbecue sauce or a salsa.

4 (6- to 8-oz.) pork sirloin steaks, about 1/2 inch thick
About 1 tablespoon Fresh Lemon Zest Chile-Herb Rub (page 216)
1/2 cup mesquite chips or other hardwood or 2 tablespoons tea leaves
4 whole allspice (optional)

Rinse pork steaks and pat dry. Using a meat mallet or cleaver, pound each steak on both sides to make them as thin as possible and place on a plate. Lightly dust each side of each steak with about 1/4 teaspoon of rub and gently and evenly rub into surface.

Place mesquite chips or tea leaves and allspice, if using, in bottom of a nonstick Dutch oven large enough to hold pork flat on a trivet. Add trivet and place pan over medium-high heat. Preheat oven to 425F (220C). When tea leaves begin to smoke, add seasoned pork, carefully placing each on rack; cover pan. Place pan in oven and smoke pork 20 minutes or until pork is firm to the touch and flesh is white, not pink, when sliced in thickest portion. Serve as desired.   *Makes 4 servings.*

Jiffy Turkey Tenders Burritos with Salsa

▼▼▼▼▼

Try mesquite chip smoking on these quick-to-do turkey tenders, which are also great served as is with vegetables. They are pretty and festive enough to serve for a luncheon party.

1-1/2 pounds turkey tenders
4 tablespoons apple cider vinegar
2 tablespoons crushed caribe chile
1/2 cup mesquite or other hardwood chips or 2 tablespoons tea leaves
2 cups thinly sliced white or red cabbage
1/2 cup chopped white onion
12 (10- to 12-inch) flour tortillas
1 recipe Fresh Cranberry Salsa (page 208) and/or 1 recipe Black Bean & Corn Salsa
    (page 206)

Rinse turkey tenders and cut larger ones so that all will be about the same size; pat dry. Pound with a meat mallet or cleaver to flatten to about 1/2-inch thickness. Place tenders on a plate and sprinkle each side first with 2 tablespoons of the vinegar and then with caribe chile, evenly coating each. Let set about 30 minutes.

Meanwhile, combine cabbage with onion and remaining 2 tablespoons vinegar in a medium bowl. Cover and set aside.

Place wood chips or tea leaves in bottom of a nonstick Dutch oven large enough to hold turkey flat on a trivet. Add trivet and place pan over medium-high heat. Preheat oven to 425F (220C). When tea leaves begin to smoke, place turkey on rack; cover pan. Place pan in oven and smoke turkey 7 minutes.

When done, turkey will be opaque, not translucent. Slice or chop into bite-size pieces. Warm tortillas in a microwave or wrap in foil and place in a hot oven for about 10 minutes. To serve, place marinated cabbage in a strip down center of each tortilla. Evenly divide turkey among tortillas, and then spoon a ribbon of salsa over turkey or just top each with a spoonful of salsa. Serve with additional salsa. *Makes 12 burritos or 6 servings.*

HERB-SMOKED PORK TENDERLOIN ON SAUTÉED MUSHROOMS

▼▼▼▼▼

Smoking tenderloin over herbs enhances its flavors. Paired with sautéed mushroom salsa, this quick-to-fix entree will become a favorite. Serve with polenta, Southwestern chile or blue corn pasta under the mushroom salsa.

1 (1-lb.) pork tenderloin
2 tablespoons dry sherry
1 teaspoon crushed pequin quebrado or 1 teaspoon ground pure hot chile
2 teaspoons fresh rosemary or 1 teaspoon dried rosemary
1/2 cup fruitwood chips or other hardwood or 2 tablespoons tea leaves
2 teaspoons unsalted butter
2 cups sliced mushrooms
1 cup chopped onion
2 cloves garlic, minced
Salt and freshly ground black pepper

Trim off any excess fat, then rinse pork tenderloin and pat dry. Place on a plate and drizzle with 1 tablespoon of the sherry. Sprinkle with chile and place rosemary sprigs over entire surface of pork.

Place fruitwood chips or tea leaves in bottom of a nonstick Dutch oven large enough to hold pork in a single layer on a trivet. Add trivet and place pan over medium-high heat. Preheat oven to 425F (220C). When wood chips or tea leaves begin to smoke, place seasoned pork on trivet; cover pan. Place pan in oven and smoke pork 20 minutes or until pork is firm to the touch and flesh is white, not pink, when sliced in fleshiest portion.

Meanwhile, melt butter in a medium skillet over medium heat. Add mushrooms, onion and garlic and cook, stirring occasionally, until onion is transparent and mushrooms have released their liquid. Drizzle with remaining sherry. Season with salt and black pepper. Cut pork into 1/2-inch-thick slices and serve over mushrooms. *Makes 4 servings.*

MESQUITE-SMOKED BEEF MEDALLIONS & SALSA

▼▼▼▼▼

Make a salsa from seasonal ingredients to accompany this steak dish—no need to heat the grill in stormy weather!

4 (6-oz.) beef top loin steaks (New York strip), cut into about 1/2-inch-thick slices
2 teaspoons freshly ground green peppercorns
2 cloves garlic, finely minced
1/2 cup mesquite chips or other hardwood chips or 2 tablespoons tea leaves
Aztec-Style Pico de Gallo with Chipotles (page 202) or other salsa

Pat steaks dry with paper towels. Combine ground pepper with garlic in a small bowl and pat into each side of steaks.

Place mesquite chips or tea leaves in bottom of a nonstick Dutch oven large enough to hold beef on a trivet. Add trivet and place pan over medium-high heat. Preheat oven to 425F (220C). When wood chips or tea leaves begin to smoke, place beef on trivet; cover pan. Place pan in oven and smoke beef 10 to 15 minutes or to desired doneness. Serve with salsa.   *Makes 4 servings.*

TEA-SMOKED TOMATOES

▼▼▼▼▼

The subtle smoky taste of these tomatoes makes them an excellent accompaniment to any of the other smoked entrees here. You can smoke them first and keep them warm while smoking meat or fish.

2 large tomatoes, cut in half crosswise
1 tablespoon coarsely chopped fresh basil or other fresh herb such as dill, thyme or
    oregano, or 1-1/2 teaspoons dried herb
2 tablespoons tea leaves

Sprinkle tomatoes with herbs. Add tea leaves to bottom of a nonstick Dutch oven large enough to hold tomatoes on a trivet. Add trivet and place pan over medium-high heat. Preheat oven to 425F (220C). When tea leaves begin to smoke, add tomatoes to trivet; cover pan. Place pan in oven and smoke tomatoes 5 minutes or until they are just softened. Serve as desired.   *Makes 4 servings.*

RUBBED SMOKED ONIONS

▼▼▼▼▼

These onions are outrageous served with any entree! You can smoke them alongside meat or, depending on the space, smoke them first.

1 large or 2 medium onions, cut crosswise into 1/2-inch-thick slices
1 teaspoon any kind of rub (pages 216 to 218)
2 tablespoons tea leaves or 1/2 cup wood chips, if smoking with an entree

Lightly dust onion slices with rub. Add tea leaves or wood chips to bottom of a nonstick Dutch oven large enough to hold onion slices flat on a trivet. Add trivet and place pan over medium-high heat. Preheat oven to 425F (220C). When tea leaves or wood chips begin to smoke, add onion slices to trivet; cover pan. Place pan in oven and smoke onion slices 5 minutes or until softened and done as desired. Serve as desired.   *Makes 4 servings.*

SMOKED EGGPLANT

▼▼▼▼▼

Depending on what material you use for smoking, this eggplant tastes rich enough to be an entree. Sliced after smoking, it is a wonderful addition to a pasta sauce, pasta salad or as part of a vegetarian burrito served with your favorite salsa. It's important to rub the salt on each side of the eggplant slices and allow them to "weep" at least 30 minutes before smoking them.

1 small eggplant
About 1/2 teaspoon salt
1 teaspoon any rub (pages 216 to 218) (optional)
2 tablespoons tea leaves or 1/2 cup wood chips, if smoking with an entree

Rinse eggplant, then using a sharp-tined meat fork, score entire outer surface of eggplant, piercing about 1/4 inch deep. Cut crosswise into about 3/8-inch-thick slices. Lightly sprinkle each side of each slice with salt and place between a double thickness of paper towels. Place between plates and let stand at least 30 minutes. Pat eggplant dry with paper towels.

Lightly dust eggplant slices with rub. Add tea leaves or wood chips to bottom of a nonstick Dutch oven large enough to hold eggplant slices flat on a trivet. Add trivet and place pan over medium-high heat. Preheat oven to 425F (220C). When tea leaves or wood chips begin to smoke, add eggplant slices to trivet; cover pan. Place pan in oven and smoke eggplant slices 5 minutes or until softened. Serve as desired. *Makes 4 servings.*

VARIATION

Zucchini, yellow or pattypan squash can be substituted for eggplant. You do not need to salt them. Just slice lengthwise, season with rub or herb salt and smoke as above.

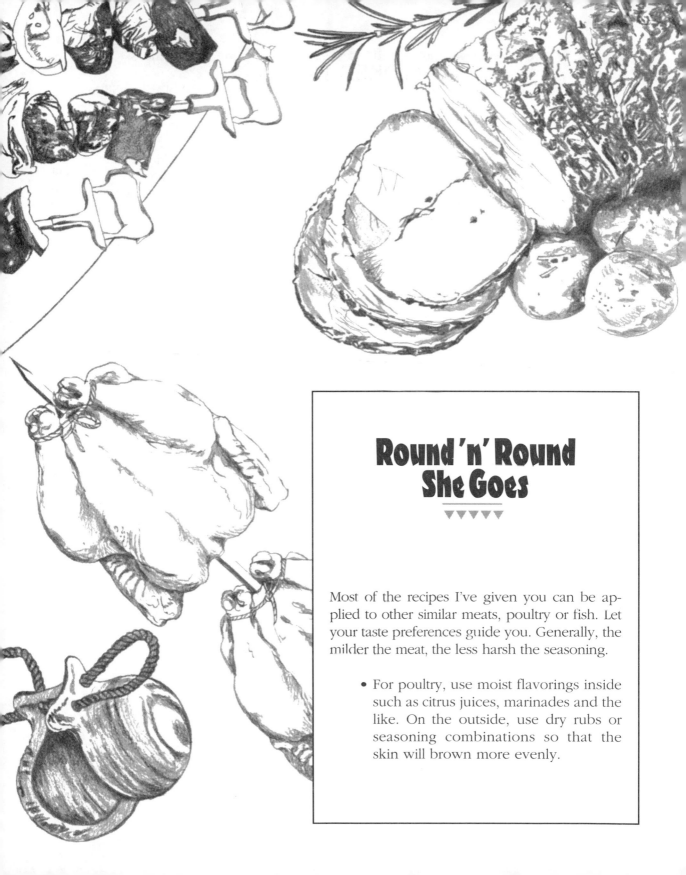

Round 'n' Round She Goes

▼▼▼▼▼

Most of the recipes I've given you can be applied to other similar meats, poultry or fish. Let your taste preferences guide you. Generally, the milder the meat, the less harsh the seasoning.

- For poultry, use moist flavorings inside such as citrus juices, marinades and the like. On the outside, use dry rubs or seasoning combinations so that the skin will brown more evenly.

- Lift the skin on poultry and insert any favorite herb, chiles, cheeses, garlic and spices under it.
- Marinating meats in seasonings for at least 2 hours ahead of time will intensify the flavors.
- For large roasts, such as a large beef tip roast, overseason the outside and allow to marinate or penetrate before roasting. Let stand at least 30 minutes before carving so that the flavors will be absorbed with the internal juices.
- If desired, you can always add soaked wood chips to the fire if using gas or electric, or green or soaked chunks to the charcoal fire. Just try what you like and have lots of fun developing your very own style!
- All the suggested cooking times allow for extra time to start a charcoal fire. You can shorten the time by up to 15 to 30 minutes if you have a fast-heating rotisserie-grill. The approximate time at which to start the cooking also allows for the roast, etc., to stand before carving and serving.

ROLLED PORK ROAST WITH MEXICAN OREGANO, ORANGE & GARLIC

▼▼▼▼▼

Fruits add a somewhat sweet overtone that always complements pork. Finish the meal with a grilled vegetable or salad.

2 teaspoons ground Mexican oregano
6 cloves garlic, minced
1 tablespoon minced orange zest
1 (4-lb.) rolled boneless pork butt or shoulder
1/2 cup freshly squeezed orange juice
1/4 cup orange marmalade (optional)

Combine oregano, garlic and orange zest in a small bowl. Unroll roast. Spread half of mixture over inside of roast. Roll and tie together with kitchen string, allowing 1 inch between each tie. Mix juice and marmalade, if using, with remaining half of herb mixture. Drizzle mixture evenly over outer surface of pork and rub in. Cover and refrigerate overnight or at least 2 hours.

About 3-1/2 hours before you wish to serve, and following the manufacturer's instructions for using your rotisserie, build a fire or turn on electric or gas rotisserie unit. For charcoal, build fire about 2 inches from back, removing grate and placing a pan for drippings centered under meat. The firebed should be about 6 inches wide and extend beyond pit about 4 inches on each end. The coals should be gray when you start cooking. Heat unit to 350F to 400F (175C to 205C).

Meanwhile, evenly skewer roast on spit, adjusting until it is well balanced, and tighten forks into meat at either end, centering roast on spit. Place on grill so that motor will turn properly. Roast, spooning pan juices over meat periodically. If using charcoal, keep adding briquettes, 6 to 10 every 30 minutes. Continue to roast until internal temperature reaches 160F (70C) or medium. Allow roast to stand 20 minutes before carving to set juices. *Makes 6 to 8 servings.*

Spit-Roasted Fresh Ham with Raisin Bourbon Sauce

▼▼▼▼▼

Spending about a day tending the fire and basting this fresh ham will be worth the effort. My mother always loved this dish and prepared it for special family affairs. One great time is Derby Day, if you are staying home and watching the races on television. Most any holiday is fine, too.

1 (11- to 13-lb.) fresh whole ham
1 tablespoon salt
Freshly ground black pepper
1/4 cup freshly minced gingerroot or 1 teaspoon ground ginger
2 tablespoons fresh sage leaves or 2 teaspoons dried sage
Raisin Bourbon Sauce (see below)
Prepared mustard
Chutney

Raisin Bourbon Sauce

2 cups raisins, preferably half dark and half golden
1 cup bourbon
1 cup packed light brown sugar
1/4 cup cornstarch
1 teaspoon freshly grated nutmeg
1/2 teaspoon ground allspice
1 tablespoon grated lemon zest
2 cups cold water
1 cup apple juice
1/4 cup freshly squeezed lemon juice

Have butcher bone ham, removing skin and excess fat layer and trimming out pockets of fat on inside. To prepare for roasting, place inside down on a cutting board and trim off any excess fat on outside, leaving at least 1/4 inch of fat layer to keep meat moist. (For ease in trimming fat, use a boning knife and insert it into fat about 1/4 inch from lean and slice off fat.) Score outside fat into 1-inch diamonds. Combine salt, pepper, ginger and sage in a small bowl and mix. Rub about half of it over entire inside surface. Then roll inside of ham tightly together. Secure tightly with kitchen twine, allowing about 1 inch between each tie. Sprinkle outer surface of ham with remaining spice mixture.

About 8 hours before you wish to serve, and following the manufacturer's instructions for using your rotisserie, build a fire or turn on electric or gas rotisserie unit. For charcoal, build fire about 2 inches from back, removing grate and placing a pan for drippings centered under meat. The firebed should be about 6 inches wide and extend beyond pit about 4 inches on each end. The coals should be gray when you start cooking. Heat unit to 350F (175C).

Meanwhile, evenly skewer roast on spit, adjusting until it is well balanced, and tighten forks into meat at either end, centering roast on spit. Position so that motor will turn properly. Roast, spooning pan juices over meat periodically. If using charcoal, keep adding briquettes, 6 to 10 every 30 minutes.

Prepare Bourbon Raisin Sauce. Continue to roast 6 to 8 hours or until internal temperature reaches 160F (70C). Allow to stand 20 minutes before carving. Serve with Raisin Bourbon Sauce, mustard and chutney.   *Makes 18 to 24 servings.*

RAISIN BOURBON SAUCE

Combine raisins and bourbon in a small bowl and macerate 2 hours or so at room temperature. Combine brown sugar, cornstarch, spices and zest in a large nonreactive saucepan. Stir in a little of the water to make a smooth paste. Gradually stir in remaining water, apple juice and lemon juice. Cook, stirring constantly, over medium heat until thickened, 2 to 3 minutes. Remove from heat and add raisins and bourbon. Serve warm.

Roasted Leg of Lamb with Fresh Spinach, Feta & Chipotle Stuffing

▼▼▼▼▼

Lamb almost any way I can get it has always been a personal favorite. The succulent juiciness of butterflied and stuffed leg of lamb when properly done is hard to beat. This recipe is really great with a rice dish and salad and perhaps some wonderful bread. Grilled Leg of Lamb à la Greque (page 86) is wonderful on the rotisserie also.

1 (5- to 7-lb.) sirloin end of leg of lamb or whole small leg, boned and butterflied
8 ounces fresh spinach leaves, washed and stemmed
4 ounces feta cheese, crumbled
4 ounces oil-packed sun-dried tomatoes
4 to 6 dried chipotle chiles, cooked and minced (page 202)
6 cloves garlic, minced
2 tablespoons dry red wine
Freshly cracked black or other favorite peppercorns

Have butcher bone lamb, if possible. If you do it, carefully trim off the parchmentlike covering on outside of fat. Trim fat to about 1/4 inch thick on outside of roast, being sure to leave a layer of fat for juiciness and flavor. Trim out hard fat that is on inside of leg. Spread leg open, inside up. Evenly cover inside surface of lamb with layers of remaining ingredients. Roll tightly, being careful to stuff any filling that escapes back into layers of lamb. Cut off about 2 feet of kitchen twine. Tie a loop about 1 inch across and slip end of twine through loop. Secure tightly around rolled leg of lamb and continue wrapping string and tying it at 1-inch intervals.

Meanwhile, about 6 hours before you wish to serve, and following the manufacturer's instructions for using your rotisserie, build a fire or turn on electric or gas rotisserie unit. For charcoal, build fire about 2 inches from back, removing grate and placing a pan for drippings centered under meat. The firebed should be about 6 inches wide and extend beyond pit about 4 inches on each end. The coals should be gray when you start cooking. Heat unit to 350F (175C).

Evenly skewer roast on spit, adjusting until it is well balanced, and tighten forks into meat at either end, centering roast on spit. Place on grill so that motor will turn properly. Roast, spooning pan juices over meat periodically. If using charcoal, keep adding briquettes, 6 to 10 every 30 minutes. Continue to roast until internal temperature is 140F (60C) for rare, 160F (70C) for medium or 170F (75C) for well done. When done, allow roast to stand at least 20 minutes before carving to set juices.   *Makes 6 to 8 servings.*

CARNE ASADA WITH CHIPOTLE RUB

▼▼▼▼▼

Fresh roasted beef, especially when it is done on a rotisserie, is so juicy and wonderful in warm, just-off-the-grill tortillas, either corn or wheat. Drizzle with a freshly made salsa. Or serve this roast however you prefer.

1 (4- to 5-lb.) beef rump roast or sirloin tip
1 recipe Chipotle Rub (page 218)
1 recipe Sunny Salsa (page 205) or other salsa
Corn or flour tortillas

About 5 hours before you wish to serve, and following the manufacturer's instructions for using your rotisserie, build a fire or turn on electric or gas rotisserie unit. For charcoal, build fire about 2 inches from back, removing grate and placing a pan for drippings centered under meat. The firebed should be about 6 inches wide and extend beyond pit about 4 inches on each end. The coals should be gray when you start cooking. Heat unit to 350F (175C).

Meanwhile, lightly rinse beef roast. Then dust lightly with rub mixture, using a spoon to dip rub out and then applying it with your hand. Allow to set about 30 minutes.

Evenly skewer roast on spit, adjusting until it is well balanced, and tighten forks into meat at either end, centering roast on spit. Place on grill so that motor will turn properly. Roast, spooning pan juices over meat periodically. If using charcoal, keep adding briquettes, 6 to 10 every 30 minutes. Continue to roast 4 to 5 hours or until internal temperature is 140F (60C) for rare, 160F (70C) for medium and 170F (75C) for well done. Allow roast to stand 20 minutes before carving to set juices. Serve with salsa and warm tortillas. *Makes 6 to 8 servings.*

SHASHLIK SHISH KABOBS

▼▼▼▼▼

After sampling several versions of shish kabobs at famous restaurants and working to develop my very own special marinade, I created this recipe. After sampling many other marinades, I still prefer this one. It has a rich, deep flavor that improves with longer marinating. Wild rice or bulgur pilaf is excellent with this.

2 cups Burgundy wine
1/2 cup minced green onions
2 bay leaves
1 tablespoon Worcestershire sauce
2 cloves garlic, minced
2 tablespoons light soy sauce
1/4 cup good-quality olive oil, preferably Spanish
1/2 teaspoon dry mustard
**2 teaspoons each chopped fresh rosemary, thyme, basil, tarragon and marjoram or 1 teaspoon
    each dried herbs**
4 pounds lean lamb, cut from leg into 2-inch squares
6 tomatoes, cut into wedges, or 1 pint cherry tomatoes
2 large green bell peppers, cut into wedges
12 small onions, peeled and cooked 10 minutes
2 tablespoons unsalted butter
2 cups fresh mushrooms

Combine wine, onions, bay leaves, Worcestershire sauce, garlic, soy sauce, olive oil, mustard and herbs in a large nonreactive bowl. Add lamb and cover. Refrigerate at least 1 day or up to 3 days.

Meanwhile, about 1 hour before you wish to serve, and following the manufacturer's instructions for using your rotisserie, build a fire or turn on electric or gas rotisserie unit. For charcoal, build fire about 2 inches from back, removing rack and placing a pan for drippings centered under meat. The firebed should be about 6 inches wide and extend beyond pit about 4 inches on each end. The coals should be gray when you start cooking. Heat unit to 450F (230C).

If your unit came with a shish kabob attachment, use it. If not, use the main rod for lamb. Center lamb so that it will rotate evenly. Use other skewers for vegetables. Place tomatoes on one skewer, parboiled onions on another and bell pepper chunks on another. Place over grill so that motor will turn properly. Place skewers on grill rack. Roast, spooning marinade over lamb occasionally. As it rotates, watch lamb and vegetables. When any item is done, such as tomatoes, remove and keep warm in oven.

Melt butter in a skillet over medium heat. Add mushrooms and cook until golden, about 10 minutes. Cool slightly and place on a skewer and grill for the last 3 to 5 minutes of cooking time. Check lamb after 15 minutes. Cook until internal temperature of lamb is 140F (60C) for rare, 160F (70C) for medium and 170F (75C) for well done. To serve, remove lamb and vegetables from skewers. Place lamb in center of a large platter and surround it with vegetables. *Makes 6 to 8 servings.*

CRISPY ROTI CHICKEN WITH
BLUE CORN–GREEN CHILE DRESSING

▼▼▼▼▼

Chickens are wonderful on the rotisserie. Generally most people get chicken too done and somewhat dry, especially the breast meat. With a rotisserie, the circulating spit keeps the meat juicier. It is still important, however, to watch and immediately remove the chicken from the heat when done.

2 (3-lb.) chickens
5 tablespoons unsalted butter
1/2 cup chopped onion
1/2 cup chopped celery
4 cups blue corn bread (make any favorite corn bread, substituting blue corn meal for yellow or white meal)
3 or 4 green chiles, parched (page 161), peeled and chopped or 1 (4-oz.) can chopped green chiles, drained
1 cup coarsely chopped toasted Brazil nuts (see Note)
2 teaspoons chopped fresh sage or 1 teaspoon dried sage
1 cup chicken broth

Rinse and clean chickens, removing pin feathers and trimming off any excess body fat. If desired, clip off tail and third joint of wing. Melt 1 tablespoon of the butter in a large skillet over low heat. Add onion and celery and cook until slightly transparent, about 10 minutes. Remove from heat and stir in corn bread, green chiles, nuts, sage and just enough broth to make a dressing that will cling together but is not soggy. Spoon stuffing into neck and body cavities of both chickens, skewering each cavity shut.

About 2 hours before you wish to serve, and following the manufacturer's instructions for using your rotisserie, build a fire or turn on electric or gas rotisserie unit. For charcoal, build fire about 2 inches from back, removing grate and placing a pan for drippings centered under meat. The firebed should be about 6 inches wide and extend beyond pit about 4 inches on each end. The coals should be gray when you start cooking. Heat unit to 350F (175C).

Meanwhile, evenly skewer chickens on spit, adjusting until they are as well balanced as possible, and tighten forks into chicken at either end, pressing very firmly. Melt remaining 4 tablespoons butter and brush evenly over both birds. Place over grill so that motor will turn properly. Roast, spooning pan juices over chickens periodically. If using charcoal, keep adding briquettes, 6 to 10 every 30 minutes. Continue to roast until internal temperature reaches 185F (85C) and drumsticks move easily. Allow birds to stand 20 minutes before carving to set juices. *Makes 4 to 6 servings.*

NOTE: Place nuts on a baking sheet and toast about 15 minutes in a 350F (175C) oven until they are lightly golden on edges, or toast about 5 minutes over medium heat in the skillet in which you will be making the dressing.

Mayan Roast Chicken, Pibil Style

▼▼▼▼▼

We regularly conduct culinary tours either to study the origins of foods or to review similarities between different yet related cultures. We took a group of Old Town Albuquerque Cooking School alumni to the Melia Mayan Hotel in Cozumel to study the similarities between the dishes of Yucatan and those of New Mexico.

Amazingly, there is a great deal of similarity. Each culture uses what it has at hand to create very parallel concepts. For example, this sauce, although composed of different ingredients, is similar to adobo sauce—so popular on pork in New Mexico. It can be used with equal success on shrimp or fish, yet is not traditionally used on pork in the Yucatan.

This recipe was very generously given to us by the chef at the Melia Mayan. He not only shared his recipes but also supervised our cooking to be sure we prepared Mayan dishes his way. In the Yucatan, where large, New Mexican–type chiles do not grow, achiote, made from annatto seeds, is often used as a substitute for the red chiles. Annatto seeds have a unique, subtle flavor, but they are not hot. In order to bring out the flavor of achiote, sour orange must be used. Because sour oranges are not usually available in the United States, you can substitute regular orange juice and fresh lime juice.

1 (4- to 5-lb.) roasting chicken
3/4 cup achiote paste (optional; see Note)
2-1/2 cups orange juice
2/3 cup freshly squeezed lime juice
2 teaspoons ground cumin
2 teaspoons freshly ground black pepper
2 tablespoons minced garlic (about 12 garlic cloves)
1/2 teaspoon ground Mexican oregano
1 tablespoon plus 1 teaspoon chicken stock base
1 teaspoon salt

Rinse chicken and place in a large bowl. In a nonreactive bowl, combine achiote, if using, with orange and lime juices and mix well. Then stir in remaining ingredients. Spoon sauce over chicken, including inner cavities. Cover and refrigerate overnight or at least 2 hours.

About 2 hours before you wish to serve, and following the manufacturer's instructions for using your rotisserie, build a fire or turn on electric or gas rotisserie unit. For charcoal, build fire about 2 inches from back, removing grate and placing a pan for drippings centered under meat. The firebed should be about 6 inches wide and extend beyond pit about 4 inches on each end. The coals should be gray when you start cooking. Heat unit to 350F (175C).

Meanwhile, remove chicken from marinade. Evenly skewer chicken on spit, adjusting until it is as well balanced as possible, and tighten forks into chicken at either end, pressing very firmly. Place on grill so that motor will turn properly. Roast, spooning pan juices over chicken periodically. If using charcoal, keep adding briquettes, 6 to 10 every 30 minutes. Continue to roast until internal temperature reaches 185F (85C) or until drumsticks wiggle. Allow chicken to stand 20 minutes before carving to set juices. *Makes 4 to 6 servings.*

NOTE: Achiote paste is available in markets featuring Mexican foods and by mail order.

Jennifer Brennan's Tandoori Chicken

▼▼▼▼▼

I got to know Jennifer in 1985, when we both shared a podium at a professional meeting about writing cookbooks. She is fascinating and an excellent author, cook and researcher. This recipe, though it looks complicated, is delicious and a great way to use a rotisserie. Amazingly, tandoori-style preparation uses several Southwestern ingredients.

1 (3- to 3-1/2-lb.) chicken
Juice of 2 lemons
1-3/4 teaspoons ground pure mild chile or paprika
1/4 teaspoon ground cayenne or pequin chile
1-3/4 teaspoons salt or to taste
About 4 tablespoons butter, melted
Red onion rings and thin lime slices for garnish

Marinade

1 small onion, chopped
4 shallots, peeled (optional)
2-inch piece gingerroot, chopped
6 cloves garlic, peeled
3 green serrano chiles or 1 large jalapeño chile
1-1/2 cups yogurt
5 tablespoons butter, melted
2 teaspoons ground coriander
1/2 teaspoon ground cinnamon
1-1/2 teaspoons ground cumin
1/2 teaspoon ground cloves
1/2 teaspoon ground cardamom
1 teaspoon ground mace
1 teaspoon freshly ground black pepper
Few drops red and yellow coloring (optional)

Remove skin from chicken, then rinse and pat dry. Score breast and thighs with a sharp knife to allow seasoning to penetrate. Mix lemon juice, chiles and salt together in a small bowl and rub over inside and outside surfaces of chicken. Place chicken in a large bowl. Allow to set at room temperature 1 hour while you prepare marinade.

Prepare marinade. Pour over chicken. Marinate at room temperature 2 hours or up to overnight in refrigerator.

About 2-1/2 hours before you wish to serve, remove chicken from marinade, reserving marinade, and place on a rack to dry out entire surface. A blow dryer such as a hair dryer on low heat could be used if time is short. Following the manufacturer's instructions for using your rotisserie, build a fire or turn on electric or gas rotisserie unit. For charcoal, build fire about 2 inches from back, removing grate and placing a pan for drippings centered under meat. The firebed should be about 6 inches wide and extend beyond pit about 4 inches on each end. The coals should be gray when you start cooking. Heat unit to 400F (205C).

When dry, evenly skewer chicken on spit, adjusting until it is as well balanced as possible, and tighten forks into bird at either end, pressing very firmly. Place over grill so that motor will turn properly. If there is an adjustment, place chicken so it is about 2 inches from heat. Sear chicken uniformly on all sides.

When cooked on outside, place further from heat and reduce heat to 375F (190C). Immediately baste with reserved marinade and roast 5 minutes. Baste again when surface has dried, about 5 minutes. Roast about 40 minutes, basting whenever chicken looks dry.

If using charcoal, keep adding briquettes, 6 to 10 every 30 minutes. After 40 minutes, increase heat back to 450F (230C). When fire is hot, brush chicken with reserved marinade, sparingly if you wish. Roast until outside of chicken has a crisp, hard crust and legs move easily. Allow to stand at least 20 minutes before serving on a platter. Garnish with purple onion rings and lime slices. *Makes 4 servings.*

MARINADE

Combine onion, shallots, gingerroot, garlic, chiles and yogurt in a food processor or blender and puree, scraping down sides of bowl as necessary. Add melted butter, spices and coloring, if using. Even though color may look overly dramatic, it will dull upon cooking and it is traditionally served reddish in color.

HUNGARIAN-STYLE ROASTED CHICKEN À LA GREAT SOUTHWEST

▼▼▼▼▼

The Hungarians have a very special way with chicken. I was first introduced to it in New York City by Ben Roth, a close Hungarian friend, at the Red Tulip, a neighborhood restaurant. The two characteristics that make this dish so special are lemon-buttered, very crisped and browned skin and richly flavored chicken liver, herb and brandy-flavored stuffing.

2 (about 2-1/2-lb.) chickens
About 4 tablespoons butter
1/2 cup minced Spanish onion
2 cloves garlic, minced, plus 10 whole cloves for pan drippings
3/4 pound chicken livers, plus livers from chickens, finely chopped
1 tablespoon minced fresh sage, or 1-1/2 teaspoons dry sage
4 teaspoons minced fresh thyme, or 2 teaspoons dry thyme
2 teaspoons minced fresh rosemary, or 1 teaspoon dry rosemary
2 fresh or dried bay leaves
1 teaspoon freshly cracked black pepper
2 tablespoons ground pure hot New Mexican chile
1/3 cup brandy or Cognac
1 large or 2 small fresh lemons, juiced
Orange, Lemon & Smoked Pineapple Salsa (page 203) or Ginger Pear Salsa (page 206)

Rinse and remove any excess fat from chickens. Then, melt 1 tablespoon butter in a large heavy skillet over medium heat. Add onion, minced garlic and chicken livers and cook until livers are browned, about 10 minutes. Add sage, 2 teaspoons thyme and remaining spices. Cook over low heat about 15 minutes to blend flavors. Remove bay leaves and transfer mixture to a food processor. Add brandy and process until smooth. Taste and adjust seasonings. Then stuff neck and body cavities of birds. Combine lemon juice and remaining 2 teaspoons thyme in a small bowl; set aside.

About 2 hours before you wish to serve, and following the manufacturer's instructions for using your rotisserie, build a fire or turn on electric or gas rotisserie unit. For charcoal, build fire about 2 inches from back, removing grate and placing a pan for drippings centered under meat. Place 10 garlic cloves in drippings pan. The firebed should be about 6 inches wide and extend beyond pit about 4 inches on each end. The coals should be gray when you start cooking. Heat unit to 350F (175C).

Meanwhile, evenly skewer chickens on spit, adjusting until they are as well balanced as possible, and tighten forks into chicken at either end, pressing very firmly. Melt remaining 3 tablespoons butter and brush evenly over chickens. Then drizzle lemon juice mixture over outer surfaces of chickens. Place on grill so that motor will turn properly. Roast, spooning pan juices over chickens occasionally. If using charcoal, keep adding briquettes, 6 to 10 every 30 minutes. Continue to roast until internal temperature reaches 185F (85C) and drumsticks wiggle. Allow birds to stand 20 minutes before carving to set juices. Add a Southwestern touch by serving with salsa, if desired. *Makes 4 servings.*

HERBED CAROUSEL CORNISH HENS WITH SALSA SURPRISE STUFFING & NEW POTATOES

▼▼▼▼▼

A medley of fresh herbs tucked into the cavity and then doused with tequila makes for a bit of a surprise flavor. You'll love it with crusty baby potatoes, roasted to a golden turn. Serve with salsa for a wonderful and cozy dinner for two.

2 Cornish game hens
Juice of 1 lime
2 medium tomatoes, chopped
1 medium onion, chopped
4 cloves garlic, minced
1/2 cup cilantro leaves
1 green jalapeño chile, minced, or 1 dried chipotle chile, cooked and minced (page 202)
1 teaspoon salt
1/4 cup tequila
3 tablespoons good-quality olive oil, preferably Spanish
12 to 24 baby new potatoes, peeled around centers (optional)
Sunny Salsa (page 205)

Rinse hens and pat dry. Trim any fat or excess skin from inside cavity. In a non-reactive bowl, combine lime juice, tomatoes, onion, garlic, cilantro, jalapeño chile and salt. Taste and add more chile if a hotter taste is desired. Stir in tequila and use mixture to loosely stuff hens.

About 2 hours before you wish to serve, and following the manufacturer's instructions for using your rotisserie, build a fire or turn on electric or gas rotisserie unit. For charcoal, build fire about 2 inches from back, removing grate and placing a pan for drippings centered under meat. The firebed should be about 6 inches wide and extend beyond pit about 4 inches on each end. The coals should be gray when you start cooking. Heat unit to 350F (175C).

Meanwhile, evenly skewer hens on spit, adjusting until they are as well balanced as possible, and tighten forks into birds at either end, pressing very firmly. Position over grill so that motor will turn properly. Very lightly brush outside of each hen with olive oil. Place baby potatoes in roasting or dripping pan underneath hens. Roast, spooning pan juices over hens occasionally. Turn potatoes occasionally to get a golden skin. If using charcoal, keep adding briquettes, 6 to 10 every 30 minutes. Continue to roast until internal temperature reaches 185F (85C) and drumsticks move easily. Allow hens to stand 20 minutes before carving to set juices.

Serve birds either whole or halved with salsa napped over top and potatoes on the side. *Makes 2 to 4 servings.*

Herb-Infused Capon or Turkey el Patio

▼▼▼▼▼

Small whole turkeys or capons roasted on the rotisserie are marvelous when prepared almost any way. I like them three ways: infused with herbs and then served with salsa, seasoned with a rub and served with a favorite barbecue sauce or done Hawaiian-style, basted in a teriyaki or shoyu-type marinade. For an even more intense herbal flavor, see the variation at end of this recipe.

1 (about 8-lb.) capon or 1 small (8- to 10-lb.) turkey
1 tablespoon salt
Green, white or rose peppercorns or a mixture of the three
2 limes
2 tablespoons minced fresh sage, or 2 teaspoons dried sage
2 tablespoons minced fresh thyme, or 2 teaspoons dried thyme
2 tablespoons crushed caribe chile
1/2 cup minced green onions
3 tablespoons good-quality olive oil, preferably Spanish
1 recipe Tropical Salsa (page 205) or Ginger Pear Salsa (page 206) (optional)

Rinse and trim fat and excess skin from inside and around cavities. Pluck any pin feathers. Rub salt into neck and body cavities only, not on skin. Grind peppercorns into cavities and rub in.

About 5 hours before you wish to serve, and following the manufacturer's instructions for using your rotisserie, build a fire or turn on electric or gas rotisserie unit. For charcoal, build fire about 2 inches from back, removing grate and placing a pan for drippings centered under meat. The firebed should be about 6 inches wide and extend beyond pit about 4 inches on each end. The coals should be gray when you start cooking. Heat unit to 350F (175C).

Cut limes in half and squeeze their juice into neck and body cavities. Then quarter each lime and place inside hens.

Combine herbs, caribe chile, green onions and olive oil in a mini food processor or blender and process until pureed. Loosen skin on capon breast, thighs and every place skin can be separated from flesh. Spoon some of mixture into these spaces, then skewer neck and body cavities shut.

Balance capon or turkey on skewer, tightening forks to hold it firmly. Position it over grill so that motor will turn properly. Roast, covered, 1 hour, occasionally spooning pan juices, when they have developed, over turkey. If using charcoal, keep adding briquettes, 6 to 10 every 30 minutes. Continue to roast, covered, until internal temperature reaches 185F (85C) and drumsticks move easily. Allow to stand 20 minutes before carving to set juices. Serve with salsa of your choice. *Makes 12 to 16 servings.*

Variation

If desired, you can place sherry, tequila or chicken broth in drippings pan along with sprigs of fresh sage and thyme and a whole red chile or two to intensify flavor infused into turkey.

CHILIED SHRIMP BROCHETTES WITH YOGURT MINT SAUCE

▼▼▼▼▼

This dish is very fast to make, especially if you buy the shrimp shelled. Serve it with a rice, quinoa or kasha dish and your favorite salad. Why not try one of our grilled salads?

2-1/2 pounds (about 30) jumbo shrimp
1 cup plain yogurt
3 cloves garlic, minced
1 teaspoon ground turmeric
2 teaspoons freshly ground cumin
1/2 teaspoon crushed pequin quebrado or to taste
2 teaspoons pure ground New Mexican mild chile
1/2 teaspoon ground coriander
3 tablespoons chopped fresh mint or to taste
3 tablespoons freshly squeezed lime juice

About 45 minutes before you wish to serve, and following the manufacturer's instructions for using your rotisserie, build a fire or turn on electric or gas rotisserie unit. For charcoal, build fire about 2 inches from back, removing grate and placing a pan for drippings centered under meat. The firebed should be about 6 inches wide and extend beyond pit about 4 inches on each end. The coals should be gray when you start cooking. Heat unit to broil or hottest heat setting, about 500F (260C).

Peel and devein shrimp, if needed. If you are peeling them yourself, leave on the tails. In a large bowl, combine all remaining ingredients and stir in shrimp. Allow to marinate 15 minutes.

Place shrimp on skewer attachment to rotisserie, reserving marinade. Grill, basting frequently with yogurt marinade, about 5 minutes or until shrimp turn pink. Serve hot, brushed with marinade. *Makes 4 to 6 servings.*

SEA SCALLOPS & PORCINI MUSHROOMS WITH LEEKS & HERB BASTE

▼▼▼▼▼

Scallops are so sweet and juicy yet also quick to cook. They are particularly good on the rotisserie as searing on all sides seals in juices. This dish is wonderful with a simple rice dish. For a luncheon, serve them over your favorite pasta, such as blue corn or green chile, or over mixed greens.

2 leeks
About 6 ounces porcini or other large flavorful mushrooms
1-1/2 pounds fresh sea scallops
2 tablespoons good-quality olive oil, preferably Spanish
2 tablespoons freshly squeezed lime juice
3 cloves garlic, minced
1 teaspoon crushed pequin quebrado chile

Trim tops and roots from leeks. Then cut almost in half lengthwise. Rinse leeks to remove all sand. Then cut in 1-inch lengths. Wipe off mushrooms and either cut in quarters or pieces that are approximately same size as scallops and leeks. Combine remaining ingredients in a nonreactive shallow dish and add leeks, mushrooms and scallops. Marinate at least 15 minutes.

About 45 minutes before you wish to serve, and following the manufacturer's instructions for using your rotisserie, build a fire or turn on electric or gas rotisserie unit. For charcoal, build fire about 2 inches from back, removing grate and placing a pan for drippings centered under meat. The firebed should be about 6 inches wide and extend beyond pit about 4 inches on each end. The coals should be gray when you start cooking. Heat unit to broil or hottest heat setting, about 500F (260C).

Using kabob attachment, thread vegetables and scallops on skewers, placing each on a separate skewer. Or, if a kabob attachment is not available, thread all of them on one rod. Place on rotisserie motor, positioning them closest to heating unit. Grill until leeks are seared and somewhat blackened and scallops are opaque, 5 to 10 minutes. You may have to remove scallops before leeks are done, so if using one skewer, thread scallops on last. If mushrooms are done, remove them also and continue to cook until all are done. Keep scallops and/or mushrooms warm until leeks are done. Serve as desired. *Makes 4 servings.*

Sea Scallop & Shrimp Brochettes over Chipotle Rotini with Champagne Alfredo Sauce

▼▼▼▼▼

This dish is a winner—elegant looking yet easy enough to whip together in about a half hour. I like to serve it with a salad of baby greens with a simple vinaigrette dressing, grilled zucchini and summer squash and perhaps some crusty bread.

1/2 cup Champagne
1 tablespoon vegetable oil
Freshly ground black pepper
12 large sea scallops (about 3/4 pound)
12 large shrimp (about 1/2 pound), peeled and deveined
1 pound chipotle fusilli or plain fusilli
1/2 cup freshly grated Parmesan

Champagne Alfredo Sauce

1 cup Champagne
1 dried chipotle chile
3/4 cup whipping cream
Freshly grated nutmeg

    In a large, shallow nonreactive bowl, combine Champagne with oil and pepper. Add seafood and stir to mix. Marinate 30 minutes. Drain seafood and place on skewers, if possible, placing all scallops on one skewer attachment and all shrimp on another or placing all together on main rod.

    Meanwhile, about 1 hour before you wish to serve, and following the manufacturer's instructions for using your rotisserie, build a fire or turn on electric or gas rotisserie unit. For charcoal, build fire about 2 inches from back, removing grate and placing a pan for drippings centered under meat. The firebed should be about 6 inches wide and extend beyond pit about 4 inches on each end. The coals should be gray when you start cooking. Heat unit to broil or hottest heat setting, about 500F (260C).

When hot, attach rod to motor and cook about 15 to 20 minutes, depending on closeness of grilling rod to heat, or until scallops are opaque and shrimp are pink. Do not overcook.

Cook pasta in boiling salted water according to package directions. Prepare sauce. Drain pasta and divide among four warmed plates. To serve, arrange 3 shrimp and 3 scallops over each pasta serving. Top with sauce and freshly grated cheese. *Makes 4 servings.*

Champagne Alfredo Sauce

Pour Champagne into a heavy skillet over medium heat. Add chipotle chile. Bring to a boil, then reduce heat to low and simmer until Champagne is reduced to 1/2 cup, removing chipotle when it is softened. Stir in cream. Mince chipotle and stir into sauce. Add nutmeg and remove from heat.

LEMON-BASTED MONKFISH NUGGETS WITH TROPICAL SALSA

▼▼▼▼▼

Monkfish, when broiled to perfection, is difficult to tell from lobster. When flavored with this fresh-tasting sauce, it is pure heaven.

1 (1-lb.) monkfish fillet
1/2 cup freshly squeezed lemon juice
2 tablespoons good-quality olive oil, preferably Spanish
2 teaspoons pure ground mild New Mexico chile
1 tablespoon crushed caribe chile
2 tablespoons coarsely chopped cilantro or flat-leaf parsley
1 recipe Tropical Salsa (page 205)

Trim any bones and skin from fish, then cut into 24 cubes. Combine remaining ingredients except salsa in a large, shallow nonreactive bowl. Add monkfish and stir. Marinate 30 minutes.

Meanwhile, about 1 hour before you wish to serve, and following the manufacturer's instructions for using your rotisserie, build a fire or turn on electric or gas rotisserie unit. For charcoal, build fire about 2 inches from back, removing grate and placing a pan for drippings centered under meat. The firebed should be about 6 inches wide and extend beyond pit about 4 inches on each end. The coals should be gray when you start cooking. Heat unit to broil or hottest heat setting, about 500F (260C).

About 15 minutes before serving, remove fish from marinade and thread on skewers. Then attach to motor and grill about 15 minutes or until fish is cooked through and golden brown on edges. Place a pool of salsa on each of 4 plates and top with 6 pieces of grilled fish. *Makes 4 servings.*

Sauces, Salsas, Marinades, Bastes & Rubs

▼▼▼▼▼

The flavors that distinguish one grilled, smoked or rotisserie-cooked recipe from another are often the result of the treatment given to the food before or after it is cooked. That is what this chapter is all about!

By the way, there are only two marinades listed here. You can find many marinades in the other chapters that can be used with other recipes.

There are two important rules for using rubs: Never place your fingers in the bowl of rub; use a clean spoon so leftover rub can be used later. Never apply a thick coating.

ADOBO SAUCE

▼▼▼▼▼

This very popular spicy red chile marinade is made locally in Northern New Mexico with 100 percent caribe chiles. I have toned this recipe down a bit because caribe chiles are so spicy that they would prevent many people from eating this sauce. The conquistadores brought the seeds and chiles given them by the Caribe Indians to Northern New Mexico. For this reason the sauce is also known as conquistador sauce or marinade. Originally this sauce was only used as a marinade for pork.

1/2 cup crushed caribe chiles
1/2 cup ground pure mild chiles
2 garlic cloves, peeled
2 tablespoons ground cumin
2 teaspoons ground Mexican oregano
1-1/2 teaspoons salt
4 cups water

Place all ingredients in a blender in the order given; process until combined. Use as a marinade for chicken, pork or seafood.   *Makes about 4 cups.*

AZTEC-STYLE PICO DE GALLO WITH CHIPOTLES

▼▼▼▼▼

The fajita favorite, pico de gallo is a very spicy salsa. Serve it on almost any highly flavored smoked or grilled dish.

Literally translated, *pico de gallo* means "tip of the cock's comb." And, if you are sensitive to chile heat, it just might make you jump higher than the tip of a cock's comb, which is how it was so named. The Aztecs smoked red ripe jalapeño chiles with banana leaves to produce what is known today as *chipotles*. The brown, wrinkled, sun-dried ones yield the very best flavor, much better than the canned ones. The reddish mora-style chipotles are mechanically dried and are far less flavorful.

4 dried chipotle chiles
1/2 cup water
2 teaspoons cider or white vinegar
1-1/2 cups diced roma tomatoes

1-1/2 cups diced white onion
3 cloves garlic, minced
3/4 teaspoon salt
1/3 cup freshly squeezed lime juice
1/2 cup coarsely chopped cilantro leaves

Place chipotles in a medium microwave-safe bowl or small pan and add water and vinegar. Cook, covered, 5 minutes in microwave or 30 minutes on low heat. Uncover and set aside.

Combine remaining ingredients in the order listed in a serving bowl. Drain chipotle chiles, reserving liquid, and finely mince. Stir chopped chiles into tomato mixture, adding some reserved liquid as needed to produce desired consistency. *Makes 3 cups or 6 to 8 servings.*

ORANGE, LEMON & SMOKED PINEAPPLE SALSA

▼▼▼▼▼

Prepare this salsa when you already have the smoker or grill operating. You can make it without smoking the pineapple, but just 10 minutes or so in the smoker adds a subtle smoky overtone and makes the pineapple juicier. In fact a greenish pineapple can be used for smoking. This salsa is terrific over fish or chicken.

1/2 medium, fresh pineapple or 1-1/2 to 2 cups canned chunks, drained
1 red bell pepper
1 large or 2 small navel oranges, peeled and sectioned
2 cups diced white onions
1/4 cup freshly squeezed lemon juice
2 tablespoons crushed caribe chile or to taste

Preheat grill or smoker if not already hot. Add wood chips to fire and replace grill rack. Peel fresh pineapple and cut lengthwise into about 1-inch-wide wedges. Rinse bell pepper and pierce with a sharp knife on opposite sides. Place pineapple and bell pepper on grill rack and cover with a lid or foil. Grill 10 to 15 minutes or until pineapple is softened. Grill bell peppers, turning often, until evenly blackened and blistered. Place grilled bell peppers in ice water to cool. Drain and peel, then cut into about 3/4-inch squares.

Combine all ingredients in a large bowl. Taste and adjust seasonings. Allow to set at least 30 minutes before serving. Serve with seafood or poultry. *Makes about 6 cups or 8 to 12 servings.*

HOT ORANGE SALSA

▼▼▼▼▼

This salsa is hot two ways—from the grill and from its spicy components. We love it on pork, seafood and poultry. Try it; it is so very easy. Start with the smaller amount of caribe chile and add more to taste.

2 navel oranges
12 green onions with tender green tops
1 lime
1/4 to 1/2 cup crushed caribe chile
1/2 cup coarsely chopped flat-leaf parsley
1/2 cup Triple Sec, Cointreau or Grand Marnier

Preheat grill if not already hot. Place oranges on grill rack, rotating every 3 to 5 minutes. Trim green onions and place on rack. Cut lime in half and squeeze half over onions. Grill onions until slightly blackened and turn. Squeeze remaining lime half over grilled side of onions. Oranges are done when there are grill marks blackening outside edges.

Working over bowl in which salsa will be mixed, peel and section oranges, removing membranes. Dice sections and add to bowl. Cut onions into 1/2-inch dice. Combine all ingredients in bowl with oranges and let set about 30 minutes before serving. Any leftovers keep several days in refrigerator.   *Makes 3 cups or 4 to 6 servings.*

Tropical Salsa

▼▼▼▼▼

The tropical flavors are wonderful with seafood and poultry such as shrimp, scallops or chicken breasts. You can omit the tamarind if you must.

1/4 cup tamarind pulp (see Note)
1 medium mango or papaya, cut into 1/2-inch cubes
2 fresh guava or red or purple plums, sliced in thin wedges
1/4 fresh pineapple, peeled, cored and cut into 1/2-inch cubes
1 small red onion, cut into 1/2-inch squares
3 kiwi fruits, peeled and cut into 1/4-inch cubes
1/4 cup freshly squeezed lime juice or Midori liqueur

Combine all ingredients in a medium bowl and allow to set at least 1 hour before serving. *Makes 4 cups or 6 to 8 servings.*

NOTE: Tamarind pulp is available in Spanish or Asian markets.

Sunny Salsa

▼▼▼▼▼

This recipe is similar to the original salsa, which is often called *salsa fresca*. Embodying the three basic colors of the flag of Mexico—red, green and white—this salsa has a political past. It seems that Mexican families had to have a dish with equal parts of red, green and white on the table to signify their loyalty to the political party in power, should *Federales* visit during mealtime. This is probably how salsa became so popular!

1 cup fresh tomatoes, cut into 1/2-inch cubes
1 cup white Spanish onion, cut into 1/4-inch squares
8 to 12 green chiles, parched (page 161), peeled and diced (1 cup), or 2 (4-oz.) cans
    diced green chiles, drained
2 cloves garlic, minced
1/2 teaspoon salt
1/3 cup coarsely chopped cilantro leaves

Combine all ingredients in a medium bowl. Let set about 15 minutes before serving. *Makes 3 cups or 4 to 6 servings.*

NOTE: Any leftovers freeze well for use in ranchero sauce, stews or eggs. Or, whisk into a simple vinaigrette for salad dressing. It can also be added to diced avocados to make guacamole.

GINGER PEAR SALSA

▼▼▼▼▼

The mellow flavor of pears goes very well with duck, pork or lamb. A salsa such as this one adds a graceful note to servings of grilled or smoked meats as it is pretty to nap over sliced meat or act as a setting for meat.

3 medium pears, such as Bartlett or Bosc, unpeeled and cut into 1/2-inch cubes
1 medium red onion, cut into 1/4-inch pieces
2 green jalapeño chiles, finely diced
1/3 cup finely diced candied ginger

Combine all ingredients in a nonreactive bowl and mix together. Allow to set for at least 15 minutes for flavors to blend, tasting to adjust flavors to suit your spiciness preference.   *Makes 2-1/2 cups or 4 servings.*

BLACK BEAN & CORN SALSA

▼▼▼▼▼

This is one of my favorite snacking salsas. I developed it for my New York City restaurant and served it with pan-sautéed chicken livers, of all things! For a good variation, substitute papaya for the corn.

1 large tomato, cut into 1/2-inch cubes
1/2 cup white or yellow onion, chopped into 1/4-inch pieces
1/2 cup coarsely diced pickled jalapeño slices
3/4 cup cooked black beans, drained
1/2 cup cooked whole kernel corn
1/2 teaspoon salt
2 cloves garlic, finely minced
1/4 cup coarsely chopped cilantro (optional)

Combine all ingredients, adding cilantro, if using, after rest of ingredients have been blended. Serve immediately or let set 15 minutes.   *Makes 4 to 6 servings or 2-1/2 cups.*

VARIATIONS

Substitute papaya or mango for corn in above recipe: Peel a ripe yellow or melon-colored papaya, remove seeds and cut into 1/2-inch cubes. For mango variation, peel mango, then make crosswise cuts on one side 1/4 inch apart from top to bottom; using a very sharp knife, slice these slices off. Repeat on other side. Then dice mango slices.

GRILLED FENNEL & FRESH MINT SALSA
▼▼▼▼▼

Grilled fennel is one of my all-time favorites and is absolutely wonderful with lamb—any cut! Poultry or seafood dishes are terrific with fennel as well.

2 medium bulbs or 1 large bulb fennel
1 teaspoon good-quality olive oil, preferably Spanish
1 cup Vidalia or other sweet onion, cut into 1/2-inch pieces
2 to 4 fresh jalapeño chiles, or to taste, minced
1/3 cup freshly squeezed lime juice
1/4 cup fresh mint leaves, coarsely chopped
2 tablespoons balsamic vinegar

Heat grill if not already hot. Cut fennel into 1/2-inch-thick slices and lightly oil. Grill on medium to high heat or 350 to 500F (175 to 260C) until lightly charred on edges, about 5 minutes per side. When done, fennel should still be somewhat crunchy. Set it aside to cool. Combine fennel and remaining ingredients in a nonreactive bowl. Allow to set at least 15 minutes before serving. *Makes 2-1/2 cups or 4 servings.*

Fresh Cranberry Salsa

▼▼▼▼▼

What better to go with turkey? I created this recipe for Thanksgiving Day dinner with our family a few years ago. We like it any time with grilled or smoked turkey, pork roast or ham. Use a food processor to chop the cranberries. For a more attractive dish, chop remaining ingredients by hand.

4 cups fresh, rinsed and sorted cranberries, coarsely chopped
2 medium apples, chopped
1 medium orange, peeled and sectioned
1 cup finely chopped celery
1 cup diced red onion
3 fresh jalapeño chiles or to taste, minced
1/2 cup freshly squeezed orange juice
Sugar (optional)

Combine all ingredients early in day. Cover and allow to set until dinner. Add sugar to taste, if desired.   *Makes 8 cups or 12 to 16 servings.*

Dried Cherry Salsa

▼▼▼▼▼

Prepare this at least 1 hour ahead of time and allow it to mellow at room temperature. This way the concentrated fruity flavor of the cherries is infused throughout the salsa.

2 cups dried cherries
1 large red Delicious apple, unpeeled and cut into 1/2-inch pieces
1 medium red onion, finely chopped
1 small fresh jalapeño chile, minced
2 tablespoons kirsch or sherry

Place cherries in a nonreactive bowl. Add all remaining ingredients and carefully stir together. Allow to set at room temperature 1 hour before serving.   *Makes about 4 cups or 8 servings.*

NOTE: Dried cherries are available at specialty stores and through gourmet mail-order catalogues.

GRILLED CORN & RED BELL PEPPER SALSA

▼▼▼▼▼

This salsa is best with beef dishes or as a dipping salsa. Of course, it makes the most sense to prepare the salsa while you are grilling meat.

2 large ears yellow or white corn
1 tablespoon good-quality olive oil, preferably Spanish
1 large or 2 small red bell peppers
1 medium white onion, cut into 1/4-inch pieces
1 tablespoon crushed caribe chile or to taste
1/4 cup red wine vinegar
1/2 teaspoon salt

Preheat grill to 400F (205C) if not already hot. Shuck corn, then brush with olive oil. Halve bell peppers and remove seeds and core. Brush outer surfaces with olive oil. Place corn and peppers on grill. Rotate corn as it chars on edges of kernels. Rotate peppers, until skin is charred. When peppers are done, place in ice water to chill. When corn is cool enough to handle, slice kernels off cobs into a nonreactive bowl. Peel peppers and cut into 1/2-inch pieces and add to corn. Add remaining ingredients, then taste and adjust seasonings, if desired. Allow to set about 30 minutes before serving. *Makes about 3 cups or 6 servings.*

VARIATION

If fresh corn is not available, frozen or canned corn can be substituted. Use 1 cup whole kernel corn, drained. Frozen corn on the cob can be grilled right from the package.

HORSERADISH DILL CREAM

▼▼▼▼▼

Though traditional with roast prime ribs, this sauce is equally great tasting with any grilled or smoked beef, lamb or veal.

1 cup regular or light sour cream
1/3 cup freshly grated or good-quality prepared horseradish
2 tablespoons freshly minced dill or 2 teaspoons dried dill weed

Combine all ingredients in a bowl, then taste and adjust flavorings. Serve chilled. *Makes about 1-1/2 cups or 4 to 6 servings.*

MINT BALSAMIC CREAM

▼▼▼▼▼

This cream is excellent on lamb, especially grilled lamb.

1 cup regular or light sour cream
2/3 cup coarsely chopped fresh mint leaves
1 tablespoon balsamic vinegar or to taste

Combine all ingredients in a small bowl, then taste and adjust flavorings. Refrigerate if made ahead.   *Makes 1-1/2 cups or 4 to 6 servings.*

GRILLED TOMATO CREAM

▼▼▼▼▼

Grilled red ripe tomatoes are one of my all-time super favorites. The charring of the outside creates a sweet roasted flavor. In the fall, I roast several tomatoes—as many as I have time for right out of the garden. The rest, I just rinse and freeze in bags. Then when I am grilling in winter, I place the frozen tomatoes in foil pans on the grill until somewhat blackened. You can oven-roast tomatoes if desired. This cream is great on any meat dish, but especially good on poultry dishes.

1-1/2 cups roasted tomato puree (page 229)
1/2 cup regular or light sour cream
Freshly ground black pepper
2 tablespoons chopped fresh basil or dill or 2 teaspoons dried herb (optional)
1 teaspoon crushed pequin quebrado chile or to taste

Combine all ingredients in a bowl. Serve as desired. Refrigerate if made ahead. *Makes 2 cups or 4 to 6 servings.*

Kansas City Barbecue Sauce

▼▼▼▼▼

Kansas City is home to some of the very best barbecue sauce! I have always loved eating finger-lickin' barbecue sauce–basted ribs in good old K.C. And, I should know, I was born only 100 miles or so due west and have visited Kansas City frequently—even lived there as a child for a while. I fortunately got to sample lots of great barbecue with the greats. Though there is really some pretty good commercially made barbecue sauce, I still think homemade is better. You can tailor yours to suit your own taste, which I have always thought a worthwhile effort.

2 tablespoons bacon drippings or butter
1/2 cup finely minced Spanish onion
2 cloves garlic, minced
1-3/4 cups ketchup or 1 (14-oz.) bottle
1/3 cup Worcestershire sauce
1/4 cup apple cider vinegar
1 tablespoon prepared mustard or to taste
1 tablespoon molasses
2 tablespoons pure ground hot New Mexican chile
1 teaspoon ground cumin
1/2 teaspoon Liquid Smoke or to taste

Melt bacon drippings or butter in a heavy saucepan over medium heat. Add onion and garlic and cook until transparent and soft, about 10 minutes. Add remaining ingredients and simmer over low heat at least 15 minutes.

If using for meat, do not add until meat is nearly done. Then lightly spoon onto ribs, chicken or whatever and cook one side and repeat. The total cooking time with sauce should never exceed about 20 minutes for the best flavor. The heat at this point should not exceed medium or 350F (175C). *Makes about 1-1/2 pints or enough for 4 to 6 servings.*

SOUTHERN BARBECUE SAUCE

▼▼▼▼▼

Though barbecue sauces vary quite a bit in the South, the sweet, hot tangy variety tends to be a pretty universal favorite.

2 cups (1-lb. can) tomato sauce
2/3 cup cider vinegar
2/3 cup sugar
2 tablespoons molasses
2 cloves garlic, minced
1/4 cup finely minced onion
1/2 teaspoon celery salt
1/2 teaspoon ground allspice
1/4 cup pure ground New Mexico hot chile
Hot pepper sauce (optional)
Freshly ground black pepper

Combine all ingredients in a heavy saucepan and simmer, stirring occasionally, over low heat at least 30 minutes or until thickened. Taste and adjust seasonings. Then use as desired.

If using for meat, do not add until meat is nearly done. Then lightly spoon onto ribs, chicken or whatever and cook one side and repeat. The total cooking time with sauce should never exceed about 20 minutes for best flavor. The heat at this point should not exceed medium or 350F (175C). *Makes about 1-1/2 pints or enough for 4 to 6 servings.*

New Mexico Barbecue Sauce

▼▼▼▼▼

In New Mexico, traditional cooks have their own unique way of preparing ribs. I learned to make them this way many years ago and have found nearly all who try them really like the variation from the sweet smoky sauces so popular elsewhere.

2 tablespoons butter or lard
1/4 cup minced Spanish onion
2 cloves garlic, minced
1/4 cup pure ground hot New Mexican chiles
1/4 cup pure ground mild New Mexican chiles
Pinch each ground Mexican oregano and cumin
1 cup water
1/2 cup red wine vinegar
1/2 teaspoon salt

Melt butter or lard in a heavy skillet over medium heat. Add onion and garlic and cook until transparent and soft, about 10 minutes. Remove pan from heat. Add ground chiles and herbs and stir until well blended. Stir in about half of the water, then return to heat, stirring constantly. When combined, add remaining water, vinegar and salt. Cook about 10 minutes, then taste and adjust seasonings. Use as desired.

If using for meat, do not add until meat is nearly done. Then lightly spoon onto ribs, chicken or whatever and cook one side and repeat. The total cooking time with sauce should never exceed about 20 minutes for best flavor. The heat at this point should not exceed medium or 350F (175C). *Makes about 1-1/2 cups or enough for 4 servings.*

Maytag's Santa Fe Blue Cheese Barbecue Sauce

▼▼▼▼▼

This special blue cheese was developed by the Maytag family, who introduced it to Santa Fe on their frequent visits. The founder of the company originally wanted to duplicate the mellow flavor of French Roquefort in this country and finally settled for this superlative blue cheese, which can be purchased in selected retail outlets or by mail order—it is truly special. This sauce was always a favorite with my father.

1 cup tomato puree
1/4 cup honey
2 tablespoons freshly squeezed lemon juice
1 tablespoon crushed caribe chile
1 tablespoon Worcestershire sauce
Freshly ground black or green peppercorns or both
1/4 cup crumbled blue cheese or to taste

In a medium saucepan, combine all ingredients except cheese and simmer over low heat 15 minutes or until sauce becomes thickened. Add cheese and simmer about 5 minutes, then taste and adjust seasonings. If using with meat, do not add until meat is done as you like it and merely heat with sauce until it bubbles. Serve immediately. *Makes about 1 cup or enough for 4 servings.*

Spicy Apple Barbecue Sauce

▼▼▼▼▼

The aroma of cinnamon and apples is what I think makes apple pie, memories of Mom and home so wonderful. Taken a step further, the combination makes an excellent barbecue sauce. Use on pork or poultry—just imagine a rolled pork tenderloin or turkey roast with this!

1 cup applesauce
1/2 cup freshly squeezed lemon juice
1/3 cup honey
1/2 teaspoon salt (optional)
1 teaspoon ground cinnamon
1/2 teaspoon freshly grated nutmeg

1/2 teaspoon ground ginger
Dash of ground cloves

Pour applesauce into a heavy saucepan, then add remaining ingredients. Simmer over low heat, stirring occasionally, at least 15 minutes or until sauce thickens slightly and flavor is balanced. Taste and adjust seasonings. This sauce can be applied to grilled meats, when almost done. *Makes about 1-1/2 cups or enough for 4 servings.*

JOE AZAR'S LEMON HERB MARINADE
▼▼▼▼▼

Virginia Azar was a beginning home economist at the same time I was in Albuquerque in the sixties, when each of us was working for a different company, she for the gas company and I for the electric company. Her husband's family had just recently arrived from Lebanon and had lots of marvelous recipes that Virginia worked on to develop measurements from original pinches and handfuls. This delightfully fresh-tasting marinade is one of those recipes. It can be mild and mellow or spiced Southwestern style. Use it with lamb or poultry.

3/4 cup freshly squeezed lemon juice or lime juice
3/4 cup dry sherry
1/2 cup good-quality olive oil, preferably Spanish
1-1/2 cups minced Spanish onion
1 teaspoon salt
1-1/2 teaspoons celery salt
1-1/2 teaspoons freshly ground black or green peppercorns
1 tablespoon minced fresh thyme, or 1-1/2 teaspoons dried thyme
1 tablespoon minced fresh Mediterranean oregano or 1-1/2 teaspoons dried oregano
1 tablespoon minced fresh rosemary leaves or 1-1/2 teaspoons dried rosemary

Combine all ingredients in a nonreactive bowl. Use to marinate lamb or chicken at least 2 hours before grilling or as directed in recipe. *Makes about 2 cups or enough for a butterflied leg of lamb, 6 pounds of lean meat or 2 chickens*

VARIATION

Spicy Southwestern Version
Use lime juice instead of lemon and Mexican oregano instead of Mediterranean. Add 2 tablespoons crushed caribe chile and 1 teaspoon crushed pequin quebrado chile or to taste.

Cajun Rub

▼▼▼▼▼

This rub is actually quite similar to Western rubs. What makes it Cajun is that there's quite a bit of mild chile, which should blacken, creating the burnt effect so popular in Cajun foods.

2 tablespoons pure ground mild chile
2 teaspoons crushed pequin quebrado chile
2 teaspoons salt
2 teaspoons onion powder
2 teaspoons garlic powder
1-1/2 teaspoons ground white pepper
1/2 teaspoon freshly ground black pepper
1 teaspoon ground thyme
1 teaspoon ground Mediterranean oregano

Mix all ingredients together in a small bowl and use immediately or place in a glass jar or resealable plastic bag and refrigerate or freeze. When using, be sure to always spoon it out and then rub a light coating over entire surface of meat or vegetables you are flavoring. Allowing rub to set on food 30 minutes or long enough for grill to heat imparts more flavor. *Makes enough for 4 pounds of ribs.*

Fresh Lemon Zest Chile-Herb Rub

▼▼▼▼▼

This rub is wonderful on pork or spareribs. You can also use it on any other cut of pork or poultry. With this rub, barbecue sauce quickly becomes optional.

1/4 cup salt
1/4 cup sugar
2 tablespoons each pure ground hot and mild New Mexican chiles
1 teaspoon ground cumin
1 teaspoon ground Mexican oregano

1 teaspoon ground coriander
1 teaspoon dry mustard
1 tablespoon minced lemon zest

Mix all ingredients together, then spoon mixture lightly onto ribs or poultry, rubbing it into surface with your fingers. Freeze any leftovers. *Makes enough for 8 to 12 pounds of meat.*

MEXICAN OREGANO & GARLIC RUB

▼▼▼▼▼

This rub is particularly delicious on poultry but can also be used on any other kind of meat or seafood. Leftovers can be made into a salad dressing by whisking into a vinaigrette, beating into butter for a spread on warm bread or frozen for later use as a rub on meats.

1/4 cup sugar
1/4 cup ground pure New Mexican mild chile
1 tablespoon ground Mexican oregano
1 tablespoon minced fresh thyme or 1-1/2 teaspoons dried thyme
1 teaspoon minced lemon zest
1 tablespoon salt
9 cloves garlic, finely minced
1 tablespoon dried minced onion
2 teaspoons ground ginger

Mix all ingredients together, then spoon out mixture lightly onto poultry or other meat or fish, rubbing it into surface with your fingers. Freeze any leftovers. *Makes enough for 8 to 12 pounds of meat.*

GORDON'S WEST TEXAS–NEW MEXICO BORDER RUB
▼▼▼▼▼

In Texas, they use ground black pepper instead of crushed caribe—the Northern New Mexican special red chile. The chile is a wonderful addition, adding heat yet not over-powering grilled or smoked meat. Once you get started using a rub on grilled meats, you'll be amazed how great they are! Also try this rub on vegetables, pot roasts in the oven and lots of other foods—even popcorn.

1/2 cup crushed caribe chile
1-1/4 cups dried minced onion
1-1/4 cups granulated garlic
1/2 cup salt

Mix all ingredients together, then spoon mixture lightly onto beef or other food, rubbing it into surface with your fingers. Freeze leftover rub.   *Makes 3-1/2 cups.*

VARIATION
For enough for one meal, mix together 2 teaspoons crushed caribe chile, 4 teaspoons each dried minced onion and granulated garlic and 1 teaspoon salt.

MESQUITE PRIME RIB RUB
▼▼▼▼▼

Gordon developed this rub especially for ribs—the big prime rib variety! The mesquite flavor comes from mesquite powder, which is generally available. There are also mesquite sprays and, of course, you can always grill or smoke over mesquite as well. For this rub, he used a salt substitute.

1/4 cup ground black pepper
1/3 cup crushed caribe chile
3/4 cup dried minced onion
4-1/2 teaspoons salt substitute
1/4 cup coarsely chopped flat-leaf parsley
1/2 teaspoon dried mesquite powder flavoring

Mix all ingredients together, then spoon mixture lightly onto beef or other food, rubbing it into surface with your fingers. Never place your fingers in the rub and never apply a thick coating. Freeze leftover rub.   *Makes about 1-3/4 cups.*

VARIATION
Chipotle Rub
Substitute 2 tablespoons ground chipotle for 1/3 cup crushed caribe chile and add 3 tablespoons ground pure New Mexican mild chile.

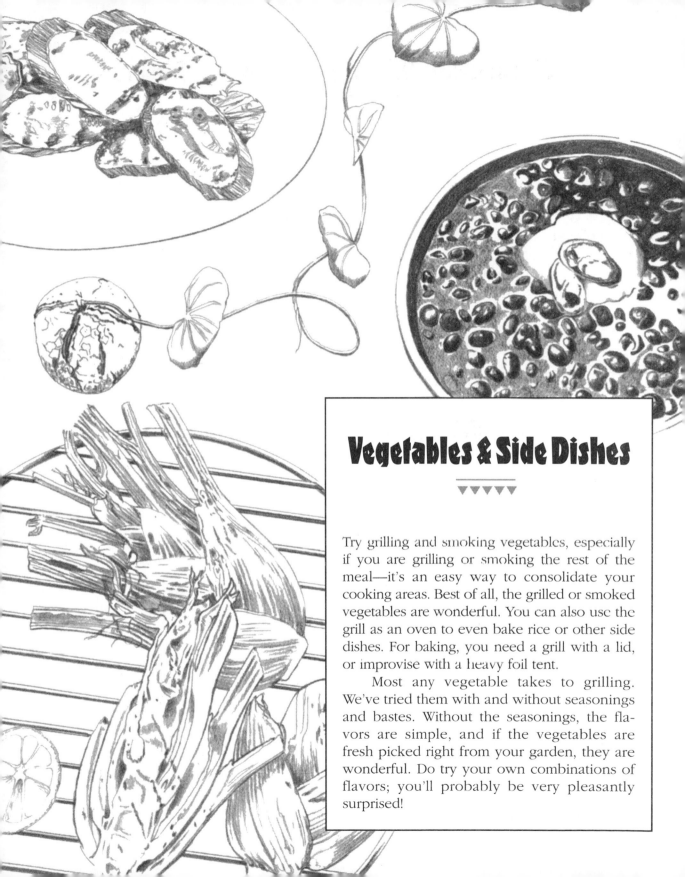

Vegetables & Side Dishes

▼▼▼▼▼

Try grilling and smoking vegetables, especially if you are grilling or smoking the rest of the meal—it's an easy way to consolidate your cooking areas. Best of all, the grilled or smoked vegetables are wonderful. You can also use the grill as an oven to even bake rice or other side dishes. For baking, you need a grill with a lid, or improvise with a heavy foil tent.

Most any vegetable takes to grilling. We've tried them with and without seasonings and bastes. Without the seasonings, the flavors are simple, and if the vegetables are fresh picked right from your garden, they are wonderful. Do try your own combinations of flavors; you'll probably be very pleasantly surprised!

Smoke-Roasted Asparagus in Garlic à la Rominger

▼▼▼▼▼

Gary Rominger, who gave us the wonderful salmon recipe on page 158, gave me this recipe for his favorite side dish to serve with the salmon. The asparagus can be smoked or grilled. Either way it is best to cook it in a pan rather than on the open grill; otherwise you'll lose the seasonings and the onion.

1 small red onion, thinly sliced
1-1/2 pounds fresh asparagus (see Note)
2 tablespoons butter
4 cloves garlic, thinly sliced
2 tablespoons freshly squeezed lemon juice
1/4 teaspoon salt
Freshly ground black pepper

Preheat grill or smoker if not already hot. Layer onion slices in an 11 X 7-inch metal or foil pan. Arrange asparagus over onion slices. Set aside.

Meanwhile, melt butter in a small pan over low heat. Add garlic and cook until tender. Remove from heat and stir in lemon juice, salt and pepper. Drizzle garlic mixture evenly over asparagus. Place pan, uncovered, on top rack of smoker or place over grill. Cover with lid and smoke 1 hour or grill about 15 minutes or until crisp-tender using either method. *Makes 4 to 6 servings.*

NOTE: The best way to get only the tender part of asparagus is to break off the tough bottoms, breaking just where the spear breaks easily.

Our Favorite Grilled Baking Potatoes

▼▼▼▼▼

Cross-hatching the potato halves and rubbing them with butter really makes these potatoes special. They definitely bake best in the little swinging baskets under a closed lid.

2 (1-lb.) potatoes
2 teaspoons butter, margarine or bacon fat
1/2 teaspoon pure ground mild chile (optional)
2 teaspoons coarsely chopped chives (optional)

Preheat grill to 400F (205C) if not already hot. Halve potatoes lengthwise. To cross-hatch, draw a sharp knife all the way across each cut surface on a diagonal at 1/2-inch intervals, cutting only through surface about 1/8 inch deep and then repeat, cutting at same angle to create diamonds all the way across each potato half. Rub each potato half with 1/2 teaspoon butter and then sprinkle with a fourth of the chile, if using, and one-fourth of the chives.

Place potatoes on vegetable shelf of grill, if available. Bake about 15 minutes, cut side up, or until top is fork tender and then turn and bake other side 10 minutes. *Makes 4 servings.*

VARIATION

Omit butter and other seasonings, and just lightly rub with any of the rubs (see pages 216 to 218).

SMOKED POTATOES

▼▼▼▼▼

One of our favorite smoked vegetables is the potato. They are easy to do and you can use almost any available space in the smoker. They are perfect for use in almost any potato dish from hash browns to potato salad. The amount of time for smoking depends on the freshness of the potato and the heat of the smoker.

Potatoes, russet or red
Rub (pages 216 to 218) (optional)

When using the smoker to cook a roast or perhaps a whole turkey, use the heat to also smoke potatoes. Scrub potatoes and lightly coat with rub, if using. Place on shelves in smoker. Smoke 4 or 5 hours or until fork tender. Serve as baked potatoes or use in another recipe. *One potato makes 1 serving.*

Baked Sweet Potatoes with Bourbon Butter

▼▼▼▼▼

These are outrageously good! They'd be terrific to serve at a Derby Day party as they are almost as good cold and can be prepared ahead and reheated.

4 (1/2-lb.) sweet potatoes or yams
4 teaspoons unsalted butter
4 teaspoons bourbon whiskey
4 teaspoons molasses
Freshly grated nutmeg
1/2 teaspoon salt
Freshly ground black pepper

Preheat grill to 400F (205C) if not already hot. Rinse sweet potatoes. Pierce once or twice with a sharp knife. Bake sweet potatoes on grill 1 hour to 1 hour and 15 minutes or until fork tender.

Remove potatoes from grill, cool slightly and halve lengthwise. Scoop out sweet potato centers to within about 1/2 inch of skins. Mash sweet potato centers with remaining ingredients. Spoon sweet potato mixture back into shells. Place on a baking sheet and bake 7 to 10 minutes on grill or until heated through.   *Makes 4 servings*.

Sweet Potato Rounds with Honey Butter

▼▼▼▼▼

These potatoes are terrific any way you can get them! We always make more than we think we will want to eat so that we'll have leftovers for snacking. They are great cold, or reheated in the microwave, regular oven, or regrilled!

2 (1-lb.) sweet potatoes, scrubbed
1/4 cup honey
1/4 cup unsalted butter, softened

    Preheat grill to 400F (205C) if not already hot. Pare out any bad spots and cut potatoes crosswise into 1/2-inch-thick slices, leaving on skin. Arrange sweet potato slices on grill. Grill 8 to 10 minutes or until grill marks show on flesh.
    Meanwhile, mix together honey and butter in a small bowl until combined. Turn sweet potatoes and spread with honey butter. Grill second side 6 to 8 minutes or until fork tender. Spread with honey butter and grill until bubbly. *Makes 6 servings.*

Grilled Jicama with Lime Chile Rub

▼▼▼▼▼

Jicama, sometimes nicknamed Mexican potato, is a flattish, large vegetable. Covered with a tan, somewhat shiny skin when fresh, it is snowy white on the inside and quite crisp. When raw, it is best served with lime juice and chile, such as a crushed caribe. It can be used instead of water chestnuts in oriental dishes and is increasingly being cooked in stir-fry combinations.

1-1/2 pounds jicama (1 large or 2 medium)
1/4 cup good-quality olive oil, preferably Spanish
1/3 cup freshly squeezed lime juice
1 tablespoon crushed caribe chile, plus additional for garnish (optional)

    Preheat grill to 400F (205C) if not already hot. Peel jicama and cut from top to bottom into 1/4-inch-thick slices. Combine olive oil, lime juice and 1 tablespoon chile in a large bowl. Add jicama slices and marinate 30 to 60 minutes, spooning marinade over tops of slices and turning occasionally. Arrange jicama slices on grill and cook 7 minutes. Turn and grill another 5 minutes or until as brown as desired. They will remain crisp. To serve, sprinkle with additional caribe for garnish, if desired. *Makes 6 to 8 servings.*

Variation
Cauliflower, broken into flowerets, can be prepared as above by placing the cauliflowerets in a foil pan or skillet on the grill.

GRILLED FENNEL

▼▼▼▼▼

This vegetable enhances anything Mediterranean, seafood, poultry or lamb. Leftovers are great in pasta mixtures, on pizza and in salsas.

2 medium bulbs or 1 large bulb fennel
2 teaspoons good-quality olive oil, preferably Spanish

Heat grill if not already hot. Cut fennel into 1/2-inch-thick slices and lightly oil both sides. Grill on medium to high heat or 350 to 500F (175 to 260C) until lightly charred on edges, about 5 minutes per side. When done, fennel should still be somewhat crunchy. *Makes 4 servings.*

HERB-BASTED GRILLED FRESH VEGETABLES

▼▼▼▼▼

These fabulous-tasting vegetables are much like a hot salad. Whatever seasonal vegetable you have on hand, you can use for grilling. Be sure not to overcook. These are best to prepare when you are using the grill for the entree.

About 2 tablespoons good-quality olive oil, preferably Spanish
1 tablespoon minced fresh rosemary or other fresh herb
1 tablespoon minced fresh thyme or other fresh herb
2 cloves garlic, minced
3 small zucchini or other seasonal squash
4 small to medium tomatoes, halved
3 medium potatoes, cut lengthwise into 1/2-inch-thick slices
2 large onions, halved and peeled

Process oil, herbs and garlic in a mini food processor or blender until pulverized and well mixed. Preheat grill to medium-hot or 400F (205C) if not already hot.

Cut zucchini lengthwise into 1/4- to 1/2-inch-thick slices. Place zucchini, tomatoes, potatoes and onions on a large baking sheet and brush cut sides of each vegetable with oil mixture.

To grill, place onions and potatoes on grill first and grill about 15 minutes or until almost fork tender. They can be covered or not up to this point. Then, turn onions and potatoes, basting with more oil mixture if any is left. Add remaining vegetables and watch carefully, turning zucchini after about 2 minutes or when they have grill marks. Do not turn tomatoes. All vegetables should be done in about 10 more minutes. *Makes 4 to 6 servings.*

VARIATIONS

Add crushed chile, such as caribe, or freshly ground peppers of any kind—black, green, red, white or a combination—to oil mixture.

If you must substitute dried herbs, use half as much or 1-1/2 teaspoons each.

QUINOA WITH CUMIN

▼▼▼▼▼

Many years ago, when I shared a podium with a professional from the Rodale Institute who was talking about future grains and new forms of old forgotten ones, he introduced quinoa. Since then I have become especially fond of it with spicy dishes.

1-1/4 cups quinoa or quinoa mixed with lentils
1 tablespoon good-quality olive oil, preferably Spanish
1 cup chopped onion
2 carrots, washed, unpeeled and chopped medium-fine
1-2/3 cups chicken broth
1/2 teaspoon salt
1 teaspoon ground cumin
2 to 3 tablespoons coarsely chopped flat-leaf parsley

Preheat grill to medium-hot or 400F (205C) if not already hot; it can be a startup fire—after the flare-up stage has passed. Place oil in a 4- to 5-quart heavy pot, then add onion and carrots. Cook on grill or on stovetop, stirring occasionally, until soft, 7 to 10 minutes.

Using a very fine sieve, rinse quinoa in hot water about 1 minute. Add quinoa to pot and immediately add broth, salt and cumin. Stir well, cover and cook 15 minutes, turning heat to low or, if on a grill, setting to side away from direct heat. Stir and cook until done as desired, adding hot water as necessary to keep the grain from sticking. *Makes about 4 to 6 servings.*

Grilled Blue Corn Polenta with Green Chile & Piñon Nuts

▼▼▼▼▼

We love this side dish even though it is a bit time consuming. It can be done inside on a griddle if space on your grill is limited.

3 cups water
1 teaspoon salt
1-1/2 cups blue cornmeal
1/2 cup parched (page 161), peeled and chopped green chiles
2 tablespoons piñon nuts, toasted and coarsely chopped
1/4 cup shredded Monterey Jack cheese
1 tablespoon good-quality olive oil, preferably Spanish

Butter a 13 X 9-inch baking pan; set aside. Combine water, salt and cornmeal in a heavy 5-quart pan. Stir until very well mixed, then place over medium heat, stirring constantly, and cook until very thick, about 15 to 20 minutes. The polenta should leave sides of pan. When polenta is quite firm, stir in green chiles, nuts and cheese. Pour polenta into prepared pan. Allow to cool slowly, then refrigerate up to 1 day.

To serve, preheat grill to 425F (220C) if not already hot. About 15 minutes before serving entree or after it has been removed and juices are settling, cut polenta into squares. Lightly brush each piece of polenta with oil, then place on grill until grill marks form, 2 to 3 minutes on each side. Keep warm until ready to serve. *Makes about 6 to 8 servings.*

Grilled Broccoli

▼▼▼▼▼

You really won't believe how delicious grilled broccoli is! And it's so quick and easy. Just think, there are no pots or pans to wash either.

4 large broccoli stalks, well trimmed and rinsed
2 tablespoons good-quality olive oil, preferably Spanish
2 tablespoons balsamic vinegar
Freshly ground black pepper

Preheat grill to medium-hot or 400F (205C) if not already hot. Halve broccoli stalks, cutting through tops. Drizzle with oil and vinegar, then place directly on grill. After 7 minutes or when broccoli is tinged with blackened areas and is beginning to become tender, turn and cook for another 7 to 8 minutes or until done as desired—it is best if cooked only until crisp-tender.   *Makes 4 servings.*

TEXAS BAKED BEANS WITH BOURBON

▼▼▼▼▼

These beans are truly best if smoked. If you do not have a smoker or are not planning to use one, they can be placed on the grill if you use wood chips. Hickory or any aromatic wood will add to the robust flavor. They are great with any barbecued meat.

4 cups cooked or canned beans, preferably small navy beans, drained
2 slices of thick country-style bacon or Canadian bacon, cut into small squares
1/2 cup diced onion
3 garlic cloves, minced
1/3 cup ketchup
1/3 cup molasses
1/3 cup bourbon
1 tablespoon Worcestershire sauce
2 tablespoons pure ground hot chile
Freshly ground black pepper
Salt to taste

Preheat grill or smoker to medium or 350F (175C) if not already hot. In a Dutch oven or heavy earthenware casserole, combine all ingredients. Place, uncovered, in smoker or on grill. If smoking, smoke at least 2 hours. If grilling, grill at least 45 minutes or until beans are crusted over and onion is soft and well cooked.   *Makes 6 to 8 servings.*

VARIATION

If baking in oven, add 1/2 teaspoon or more Liquid Smoke before baking them to create desired smoky flavor.

GRILL-ROASTED LEEKS & GREEN ONIONS

▼▼▼▼▼

Our family has always loved leeks most any way they are prepared, and this recipe is no exception. We use grilled green onions as a frequent garnish crisscrossed on top of a grilled steak or chop and in fajitas.

4 leeks
2 tablespoons honey
Freshly grated nutmeg
8 green onions
1 lime, halved

Preheat grill to medium-hot or 400F (205C) if not already hot. Prepare leeks by cutting off all of dark green tops as well as roots and slicing lengthwise down centers into halves. Place leek halves in cold water to cover, loosening layers of leek to be sure to clean out all sand, then rinse under running water.

To grill, lay halves of leeks cut side down on grill. Drizzle with a little of the honey and sprinkle with freshly grated nutmeg. Grill 8 to 10 minutes or until leeks are blackened a little with grill marks and are almost fork tender. Turn and drizzle with honey and sprinkle with nutmeg. Grill 8 to 10 minutes or until done as desired. Place green onions on grill, being very careful not to allow them to fall through grate. If desired, place several horizontally on a skewer, stabbing each just once through middle. Drizzle with lime juice. Grill 2 to 3 minutes on first side, then turn and cook second side 2 to 3 minutes or until done as desired.   *Makes 4 servings*.

WINTER'S PLEASURE GRILLED TOMATOES

▼▼▼▼▼

This process is one of the world's best kept secrets! Since I began grilling tomatoes—either fresh ones during the season or frozen ones in the winter—I have never used just plain tomatoes. The resulting taste is similar to the flavor enhancement that sun-drying yields.

12 to 15 tomatoes
1 to 2 teaspoons good-quality olive oil, preferably Spanish

Preheat grill to medium-hot or 400F (205C) if not already hot. Rinse tomatoes well and place them in a baking pan, covering outside of pan with foil to prevent its discoloration from grill. (Or use a foil pan.) Lightly rub top of each tomato with oil, using as little as possible. Then place pan of tomatoes on grill as it preheats for an entree you plan to cook, or place it beside entree if you have room. Grill about 45 to 60 minutes or until tomatoes are blackened on top and are dried and somewhat shriveled-looking. Allow to cool at room temperature until cool enough to handle, then peel, removing core. Store in freezer bags or containers if not using immediately. *Makes about 1 quart puree for sauces or stews.*

GRILLED SPAGHETTI SQUASH

▼▼▼▼▼

Spaghetti squash has more character when grilled or smoked. The smokiness from either method is a great complement to its otherwise mild flavor.

1 medium spaghetti squash
2 tablespoons butter or olive oil
2 teaspoons minced fresh herbs, such as thyme, tarragon or basil
1 teaspoon crushed pequin quebrado chile
1/2 teaspoon salt or to taste

Preheat grill to medium-hot or 400F (205C) if not already hot. Rinse squash and, using a meat fork, poke several deep holes into squash at various angles to prevent it from exploding during cooking. Place squash on grill and cook about 15 minutes on each side or until squash sinks in somewhat when pressed and is fork tender, then turn and grill about 10 more minutes or until done. If smoking, smoke about 2 hours or until fork tender. Cut squash in half lengthwise and scoop out all flesh; discard shell. Combine squash, butter, herbs, pequin quebrado and salt in a large bowl. Taste and adjust seasonings. Serve warm. *Makes 4 servings.*

Breads & Spreads

▼▼▼▼▼

Breads aren't often thought of as being baked on the grill; but they're wonderfully delicious grilled, it saves heating the oven and they can be tended as the rest of the meal is being cooked. The lingering smokiness adds a fresh flavor that all my guests find fabulous. Most breads need a grill with a lid for baking. The ones I've included here are all favorites that we've perfected for outdoor cooking. Try them with some of the flavored butters we've included at the end of this chapter.

Brunch Skillet Biscuits

▼▼▼▼▼

These bring back many camping memories. The origin of campfire biscuits was necessity. On the many major treks our forefathers made across the endless miles when they migrated Westward, biscuits were one of the only breads they could make. There was no time for yeast.

The only tricky aspect in baking these in a skillet over the grill is getting the heat just right so they don't bake too fast or too slow! The melted butter on the bottom of the skillet enriches the flavor, but it can be reduced or left out. Both old-fashioned bacon and egg or innovative brunch menus are great with these biscuits! Use your grill for the entire menu. You can even fry bacon, turning frequently, while the grill is heating. If you lack a skillet you want to use on the grill for the bacon, just use a foil one. The eggs can even work in this foil pan. Just wait until the biscuits are done, turn the grill off and quickly cook the eggs in the foil pan. We love green chile–scrambled eggs done this way.

2 cups all-purpose flour (see Note, page 234)
2 teaspoons baking powder
1 teaspoon salt
1/2 teaspoon baking soda
1/4 cup unsalted butter, chilled
1-1/2 teaspoons honey
3/4 cup buttermilk (see Note)
2 tablespoons unsalted butter, melted in bottom of 9-inch skillet

Preheat grill to high or 400F (205C). Combine dry ingredients in a medium bowl. Using a pastry blender or your hands, cut in 1/4 cup butter until mixture resembles coarse meal. Add honey and buttermilk and stir to combine. Place dough on a lightly floured board and knead a few times to combine ingredients, adding a little flour if needed. Roll out or pat dough into about 1/2-inch thickness and cut biscuits with a floured 2-inch round cutter.

Place remaining 2 tablespoons butter in a cast-iron or other heavy skillet with a heatproof handle. Cover outside of skillet with foil to protect it, if desired. Place skillet on grill rack until butter is just melted but not browned. Add biscuits, placing them close together for soft sides. Cover grill and bake 8 to 12 minutes or until done when pressed. Tops will not be very brown. Remove from heat and turn each biscuit over and leave in pan to brown other side. Serve right from skillet. *Makes 18 biscuits.*

Variations

Bacon Biscuits

Stir in 1/2 cup crumbled crisp bacon with buttermilk.

Cheese Biscuits

Add 1/2 cup shredded cheese with buttermilk.

Herb Biscuits

Add 2 teaspoons dried herbs, such as 1 teaspoon dried basil, 1/2 teaspoon dried Mexican oregano or 1/2 teaspoon dried tarragon, to dry ingredients. Other herbs and spices that are good combinations are rosemary, cumin, sage, caraway seeds, dried mustard, marjoram and flat-leaf parsley.

NOTE: For a buttermilk substitute, remove 1 teaspoon of the milk from 3/4 cup milk and replace it with 1 teaspoon white or cider vinegar. Stir to combine.

SKILLET CORNBREAD

▼▼▼▼▼

This is our family favorite for skillet baking. It is not too rich yet moist and flavorful with honey and whole-wheat flour. This recipe came to us from a student at our cooking school who shared information about her husband's gristmill in War Eagle, Arkansas. Naturally it is best with War Eagle cornmeal—we usually use their yellow cornmeal and their whole-wheat flour. Both are available by mail through our Pecos Valley Spice Company.

2 tablespoons bacon drippings or butter
1 cup yellow, white or blue cornmeal
1/2 cup whole-wheat flour
2 teaspoons baking powder
3/4 teaspoon salt
1 cup skim milk
1 egg
3 tablespoons honey

Preheat a covered grill to medium or 375F (190C). Place bacon drippings in an 8- to 9-inch cast-iron or heavy skillet and place on grill just until drippings melt. Combine cornmeal, flour, baking powder and salt in a medium bowl. Whisk milk, egg and honey together in another bowl. Beat in melted drippings. Add liquid ingredients to dry and stir only until dry ingredients are moistened. Add mixture to skillet. Place skillet on grill rack, cover grill and bake 30 to 35 minutes or until a wooden pick inserted in center of bread comes out clean. Serve warm. *Makes 2 to 3 servings.*

Variation

Foil can be used to cover bread when a covered grill is not available, but the bread will not be as brown.

HEARTH BREAD

▼▼▼▼▼

This bread when freshly baked is marvelous! It is great both to serve with a meal or to use in making sandwiches.

1-3/4 cups warm water (110 to 115F or 45C)
2 packages or 2 scant tablespoons instant dry yeast
1 teaspoon sugar
1-1/2 teaspoons salt
1 teaspoon cumin (optional)
4-1/2 cups unbleached all-purpose flour (see Note)
Yellow or white cornmeal

Place 1/2 cup warm water in a small bowl, then add yeast and sugar and stir until dissolved. Let stand until foamy. Add remaining 1-1/4 cups warm water to the bowl of a heavy-duty mixer with a dough hook or other large bowl. Add 2 cups of the flour, salt and cumin, if using. Using dough hook or by hand, beat until smooth. Beat in yeast mixture and enough remaining flour to make a stiff dough. Turn out dough on a lightly floured board and knead until dough is smooth and gluten is well formed, about 8 minutes. Grease a large bowl. Place dough in bowl, turning to coat entire surface. Cover with a damp towel and leave in a warm place about 1 hour or until doubled in size.

Punch down dough and form into 2 balls. Dust 1 large baking sheet with cornmeal. Place balls on baking sheet and slightly flatten, pushing bottom of loaves into meal. Cover again with damp towel and let rise until doubled in size, about 45 minutes, while grill is heating.

Preheat a covered grill to high or 425F (220C). Almost cover grill rack with foil. Place baking sheet on foil. Bake until loaves are golden and sound hollow when thumped on bottoms, about 40 minutes. Place on cooling racks to cool. *Makes 6 to 8 servings.*

NOTE: Carefully spoon flour when measuring; do not scoop cup into flour container, or you will have too much flour. Level off with a spatula.

MY FAVORITE SOUTHWESTERN FOCACCIA

▼▼▼▼▼

I often serve this right from the grill while guests are gathering. I find it very popular with all who sample it. You can decrease the olive oil even more than I did from my original recipe, but the flavor suffers in direct proportion.

1 cup warm water (110 to 115F or 45C)
1 package or 1 scant tablespoon dry yeast
1 teaspoon sugar
3-1/2 cups all-purpose flour (see Note, opposite)
3/4 teaspoon salt
1 tablespoon good-quality olive oil, preferably Spanish

TOPPING

1/4 cup good-quality olive oil, preferably Spanish
2 large red onions, halved lengthwise then very thinly sliced crosswise
4 large cloves garlic, minced
1/4 cup white wine vinegar
2 tablespoons chopped fresh Mexican oregano or sage or 2 teaspoons dried herb
1/2 cup *queso blanco* or feta cheese (optional), crumbled

Add warm water to bowl of heavy-duty mixer or other large bowl, then add yeast and sugar and stir until dissolved. Let stand until foamy. Add half of the flour, salt and olive oil. Using a dough hook or by hand, beat until smooth. Beat in enough remaining flour to make a stiff dough. Turn out dough on a lightly floured board and knead until dough is smooth and gluten is well formed, about 8 minutes.

Divide dough in half and form each half into a thin round, making a slight edge around sides. Poke dough with your fingers to make indentations. Prepare topping.

Preheat a covered grill to medium or 375F (190C). Evenly divide topping between dough rounds. Cover grill rack with foil to slow baking. Place bread on foil. Cover grill and bake about 20 minutes or until lightly golden. Sprinkle with cheese and serve warm in squares or wedges. *Makes 6 to 8 servings.*

TOPPING

Heat olive oil in a medium saucepan over medium heat. Add onions and garlic and cook until transparent and almost soft, about 10 minutes. Add remaining ingredients except cheese to onion mixture.

COFFEE-CAN MUSHROOM BREAD

▼▼▼▼▼

This bread looks like a mushroom when it rises enough outside the can. With a smaller-sized can, there is enough dough to form a pronounced mushroom cap. In fact, if you prefer, you can even place a foil collar made of doubled foil around the top of the can to support the mushroom.

2 tablespoons butter
1/2 pound mushrooms, finely minced
2 tablespoons minced shallots, onion or green onions
1 cup warm water (110 to 115F or 45C)
1 package or 1 scant tablespoon dry yeast
1 tablespoon sugar
1 cup skim milk
1-1/2 teaspoons salt
1 teaspoon coarsely ground black pepper
1 tablespoon fresh minced sage, or 1-1/2 teaspoons dried sage
6 cups unbleached all-purpose flour (see Note, page 234)

Melt butter in a skillet over medium-low heat. Add mushrooms and shallots and cook until lightly browned and liquid has been absorbed.

Add warm water to bowl of heavy-duty mixer or other large bowl, then add yeast and sugar and stir until dissolved. Let stand until foamy. Add milk, salt, pepper and sage. Add 3 cups of the flour. Using dough hook or by hand, beat until smooth. Beat in mushroom mixture and enough remaining flour to make a stiff dough. Turn out dough on a lightly floured board and knead until dough is smooth and gluten is well formed, about 8 minutes. Grease a large bowl. Place dough in bowl, turning to coat entire surface. Cover with a damp towel and leave in a warm place about 1 hour.

Butter 2 (1-lb.) coffee cans. Punch down dough and form into 2 balls. Place 1 ball in each coffee can, cover with a damp towel or plastic wrap and let rise in a warm place until doubled in size, about 45 minutes, while grill is heating.

Preheat a covered grill to medium or 375F (190C). Cover part of grill rack with foil pieces large enough to accommodate cans for baking and to allow some room around them. Place coffee cans on foil, cover grill and bake about 50 minutes or until bread is lightly browned and a long skewer inserted in bread comes out clean. Remove cans from heat and immediately remove bread from cans; place on a wire rack to cool. *Makes 2 loaves.*

Beer Dill Bread

▼▼▼▼▼

This bread is quite dense and heavy. While very European in character, it is wonderful served with butter with meals or as a snack or breakfast.

2-1/2 cups (20 oz.) dark beer
1/4 cup dark honey such as mesquite or wildflower
1/4 cup butter or vegetable oil
1/2 cup warm water (110 to 115F or 45C)
2 packages or 2 scant tablespoons dry yeast
About 5 cups whole-wheat flour (see Note, page 234)
1 cup buckwheat flour
2 cups gluten flour (see Note)
1-1/2 teaspoons salt
2 teaspoons dried dill weed

Combine beer, honey and butter in a microwave-safe bowl or a small pan and microwave on HIGH or place over medium heat until butter melts. Cool to warm. Add warm water to bowl of heavy-duty mixer or other large bowl, then add yeast and stir until dissolved. Let stand until foamy. Add honey mixture and beat to combine. Add 2-1/2 cups of the whole-wheat flour, buckwheat flour, gluten flour, salt and dill. Using a dough hook or by hand, beat until smooth. Beat in enough remaining whole-wheat flour to make a stiff dough. Turn out dough on a lightly floured board and knead until dough is smooth and gluten is well formed, about 8 minutes. Grease a large bowl. Place dough in bowl, turning to coat entire surface. Cover with a damp towel and leave in a warm place about 1 hour.

Punch down dough and form into 2 round loaves. Grease 2 baking sheets. Place loaves on baking sheets, cover with damp towel and let rise until doubled in size, about 45 minutes, while grill is heating.

Preheat a covered grill to medium or 350F (175C). Almost cover rack with foil. Place baking sheets on foil. Bake until loaves are golden and sound hollow when thumped on bottoms, about 40 minutes. Cool slightly on cooling racks and serve warm. *Makes 6 to 8 servings.*

NOTE: Gluten flour is sold at natural-food stores. If unavailable, reduce whole-wheat flour to 3-1/2 cups and use 3-1/2 cups bread or all-purpose flour.

Honey Whole-Wheat Bread

▼▼▼▼▼

This bread is somewhat dense, very healthy and tasty.

2 cups warm water (110 to 115F or 45C)
2 packages or 2 scant tablespoons dry yeast
1/4 cup honey
1/4 cup butter, melted
2 teaspoons salt
About 5-1/2 cups whole-wheat flour (see Note, page 234)

Add warm water to bowl of heavy-duty mixer or other large bowl, then add yeast and stir until dissolved. Let stand until foamy. Add honey, butter and salt and beat to combine. Add 2 cups of the whole-wheat flour. Using a dough hook or by hand, beat until smooth. Beat in enough remaining whole-wheat flour to make a stiff dough. Turn out dough on a lightly floured board and knead until dough is smooth and gluten is well formed, about 8 minutes. Grease a large bowl. Place dough in bowl, turning to coat entire surface. Cover with a damp towel and leave in a warm place about 1 hour.

Grease 2 (9 X 5-inch) loaf pans. Punch down dough and form into 2 loaves; place in prepared pans. Cover with damp towel or plastic wrap and let rise until doubled in size, about 45 minutes, while grill is heating.

Preheat a covered grill to medium or 350F (175C). Almost cover rack with foil. Place pans on foil. Bake until loaves are browned and sound hollow when thumped on bottoms, about 40 minutes. Remove from pans and cool on cooling racks. *Makes 6 to 8 servings*.

ANADAMA BREAD

▼▼▼▼▼

A bread with personality—somewhat crunchy and sweet—it is great fresh or toasted. Of all anadama bread recipes, I seem to always prefer this one. Legend has it that it was named by a New England fisherman whose wife, Anna, did not cook for him. In disgust he threw a molasses and cornmeal mush experiment into the fire cursing her, "Anna—damn you," and the name stuck!

2 cups warm water (110 to 115F or 45C)
2 packages or 2 scant tablespoons dry yeast
1/2 cup honey or light molasses
3 tablespoons vegetable oil
2 teaspoons salt
5 cups unbleached all-purpose flour (see Note, page 234)
1/2 cup yellow cornmeal
1/4 cup wheat germ
1/4 cup whole-wheat flour

Add warm water to bowl of heavy duty mixer or other large bowl, then add yeast and stir until dissolved. Let stand until foamy. Add honey, oil and salt and beat to combine. Add 3 cups of all-purpose flour, cornmeal, wheat germ and whole-wheat flour. Using a dough hook or by hand, beat until smooth. Beat in enough remaining all-purpose flour to make a stiff dough. Turn out dough on a lightly floured board and knead until dough is smooth and gluten is well formed, about 8 minutes. Grease a large bowl. Place dough in bowl, turning to coat entire surface. Cover with a damp towel and leave in a warm place about 1 hour.

Grease 2 (9 X 5-inch) loaf pans. Punch down dough and form into 2 loaves; place in prepared pans. Cover with damp towel or plastic wrap and let rise until almost doubled in size, about 45 minutes, while grill is heating.

Preheat a covered grill to medium or 375F (190C). Almost cover rack with foil. Place pans on foil and bake until loaves are browned and sound hollow when thumped on bottoms, about 45 minutes. Remove from pans and cool on cooling racks. *Makes 2 loaves.*

ULTIMATE GRILLED GARLIC BREAD

▼▼▼▼▼

After savoring a similar style of garlic bread many years ago in Pete's Tavern, near where I worked in New York City, I began to develop this recipe. Everyone loves it except for devout fat watchers.

1/4 cup (1/2 stick) unsalted butter
1/4 cup good-quality olive oil, preferably Spanish
2 tablespoons coarsely chopped garlic (about 12 cloves)
1 fresh loaf crusty Italian or French bread, unsliced
2 to 3 tablespoons coarsely chopped flat-leaf parsley (optional)
2 to 3 ounces prosciutto (optional), chopped
1/4 cup freshly grated Parmesan (optional)
1 teaspoon ground mild chile (optional)

Melt butter on grill as grill preheats for rest of your meal or over medium-low heat. Add oil and garlic. Cook until garlic is light golden. Remove from heat.

Cut bread on diagonal into 3/4-inch slices. Place slices on a baking sheet or piece of foil. Drizzle with garlic mixture, evenly dividing among all pieces. Sprinkle with any or all of the optional ingredients, except chile, which can burn. Heat on a medium grill about 5 minutes or smoke about 20 minutes or until tops are crisped and light golden. Sprinkle with chile, if using. Cover and keep warm until served. *Makes 6 to 8 servings.*

VARIATION

Top each bread slice with a slice of mozzarella cheese before cooking.

SOUTHWESTERN PESTO BREAD BRAID

▼▼▼▼▼

Using any favorite bread dough—even the refrigerated bread loaves from the freezer section in your grocery store—you can create this festive loaf rather quickly. I prefer to go ahead and make my own bread. Hearth bread (page 234) is a good dough—just omit the cumin when preparing it for this recipe. Most any meal will be complemented by this bread. It even works well as an appetizer. This recipe bakes relatively fast and is great for a preheating grill.

Bread dough for 1 loaf
4 ounces (about 1/2 cup) prepared pesto
2 tablespoons freshly grated Parmesan or Romano cheese

Preheat grill to medium or 350F (175C) if not already hot. Grease a large baking sheet. Bread dough should be at room temperature and have risen once. On a board, roll out dough into a rectangle about 10 inches long, 8 inches wide and 3/4 inch thick. Using a sharp knife or utility scissors, cut bread from each long side toward center at a slight angle into strips, cutting about 2 inches in from each side and leaving center uncut. In center, spread pesto. Sprinkle with cheese. Overlap strips to cover filling. Place on prepared baking sheet. Partially cover rack with foil. Place baking sheet on foil. Cover grill and bake 25 to 30 minutes or until light golden.   *Makes 6 to 8 servings.*

SOURDOUGH STARTER

▼▼▼▼▼

Plan to make this at least a day before you wish to bake bread. Never use anything but glass, stainless steel or wooden utensils with sourdough.

2 packages or 2 scant tablespoons dry yeast
2 teaspoons sugar
2 cups warm water (110 to 115 F or 45C)
4 cups all-purpose flour

Dissolve yeast and sugar in warm water in a large bowl. Let stand until foamy. Add flour and beat to mix well. Cover loosely and place in a warm place to rise. Let stand overnight before using. Refrigerate leftover starter, loosely covered, until next use.

Always refresh starter immediately after removing all but 1 cupful. Add 1 cup warm water and 1 cup flour and stir—not necessary to be smooth. Allow to rest at room temperature at least 3 hours or overnight before using.   *Makes about 3 cups.*

GRILLED GREEN CHILE SOURDOUGH BREAD

▼▼▼▼▼

Sourdough bread used to be the darling of San Francisco and now it is much better known. You can use an old favorite starter, a borrowed one, a mix you buy or you can make it yourself with the recipe that follows this one.

1 cup warm water (110 to 115F or 45C)
1 package or 1 scant tablespoon dry yeast
2 teaspoons sugar
1 cup Sourdough Starter (page 241)
1/2 cup chopped, parched (page 161) and peeled green chiles
6 cups all-purpose flour
2 teaspoons salt
1/2 teaspoon baking soda

Add warm water to bowl of heavy-duty mixer or other large stainless or glass bowl, then add yeast and sugar and stir until dissolved. Let stand until foamy. Add starter and chiles and beat 3 minutes. Add 4 cups of the flour. Using a dough hook or by hand, beat until smooth. Remove from mixer and cover with a damp towel or plastic wrap. Allow to double in size in a warm place, about 1 hour.

Mix salt and soda with 1 cup remaining flour and beat into dough mixture. Beat in enough remaining flour to make a stiff dough. Turn out dough on a lightly floured board and knead until dough is smooth and gluten is well formed, about 8 minutes.

Grease a large baking sheet. Divide dough and form into 2 round loaves. Place on prepared baking sheet. Cover with damp towel or plastic wrap. Let rise until doubled in size, about 45 minutes, while grill is heating.

Preheat a covered grill to medium or 350F (175C). Partially cover rack with foil. Using a razor or sharp knife, slash top of each loaf about three times, using shallow cuts. Place a shallow pan of water on rack, near where you'll be placing bread. Place pan on foil. Bake loaves 30 to 40 minutes or until loaves are browned and sound hollow when thumped on bottoms. Cool on cooling racks. *Makes 6 to 8 servings.*

GRILLED PUMPKIN PANCAKES

▼▼▼▼▼

Wanting a different flavor for brunch one fall Sunday and overrun with pumpkins we'd grown, we decided to try these and loved 'em. I just didn't make enough the first time. Over the same grill, you can also cook breakfast meat—ham, bacon, sausage or whatever you prefer.

4 eggs, lightly beaten
1-1/3 cups skim milk
3 tablespoons vegetable oil
2 cups canned or cooked pureed pumpkin (see Note)
1 cup yellow cornmeal or whole-wheat flour
1 cup all-purpose flour
1/4 cup sugar
2 teaspoons baking powder
1 teaspoon baking soda
1/2 teaspoon ground cinnamon
1/2 teaspoon freshly grated nutmeg
1/2 teaspoon ground ginger or 2 teaspoons finely chopped candied ginger
Vegetable oil for cooking

Preheat grill to medium or 375F (190C). In a large bowl, whisk together eggs, milk and oil. Stir in pumpkin. Combine dry ingredients in another bowl and add to pumpkin mixture. Stir just until dry ingredients are moistened.

Meanwhile, place a heavy griddle on grill rack. Brush lightly with vegetable oil. Spoon batter onto hot griddle and cook until tops are bubbly. Turn and cook remaining side. Serve warm with honey or maple syrup. *Makes 4 servings.*

VARIATION

If desired, use only all-purpose flour.

NOTE: If starting with fresh pumpkin, bake or grill pumpkin pieces at 350F (175C) about 1 hour or until pumpkin is very tender. Peel flesh from rind and blend or process with a food processor until pureed. Strain if desired.

DOUBLE-BLUE BLUEBERRY PANCAKES

▼▼▼▼▼

What could be better than a pairing of fresh blueberries with blue corn? Nothing, in our book! These are absolutely wonderful for brunch or breakfast. To us, they must be served with blueberry compote spiked with Cointreau or Triple Sec. Or served with a fruited yogurt made by starting with a berry yogurt and adding fresh seasonal fruit. Spoon it over pancakes and top with honey.

2 eggs, slightly beaten
2 cups buttermilk
3 tablespoons vegetable oil
1 cup all-purpose flour
1 cup finely ground blue corn flour
2 tablespoons sugar
2 teaspoons baking soda
1 teaspoon salt
1 teaspoon finely minced orange zest
Vegetable oil for cooking
1 cup fresh blueberries
Blueberry Compote (opposite)

Preheat grill to medium or 375F (190C). In a large bowl, whisk together eggs, buttermilk and oil. Combine dry ingredients and orange zest in another bowl and add to buttermilk mixture. Stir just until dry ingredients are moistened. Meanwhile, place a heavy griddle on grill rack. Brush lightly with vegetable oil. Spoon batter onto hot griddle and place several blueberries on each pancake. Cook until tops are bubbly, then turn and cook remaining side. Serve warm with Blueberry Compote. *Makes 4 servings.*

Blueberry Compote

▼▼▼▼▼

This can be made ahead and warmed just before serving.

1 cup fresh blueberries
1/2 cup sugar or to taste
1/2 cup water or orange juice
1 teaspoon minced orange zest
1 tablespoon Cointreau or Triple Sec (optional)

Combine all ingredients except Cointreau in a heavy saucepan over medium heat and cook, stirring frequently, until sugar is dissolved and mixture thickens slightly, about 10 minutes. Add Cointreau just before serving, if using. Serve warm. *Makes 4 servings.*

Jalapeño Cilantro Spread

▼▼▼▼▼

This Mexican-accented spread is great on both breads and meats. You can lighten the fat calories by using whipped low-fat spread.

1/4 cup unsalted butter, softened
1/4 cup good-quality olive oil, preferably Spanish
1 medium fresh jalapeño, very finely minced, seeded if desired
2 tablespoons coarsely chopped cilantro

In a small bowl, whip butter and oil. Stir in remaining ingredients. Use immediately or refrigerate, covered, for later use. *Makes 4 to 6 servings or 1/2 cup.*

HOT HERBED OIL

▼▼▼▼▼

Quick bastes, salad dressings and as a table condiment are but a few of the uses for which this oil is great!

2 cups good-quality olive oil, preferably Spanish
1/2 cup crushed pequin quebrado chile
1/4 cup minced fresh herbs such as rosemary, basil and thyme

Place oil and chile in a heavy saucepan. Heat just until warm, then remove from heat. Cover and cool to room temperature. Allow to steep at least 2 hours, then strain out chile. Stir in herbs. Refrigerate leftovers. *Makes 1 pint.*

SMOKED CUMIN CORIANDER OIL

▼▼▼▼▼

This oil is wonderful as an ingredient in bastes and marinades and as a dipping sauce for breads. Make it when using the smoker to cook an entree.

2 cups walnut, sesame or peanut oil
2 tablespoons ground cumin
2 tablespoons ground coriander
1 tablespoon crushed caribe chile
2 tablespoons minced flat-leaf parsley

Whisk oil with cumin and coriander until blended in a heatproof bowl. Place on top shelf in smoker. Allow to smoke 30 minutes, then sample. The flavor of the smoke should be pleasant. If too subtle, return to smoke, checking every 5 minutes. Stir in chile and parsley. Refrigerate leftovers. *Makes about 2 cups.*

VARIATION

To quick-smoke, preheat unit to medium or 325F (165C). Place a few wood chips, preferably fruitwood, in bottom of a heavy covered pan and place pan over medium heat. Allow to heat until smoking, 7 to 10 minutes. When chips are smoking, place oil mixture in heatproof bowl on a rack over chips and cover. Place pan in oven and smoke 30 minutes.

CHILE GARLIC BUTTER

▼▼▼▼▼

Besides making wonderful garlic bread, this butter is great in salad dressings and as a baste for almost all meats, poultry and fish.

1/2 cup (1 stick) unsalted butter, softened
3 tablespoons good-quality olive oil, preferably Spanish
6 cloves garlic, minced
1/4 cup crushed caribe chile

Using a wooden spoon, combine all ingredients in a small bowl.   *Makes about 3/4 cup.*

DOUBLE MUSTARD BUTTER

▼▼▼▼▼

The crunch of mustard seeds gives this butter an interesting texture. It dresses up hamburgers and sandwich buns and makes a good table spread.

1/2 cup (1 stick) unsalted butter, softened
3 tablespoons Dijon mustard
1-1/2 tablespoons mustard seeds

Using a wooden spoon, combine all ingredients in a small bowl.   *Makes about 3/4 cup.*

Tri-Pepper Herb Butter

▼▼▼▼▼

Red and green chiles sparked with pequin and flavored with Southwestern herbs make this butter a natural for dressing up hamburgers, sandwich buns, steaks, chops and chicken.

1/2 cup (1 stick) unsalted butter, softened
1/4 cup crushed caribe chile
1 tablespoon crushed pequin quebrado chile
2 green chiles, parched (page 161), peeled and chopped, or 1/4 cup canned chopped
    green chiles, drained

    Combine butter with dried chiles in a small bowl until blended. Then fold in green chiles and serve at room temperature. Refrigerate leftovers. *Makes about 1 cup.*

Rosemary Butter

▼▼▼▼▼

The combined fragrance of rosemary and the flavor of butter makes any steak more succulent. Try this butter on grilled beef, lamb, game, turkey or chicken breast. If you don't have time to marinate meat, this really takes its place—almost.

1/2 cup (1 stick) unsalted butter, softened
1 tablespoon fresh rosemary leaves, coarsely minced

    Using a wooden spoon, whip ingredients together in a small bowl. Form into teaspoon-size balls, if desired, and chill. *Makes about 24 balls or 1/2 cup.*

Desserts from the Grill

▼▼▼▼▼

Once the grill is hot, why not use the heat as an oven for preparing your dessert. I think fruity or simple desserts, such as Hot-off-the-Grill Biscotti, are best. Rich, soothing desserts are fun, too.

For baking on the grill, it is always best to have a grill with a lid; lacking one, you have to fashion one from heavy foil. Several of the following desserts were done on the grill while we ate the main course.

Strawberry Rhubarb Crumble

▼▼▼▼▼

The combination of strawberries and rhubarb is difficult to top. This dessert can just bubble along when you are grilling the entree and whatever side dishes. Or, bake it while you eat the main course, if the grill is too full. It can be rewarmed in the oven. It is definitely best served hot and simply fabulous with any kind of cream—whipped, ice cream, crème fraîche or thick cream.

2 cups fresh or frozen unsweetened rhubarb
3 cups fresh or frozen unsweetened strawberries
1 cup sugar
1/2 cup all-purpose flour
1/2 cup rolled oats
1/2 teaspoon ground cinnamon
Freshly grated nutmeg
1/2 cup unsalted butter, chilled and cut into small pieces

Preheat grill to medium or 350F (175C) if not already hot. Butter an 8 X 8-inch baking pan that will not get damaged on the grill or cover the bottom with foil. Arrange fruit in pan. Combine all remaining ingredients in a medium bowl and mix until crumbly. Evenly sprinkle mixture over fruit. Cover with foil and place on a grill rack. Cover grill and bake 20 minutes. Remove foil from pan and bake another 10 minutes or until top is golden and somewhat dry and fruit is tender when pierced with a knife. *Makes 4 to 6 servings.*

Grilled Pineapple Kabobs with Mai Tai Baste

▼▼▼▼▼

Pineapple is even better when it is grilled with these wonderfully compatible flavors. Pineapple, unlike many fruits, does not get mushy when cooked, so kabobs hold their texture nicely. For color, you may wish to use orange slices and candied whole cherries, or you may leave them out.

1 fresh pineapple
2 fresh oranges (optional), unpeeled, cut into 1/4-inch-thick slices
6 whole maraschino cherries with stems on (optional)
1/4 cup unsalted butter
1/4 cup light brown or granulated sugar
1/2 cup light rum

Preheat grill to medium-high or 400F (205C) if not already hot, then prepare pineapple. Using a very sharp heavy chef's knife or electric knife, slice about 1 inch off the top. Then peel, cutting deep enough to trim off most of "eyes." If any remain, remove with a sharp paring knife. Halve lengthwise, then cut lengthwise in sixths and then into 2-inch pieces. Skewer pineapple, alternating with orange slices and cherries, if using. Place kabobs on grill.

Combine remaining ingredients in a small pan and place either on burner attached to grill or on grill itself. Cook, stirring occasionally, until butter melts. Brush fruit with mixture and continue to grill until it chars a bit. Turn and baste with remaining mixture and grill until kabobs are charred a bit and done as desired—they are best if they are allowed to darken somewhat from grilling as this enhances flavor.   *Makes 6 servings.*

ITALIAN GRILLED PEACHES
▼▼▼▼▼

The ingredients here are most unlikely but amazingly delightful when combined. You can use any cheese you like, if you do not like blue cheeses.

2/3 cup good-quality balsamic vinegar
3 tablespoons sugar
2 teaspoons freshly ground rose or other peppercorns
2 large fresh freestone peaches or nectarines, unpeeled, halved and pitted
2 to 3 ounces Gorgonzola cheese, crumbled

Earlier in day, simmer balsamic vinegar in a small nonreactive saucepan with sugar and pepper until reduced by about half and slightly thickened for a glaze.

Preheat grill to medium-high or 350 to 400F (175 to 205C) if not already hot. Place peach halves on grill, cut side down, and grill about 5 minutes or until flesh has slightly charred. Brush top sides with glaze and cook 1 to 2 minutes. Turn, brush with glaze and cook another 2 to 3 minutes. Transfer to individual serving dishes and spoon any remaining glaze over tops. Serve with crumbled cheese on top.   *Makes 4 servings.*

GRILLED STUFFED PEACHES

▼▼▼▼▼

Hot peaches right from the grill are delectable. They can be cooked ahead of time and served hot or cold or they can cook while you are eating. Just leave the grill on and if you're using charcoal, add enough charcoal to sustain a moderate heat for 30 minutes in a small area.

5 large, fresh freestone peaches
1 tablespoon honey or brown sugar
1/4 cup crisp cookies, such as oatmeal, sugar or any flavor compatible with peaches, broken
2 tablespoons plain or vanilla yogurt
2 teaspoons hazelnut, orange or even peach liqueur

Preheat grill to medium or 350F (175C) if not already hot. Butter a 9 X 13-inch baking pan that will not get damaged on the grill or cover the bottom with foil. Peel and pit 1 peach; place in a blender or food processor. Halve remaining 4 peaches lengthwise and remove pits. Scoop out about 1/2 inch of flesh from each peach center and add to flesh in blender. Arrange peach halves in prepared pan. Add honey, cookies, yogurt and liqueur to blender. Process until combined and spoon mixture into hollow of each peach half, mounding it up. Place pan on grill rack and cover grill. Bake until peaches are fork tender, about 15 minutes.   *Makes 4 large or 8 small servings.*

GRILLED HOT BAKED PEARS

▼▼▼▼▼

Pears lend themselves so well to most any flavor—from strong cheeses to scintillating spices such as ginger. I have always adored pears baked in wine, and they are so easy to do on the grill.

2 ripe Bartlett, Anjou or similar-type pears
1/2 cup cabernet sauvignon wine
1 tablespoon sugar
2-inch cinnamon stick
Freshly ground nutmeg
1/2 to 1 teaspoon crushed pequin quebrado chile or to taste

Preheat grill to medium or 350F (175C) if not already hot. Butter an 8 X 8-inch baking pan that will not get damaged on the grill or cover the bottom with foil. Halve and core pears; place pears, cut side down, in pan. Combine remaining ingredients and pour over pears. Cover baking pan with foil and place on grill rack. Bake about 15 minutes or until pears are fork tender and have absorbed wine color. *Makes 4 servings.*

LOW-FAT BANANA ZUCCHINI CAKE

▼▼▼▼▼

This baked-on-the grill cake is so good that it is hard to believe it is low fat! The fruits and zucchini add moistness. It will bake fine right on the grill when you are preparing a meat such as ribs or halves of chicken that take a moderate 350F (175C) temperature.

1 cup mashed ripe bananas (1 large or 2 small)
1/4 cup vegetable oil
1-1/2 cups granulated sugar
3 eggs
3-1/2 cups shredded zucchini
1/2 cup (8-oz. can, drained) crushed pineapple
1 teaspoon Mexican vanilla
2 cups unbleached all-purpose flour
1 teaspoon baking soda
1 teaspoon baking powder
1 teaspoon ground cinnamon
1/2 teaspoon salt
Freshly ground nutmeg
Powdered sugar for dusting top (optional)

Preheat grill to medium or 350F (175C) if not already hot. Butter a 9 X 13-inch baking pan that will not get damaged on the grill or cover the bottom with foil. Or use a foil pan.

Combine bananas, oil and sugar in a large bowl. Using an electric mixer, beat until sugar dissolves. Beat in eggs, one at a time. Mix in zucchini, pineapple and vanilla. In another bowl, combine remaining dry ingredients and stir until blended. Then add the dry ingredients one-quarter at a time, mixing after each addition. Mix only until all ingredients are well combined.

Turn batter into prepared baking pan. Place on grill rack and cover grill. Bake about 45 minutes or until a wooden pick inserted in center comes out clean and cake springs back when gently pressed. Cool on a cake rack. Dust with powdered sugar, if desired. *Makes 12 servings*.

VARIATION

Substitute carrots for zucchini if desired.

JAN'S HONEY-NUT FRUIT BROCHETTES

▼▼▼▼▼

The nuts toast nicely, adding crunch and flavor. These are easy to do and best if you prepare them just before you're planning to eat them. Just leave the grill on or add extra charcoal, enough for about 10 minutes' grilling time for the fruit.

1 large or 2 medium bananas
2 oranges, peeled
2 cups strawberries (1 small box)
1/4 fresh pineapple or 1/2 cantaloupe or honeydew, peeled
1/4 cup honey
1/3 cup finely chopped nuts

Preheat grill to medium or 350F (175C) if not already hot. Cut bananas crosswise into 2-inch lengths. Cut oranges into quarters and then cut quarters in half crosswise. Cut pineapple into 2-inch pieces. Then place fruit, alternating types, on 4 skewers. Place honey in a flat dish and nuts in another. Roll skewers first in honey, then in nuts. Place skewers on grill rack, rotating frequently. When nuts are toasted and fruit shows some grill charring, about 20 minutes, remove and serve. *Makes 4 servings.*

VARIATION

If preferred, omit the honey and nuts. Serve doused with a liqueur or with a fruit puree that has been flavored with a compatible liqueur. Use any fruit substitutions that will cook in about the same time and can be skewered.

NOTE: If you use wooden skewers, soak them first in water to prevent them from burning.

HOT-OFF-THE-GRILL BISCOTTI

▼▼▼▼▼

Biscotti can be kept, if tightly sealed, for at least a few weeks and frozen for at least 3 months. They are great cookies to have to accompany sherbets, sorbets, fruit desserts or to enjoy with coffee and/or a liqueur. They are fun to cook on the grill, but can obviously be baked in the oven. If the grill is not already hot, the oven is probably more convenient.

1 cup whole blanched almonds
1 cup unsalted butter, softened
1-1/2 cups granulated sugar
4 large eggs
1/4 cup anisette, marsala or brandy
2 tablespoons anise seeds
4 cups plus 2 tablespoons all-purpose flour
3/4 teaspoon baking powder
1/2 teaspoon salt

Preheat grill to medium or 350F (175C) if not already hot. Place almonds on a baking sheet and toast on grill about 15 minutes while grill is heating. Watch and stir every 5 minutes. When lightly toasted, pour almonds onto a cutting board. Reduce heat to 325F (165C).

Beat butter and sugar on low with an electric mixer or food processor. Add eggs one at a time, beating well after each addition and scraping down sides of bowl. Add anisette and anise seeds and beat again. In a separate bowl stir together flour with baking powder and salt. Add flour mixture, about one-quarter at a time, mixing after each addition. Beat until a very stiff dough results. Coarsely chop almonds, then mix them in until well blended. Pour dough out onto a board and knead until smooth. Form into rolls about 2 inches in diameter and as long as the baking sheet you will be using for baking them.

While forming rolls, double-check heat in grill. If you do not have a cover for grill, create a tentlike cover from heavy foil. Place rolls of cookie dough on a baking sheet about 2 inches apart. Place on grill and cover grill. Bake 25 minutes or until lightly browned. (If your cover is not very tight, turn roll of dough after about 15 minutes or when it starts to brown on bottom.) Cool 5 minutes, then cut rolls into 1/2-inch-thick slices. Place slices cut side up on baking sheets and return to grill 5 minutes to lightly brown. Turn and dry another 5 minutes, then serve. Store remaining cookies in airtight containers when cooled. *Makes 72 (3-inch) cookies.*

SUMMER BERRY BOWL

▼▼▼▼▼

After any grilled summer meal or, for that matter, any time you can get fresh, great-tasting berries, enjoy them simply! The fresh flavors of berries can hardly be improved upon. You can serve this medley hot or cold. Serve with frozen yogurt, sherbet or with a crisp cookie such as Hot-off-the-Grill Biscotti (opposite).

1/2 pint each of 3 kinds of berries, if possible, such as strawberries, raspberries, blueberries or blackberries or any other special local berry
2 tablespoons orange-flavored liqueur
1-1/2 teaspoons minced lemon zest
1/4 cup sugar or to taste

Combine berries in a medium heatproof serving dish, then add remaining ingredients and macerate 1 hour at room temperature.

Preheat grill to medium or 350F (175C) if not already hot. Cover bottom of dish with foil and place on grill rack while you are eating. Grill until hot.   *Makes 4 to 6 servings.*

Guide to Manufacturers

GRILLS

The new popularity of heavy restaurant-style ranges for the home kitchen has spawned a whole new generation of fully featured, ultimate grills.

The climate where you live as well as how often you plan to cook out will have an impact on which grill or smoker is best for you or your family. As a general rule, the better-quality units will hold up much longer and give you many, many trouble-free cookouts. A few years back some poor-quality electric, gas and charcoal units were sold. Their short-lived poor performance and lack of flexibility disappointed many cooks. Do look into these new fully featured models when you can!

What separates the ultimate models from the others are features such as a rear burner behind the rotisserie. With these new models, there are no flare-ups. The cooking is direct, on a vertical plane, which produces the most even results. Most are meant for a permanent outdoor installation and some models are only manufactured for natural gas. In comparison with older models, they are much heavier and have a much higher BTU capacity for faster, hotter grilling as well as for low controlled heat. They are designed to be a full outdoor kitchen.

FEATURES TO LOOK FOR

Following is a review of features available as of the writing of this book. Some are optional; others are standard. They vary, depending on the manufacturer.

FIREBOX

Look for a body that is heavy-gauge steel, rustproof and deep enough to allow flexibility of cooking height.

GAS BURNERS

The burners should also be of heavy material and possess a number of ports or holes for releasing the gas so that there will be even temperature control. The higher the BTU rating, the more capable of high-temperature, high-performance grilling. Also look for low BTU input for low controlled temperatures. For flexibility of place of use, LP units are better; for permanent installations, however, natural gas is better and, according to some, safer.

ELECTRIC GRILLS

These units should have heavy, calrod-type steel-sheathed burner units designed for operation on 220-volt current. The lower wattages do not have the power to generate hot, searing grilling heat and are very slow.

CHARCOAL GRILLS

Look for a rack that can be easily adjusted. It is always best to have a lid. A method to remove the charcoal ashes is needed.

DELUXE FEATURES

ROCK LAYER

Lava rock is considered by many to be the real answer to getting the charred taste with gas or electric units. The "rocks" absorb the fats and juices. Then the heat from the burners smokes it off when they get hot, flavoring the foods being grilled.

SIDE BURNERS

These are wonderful to have for sauces and side dishes. They add to overall flexibility of use, meaning that all the cooking for a meal can be done at the grill.

SMOKER DRAWER OR TRAY

Available on several models, this feature is designed to hold wood chips for adding smokiness to foods. When the tray or drawer is contained in one area, as it is on deluxe models, then cold smoking of fish and cheese can be done.

ROTISSERIES

The best units have a vertical back burner that attaches to the back of the grill above the burners and on a level with the meat being cooked. This yields better, crisper browning and no flare-ups.

SWING-OUT SHELVES

These add convenience, supplying handy work surfaces for preparing and serving the grilled foods.

GRATES

Look for porcelain coating as it is the easiest by far to clean. At the least, grates should be made from heavy steel or cast iron, which require more maintenance. Lightweight grates warp, rust and do not last.

SMOKER FEATURES TO LOOK FOR

- A large fire-tending door or separate compartment for the fire makes tending the fire easier without reducing the heat greatly.
- Multiple racks allow for greater flexibility of use.
- Look for optional use as a grill—even a steamer.
- Choose models made from heavy steel or other material, so that the high fire-box heat will not deteriorate the unit.

GRILL MANUFACTURERS

BROIL KING
ONWARD MULTI-CORP.
Product Line: Deluxe multifeatured gas units with rear burner for rotisserie as well as standard gas units and a tabletop portable gas model.
Contact: Kelly Boutelier
932 Victoria St., N.
Kitchener, Ontario
Canada N2B 1W4
519-578-3770; Customer Service 800-265-2150

BROILMASTER
Division of MARTIN INDUSTRIES
Product Line: Deluxe, heavy-duty gas grills for natural or LP gas on posts or roll-about carts. Racks adjust up to three different levels at same time. Has retract-a-rack grilling accessory that can increase grilling area up to 50 percent. Features a double cart, allowing for rotisserie cooking on one unit and grilling on the other. Many accessories, such as side burners and cooking gadgets.
Contact: Rachel Webster
P.O. Box 128
Florence, AL 35630
800-255-0403 or 205-767-0330

CAJUN GRILL
PERCY GUIDRY, INC.
Product Line: Has two models of heavy-duty steel charcoal cookers on wheels. Have adjustable air-draft intake, removable ash pan and lid. Accessories include rotisserie, indirect back burner, utensils and covers.
Contact: Customer Service
204 Wilson St.
Lafayette, LA 70501
800-822-4766 or 318-233-6808

CHAR-BROIL
Division of W. C. BRADLEY CO.

Product Line: Gas roll-about carts in cabinets, with side burners and shelves; smaller electric grills on stands; portable gas and charcoal tabletop and charcoal cookers in cabinets with side shelves; full line of accessories and smokers (see smokers).

Contact: Customer Service
P.O. Box 1240
Columbus, GA 31993
800-352-4111 or 706-571-7000

COLEMAN

Manufactured under license from The COLEMAN Company by CHAR-BROIL (see above for contact, telephone and address).

Product Line: Gas roll-about carts for LP Gas. Offer choice of cast-iron or heavy-duty porcelain steel cooking surfaces. Have side shelves, hoods, some with windows. Bonus burners offered on some models. Also have smokers (see smokers).

DUCANE

Product Line: Deluxe ultra line of heavy-duty outdoor gas grills for operation on LP or natural gas. Have a vertical rotisserie and complete outdoor kitchen accessories for an ice compartment and serving area.

Contact: Scott Walters, Director of Marketing
800 Dutch Square Blvd.
Columbia, SC 29210
800-489-6543

DYNAMIC COOKING SYSTEMS

Product Line: Deluxe ultra line of heavy-duty LP and natural gas outdoor grills available with a vertical rotisserie burner, range top, side burners and accessories such as a built-in wok. Entire units can be free-standing on a cart or built-in. Also manufacture professional restaurant grills, fryers, ranges, etc.

Contact: Bob Wood, Sales Manager
10850 Portal Dr.
Los Alamitos, CA 90720
714-220-9505

DYNASTY
Division of JADE RANGE, INC.

Product Line: Ultra deluxe heavy-duty LP or natural gas outdoor grills with smoke ejector system, heavy-duty vertical rotisserie and other features. Comes with a smoking system with hood. The units were formerly made only for commercial use. Can come on roll-about heavy cart or built-in.

Contact: Marty Leskin, National Product Manager
7355 E. Slauson Ave.
City of Commerce, CA 90040
213-728-5700

FALCON (EMBERMATIC)
Division of SUNBEAM OUTDOOR PRODUCTS
Product Line: Competitively priced gas grills on carts. Minimum features. Sold exclusively through distributors, utility companies and specialty retailers.

Contact: Customer Service
1600 Jones Rd.
Paragould, AR 72450
800-346-8960

FIREMAGIC
Division of ROBERT H. PETERSON CO.
Product Line: Deluxe, ultra line of built-in or free-standing gas grills, griddles and ovens. Have side burners, rotisseries with drip pan and counterbalances, charcoal grills and smoker oven attachment for grills. They also have accessories, primarily for built-in grills.

Contact: Sales Manager
530 Baldwin Park Blvd.
City of Industry, CA 91746
818-369-5085

FLAME-BROIL BBQS
K & W MFG. CO.
Product Line: Built-in LP, natural gas or charcoal barbecue units, either single or double control; barbecue ovens and side cookers. Also many have barbecue doors and other accessories for a completely built-in outdoor barbecue.

Contact: Denise Jure, Vice President
23107 Temescal Canyon Rd.
Corona, CA 91719
909-277-3300

MAVERICK IND., INC.
Product Line: Has line of electric, portable countertop grills made of stoneware. Promoted to be smoke-free and stay cool on the bottom and sides when heated. Also have a larger unit made of aluminum.

Contact: Customer Service
94 Mayfield Ave.
Edison, NJ 08837
800-526-0954 or 908-417-9666

MECO
Product Line: Competitively priced free-standing charcoal units with hoods that tilt away and adjustable racks. Also have tabletop electric grills.
Contact: Customer Service
P.O. Box 1000
1500 Industrial Rd.
Greenville, TN 37744
800-251-7558 or 615-639-1171

MINUTE GLOW Gas Barbecue
L-M, INC.
Product Line: Covered, gas barbecue on wheels, constructed of stainless steel, operating on natural or LP gas. Have built-in models with optional cover.
Contact: Customer Service
616 Hardwick St.
P.O. Box 327
Belvidere, NJ 07823
908-475-5313

MODERN HOME PRODUCTS
Product Line: BBQer CHOICE, SEAR MAGIC gas grills that are made of solid aluminum and stainless steel and are warranteed for life. They are fueled by either LP or natural gas and have dual burner controls. All have lids. Rotisseries and side burners are add-on features available for all models. They have an exclusive gas low fuel indicator that lets you know when fuel is low and a leak detector—a good safety feature. Modern Home Products originated the first gas grill under the name CHARM GLOW.
Contact: Kevin Knight, Vice President Sales
150 S. Ram Rd.
Antioch, IL 60002
847-395-6556

NAPOLEON BARBECUES
Product Line: Heavy-duty, deluxe, highly featured new manufacturer of gas barbecues with electric ignition. Has wide range of heat control with three independently controlled high BTU to very low burner systems, a warming rack, and smoking tray. Comes with smoker lid, rotisserie, wooden side work surfaces and electric ignition.

Has porcelainized roasting pan. Controlled flare-ups with stainless steel sear plates so that drippings vaporize. New Canadian company just started manufacture in 1995. Has distribution in Canada and the United States.

Contact: Customer Service
R.R. #1 (Hwy. 11 & 93)
Barrie, Ontario
Canada L4M 4Y8
705-721-1212

NEW BRAUNFELS SMOKER CO.

Product Line: Known for their smokers, they now have the barrel-style steel grills in medium, large and small camper sizes.

Contact: Customer Service
P.O. Box 310698
New Braunfels, TX 78131
800-232-3398 or 210-629-5742

NOMAD
RELIANT INDUSTRIES, INC.

Product Line: Electric barbecue on stand that is portable, operating on cigarette lighter plug-in as well as 12-volt battery. Optional solar power attachment. Has adjustable grill height and sets on a stand. Works with wood pellets available from manufacturer. Pellets come in a range of twelve varieties including hickory, mesquite, fruitwoods and grape cuttings.

Contact: Customer Service
333-3 Industrial Dr.
Placerville, CA 95667
916-622-5887

PACIFIC GAS SPECIALTIES

Product Line: Deluxe ultra line of gas units for outdoor installation, either built-in as a barbecue system or on a post or movable cart. Have an Infra-broil rotisserie back burner system, commercial grade burners, side burners and continuous electric ignition (automatic electric starting system). Also, additional add-on features such as a kabob attachment.

Contact: Customer Service
P.O. Box 1609
2641 DuBridge Ave.
Irvine, CA 92713
714-757-7723

PROCHEF

Product Line: Deluxe ultra gas units with a unique insert pan in center for sautéing, simmering and even deep-frying. Has porcelain on cast-iron grates. Available for built-in natural gas or LP gas on roll-about carts. Also offer a portable, camping model that folds up for transport. Accessories include side burners, lid for the center pan, rotisserie and fry basket.

Contact: Customer Service
2440 Railroad St.
Corona, CA 91720
714-278-4321

ROTISSERIE MASTER
by SWISHER MOWER & MACHINE Co., Inc.

Product Line: Have two charcoal rotisserie grilling models, one portable. Each has four separate swinging shelves that rotate with up to 10 pounds each for even distribution of heat and smoke. Has feature for indirect cooking to prevent flare-ups and control heat. Portable models come with 12-volt battery option or for use with car cigarette lighter or solar power. Has wood workshelf in front.

Contact: Customer Service
P.O. Box 67
Warrensburg, MO 64093
800-222-8183

STERLING

Product Line: Have full line of deluxe free-standing gas grills for operation on either LP or propane. Some models have many features, including rear burner rotisseries, side burners, and work surfaces and cutting boards. Also have portable tabletop gas units and accessories.

Contact: Kelly Boutilier or Customer Service
932 Victoria St., N.
Kitchener, Ontario
Canada N2B 1W4
800-265-2150 or 519-578-3770

SUNBEAM

Product Line: Have extensive line, including LP gas and electric grills on carts, charcoal grills on carts and portable LP gas, electric and charcoal models. Their line also includes accessories such as electric starters, chimney starters and various covers, lava rock and cooking and cleaning equipment.

Contact: Customer Service
Howard Bush Dr.
Neosho, MO 64850
800-641-2100 or 417-451-4550

TEC
THERMAL ENGINEERING CORP.
Product Line: Have two lines—deluxe Sterling Infra-Red grills and the Patio series—both with a ceramic cooking surface with many ports for the flame for controlled heat. There are twin burners, each with its own temperature control. Comes with two racks on a roll-about pedestal cart for LP or natural gas. Has optional wood chip smoker, rotisseries, griddle and deep-fat fryer accessories.
Contact: Customer Service
P.O. Box 868
Columbia, SC 29202
800-331-0097 or 803-783-0750

THERMOS
Product Line: Have 110-volt electric unit with a nonstick grid, shelves and lid, recently designed to operate on less energy than the average hair dryer—not for heavy cooking. Also manufactures a two-burner LP gas grill with fold-down shelves.
Contact: Customer Service
Route 75
Freeport, IL 61032
1-800-435-5194

WEBER
WEBER-STEPHEN PRODUCTS CO.
Product Line: Known for their best-selling, very durable charcoal-burning kettle grills. They have a very extensive product line, including new ultra deluxe units. Have various series of gas barbecues, including the Genesis, Spirit and the new Ultra Genesis intended for permanent installation outdoors. Operating on LP or natural gas, their units have side burners, swing-up work surfaces, steam-'n'-chips feature for steaming in the grill and three individually controlled burner units. Their easy-clean charcoal units come in a range of sizes, even including a roll-about worktable with storage. Also offer a complete line of portable units operating with charcoal or LP cylinders. Have extensive line of accessories, including chimney starters, cooking accessories such as a griddle, shish kabob racks, vegetable vertical cookers, side racks, roast holders and even hardwood briquettes, chips and chunks.
Contact: Customer Service
250 South Hicks Rd.
Palatine, IL 60067-6241
800-446-1071 or 708-934-5700

SMOKER MANUFACTURERS

BRINKMANN

Product Line: Feature both vertical and horizontal smokers. The verticals are space-saving and are fueled with either electric, gas or charcoal. All their vertical models can double as a grill. Their most deluxe model has three racks and a vertical door allowing complete access for fire or food tending. Also have small portable grills. Their horizontal smokers are designed with an adjacent firebox very similar to that of the New Braunfels models. The benefit of the separate firebox is that the fire can be tended without interrupting the heat in the smoker. Horizontal models are capable of much more capacity. They carry an extensive line of accessories, from meat holders to replacement parts to charcoal and seasonings, all available through mail order. They also have a club for members featuring several benefits such as free freight and bonuses such as free charcoal.

Contact: Customer Service
4215 McEwen Rd.
Dallas, TX 75234
800-468-5252

CHAR-BROIL
Division of W. C. BRADLEY CO.

Product Line: Electric and charcoal vertical smokers that convert easily to portable grills. They have dual racks and water pans. Their access door is small, intended basically for fire tending. They do feature parts and accessories.

Contact: Customer Service
P.O. Box 1240
Columbus, GA 31993
800-352-4111 or 706-571-7000

COLEMAN
Division of CHAR-BROIL (above)

Product Line: Have electric and charcoal models. Can smoke, roast, steam and bake with them. Some models can be used as a tabletop grill. For information, contact CHAR-BROIL Customer Service, above.

KAMADO
NAGATO SHOKAI, INC.

Product Line: Heavy clay smokers that are oval in shape. They are basically intended for smoking and slow barbecuing. They hold the heat very well, but are cumbersome and difficult to clean. Being clay, they can crack when moved, as ours did.

Contact: Customer Service
Box 311
Yokohama Port 231-91
JAPAN

NEW BRAUNFELS SMOKER CO.

Product Line: Barrel-style horizontal smokers with side offset firebox designed for fuel efficiency and even heat distribution. Fire can be tended without cooling down the smoking. Smoker can be used for direct or indirect grilling and comes with grate.
Contact: Customer Service
P.O. Box 310698
New Braunfels, TX 78131
800-232-3398

SMOKEY MOUNTAIN COOKER SMOKER
by WEBER-STEPHEN PRODUCTS Co.

Product Line: Outdoor smokers operate on charcoal and/or wood chunks. Has firebox access, water holder and 2 grates. Can be used for grilling or steaming by re-arranging the grates.
Contact: Customer Service
250 South Hicks Rd.
Palatine, IL 60067-6241
800-446-1071 or 708-705-8660

Mail-Order Sources

AMERICAN WOOD PRODUCTS
Product Line: Features logs, chunks, chips, slabs and wood charcoal of a number of types of hardwoods. Requires a minimum order of $50.00.
9540 Riggs
Overland Park, KS 66212
800-223-9046 or 913-648-7993; fax 913-648-8019

THE BRINKMANN CORPORATION
Product Line: Features their line of smokers and accessories (see page 267).
4215 McEwen Rd.
Dallas, TX 75244
Attn.: Mail Order Department
800-468-5252 or 214-770-8555; fax 800-780-0109

PECOS VALLEY SPICE CO.
Product Line: Offers a complete line of pure New Mexican chiles, herbs and spices for Southwestern cooking. Also, mesquite chunks and chips, cookbooks and videos.
2429 Monroe, NE
Albuquerque, NM 87110
800-473-TACO (8226) or 505-888-4086; fax 505-888-4269

PEOPLES CHARCOAL WOODS
Product Line: Features a wide variety of wood logs, chunks, chips and charcoal. Also sells grills, smokers, accessories and books. Requires a minimum order of $50.00.
55 Mill St.
Cumberland, RI 02884
800-729-5800 or 401-725-2700

SAUSAGE MAKER
Product Line: Handles an extensive line of cookbooks, videos and equipment for the smoking enthusiast, sausage maker or those interested in meat curing.
26 Military Rd.
Buffalo, NY 14207-2875
716-876-5521; fax 716-875-0302

General Information
NATIONAL BARBECUE ASSOCIATION
P.O. Box 29051
Charlotte, NC 28229
704-365-3622; fax 704-365-3622

Metric Conversion Charts

When You Know	Comparison to Metric Measure Symbol	Multiply By	To Find	Symbol
teaspoons	tsp	5.0	milliliters	ml
tablespoons	tbsp	15.0	milliliters	ml
fluid ounces	fl. oz.	30.0	milliliters	ml
cups	c	0.24	liters	l
pints	pt.	0.47	liters	l
quarts	qt.	0.95	liters	l
ounces	oz.	28.0	grams	g
pounds	lb.	0.45	kilograms	kg
Fahrenheit	F	5/9 (after subtracting 32)	Celsius	C

Fahrenheit to Celsius

F	C
200–205	95
220–225	105
245–250	120
275	135
300–305	150
325–330	165
345–350	175
370–375	190
400–405	205
425–430	220
445–450	230
470–475	245
500	260

Liquid Measure to Liters

1/4 cup	=	0.06 liters
1/2 cup	=	0.12 liters
3/4 cup	=	0.18 liters
1 cup	=	0.24 liters
1-1/4 cups	=	0.3 liters
1-1/2 cups	=	0.36 liters
2 cups	=	0.48 liters
2-1/2 cups	=	0.6 liters
3 cups	=	0.72 liters
3-1/2 cups	=	0.84 liters
4 cups	=	0.96 liters
4-1/2 cups	=	1.08 liters
5 cups	=	1.2 liters
5-1/2 cups	=	1.32 liters

Liquid Measure to Milliliters

1/4 teaspoon	=	1.25 milliliters
1/2 teaspoon	=	2.5 milliliters
3/4 teaspoon	=	3.75 milliliters
1 teaspoon	=	5.0 milliliters
1-1/4 teaspoons	=	6.25 milliliters
1-1/2 teaspoons	=	7.5 milliliters
1-3/4 teaspoons	=	8.75 milliliters
2 teaspoons	=	10.0 milliliters
1 tablespoon	=	15.0 milliliters
2 tablespoons	=	30.0 milliliters

Index

▼▼▼▼▼

A

Achiote paste
Mayan Roast Chicken, Pibil Style, 188
Adobo Sauce, 202
Anadama Bread, 239
Antelope
Grilled Antelope Stew with Tomatoes, Onion & Butternut Squash, 54
Smoked Chile-Sparked Game Jerky, 26
Smoked Venison, Antelope or Elk, 142
Appetizers, 23–42
Apples
Fresh Cranberry Salsa, 208
Fruitwood-Smoked Chicken with Smoked Apple Chipotle Salsa, 148
Grilled Pork Steak with Apples & Onions, 98
Raspberry Vinegar-Marinated Scallop Kabobs, 130
Applesauce
Spicy Apple Barbecue Sauce, 214
Applewood-Smoked Salmon Steaks, 159
Applewood-Smoked Turkey with Honey Glaze, 145
Asian Smoked Duck Breast Salad, 156
Asparagus
Smoke-Roasted Asparagus in Garlic à la Rominger, 220
Spring Asparagus Pizza Topping, 31
Avocados
Guacamole, 24
Southwestern Grilled Turkey Salad, 67
Aztec-Style Pico de Gallo with Chipotles, 202

B

Bacon Biscuits, 233
Baked Sweet Potatoes with Bourbon Butter, 222
Bananas
Jan's Honey Nut Fruit Brochettes, 255

Low-Fat Banana Zucchini Cake, 254
Barbecue sauces
Kansas City Barbecue Sauce, 211
Maytag's Santa Fe Blue Cheese Barbecue Sauce, 214
New Mexico Barbecue Sauce, 213
Southern Barbecue Sauce, 212
Spicy Apple Barbecue Sauce, 214
Barley
Grilled Lamb Stew with Mint & Barley, 46
Basil
Fresh Tomato Basil Salad with Mozzarella Cheese & Grilled Garlic Dressing, 69
Grilled Salad, Italiano, 62
Bayou Gumbo with Roasted Tomatoes, 50
Beans
Black Bean & Corn Salsa, 207
Grilled Lobster Chili, 127
Grilled Marinated Chicken & Pasta Salad with Garbanzos, 108
Grilled Pork Pinwheels with Fennel Salsa, 100
Southwestern Grilled Turkey Salad, 67
Texas Baked Beans with Bourbon, 227
Beef
Bayou Gumbo with Roasted Tomatoes, 50
Beef Stock, 57
Carne Asada with Chipotle Rub, 185
Dallas-Style Grilled Flank Steak, 83
Fajitas with Red Onion & Tricolored Peppers, 82
Family-Style Smoked Arm Roast, 137
Gordon's Favorite Fourth of July Brisket, 138
Gordon's Grilled Brisket, 81
Gordon's Special New York Steak with Grilled Onions, Leeks & Mushrooms, 89
Grilled Barbecue Burritos, 80
Grilled Burgers, 84

Grilled New York Strips with Peppercorn-Roasted Garlic Baste, 87
Grilled Pacific Rim Steaks, 82
Grilled Porterhouse Steak, Corpus Christi Style, 90
Grilled Short Ribs, New Mexico Style, 91
Grilled Tenderloin à la Houston Jet Set, 85
Hamburger Harry's North of the Border Burgers, 84
Mesquite-Smoked Beef Medallions & Salsa, 176
My Pecos River Cafe Burger, 84
Mystery Marinated Chuck Roast, 88
New Mexican Burgers, 84
Our Favorite Mesquite-Smoked Sirloin Tip, 136
Prime Rib Beef Bones, 140
Roast on the Rocks, 90
Smoked Prime Rib Roast with Horseradish Dill Cream, 139
Southwest Stack & Rack, 92
Beer Dill Bread, 237
Bell pepper
Grilled Corn & Red Bell Pepper Salsa, 209
Fajitas with Red Onion & Tricolored Peppers, 82
Grilled Vegetable Salad with Warm Herb Oil Dressing, 62
Biscotti
Hot off the Grill Biscotti, 256
Biscuits
Bacon Biscuits, 233
Brunch Skillet Biscuits, 232
Herb Biscuits, 233
Black Bean & Corn Salsa, 206
Blueberries
Blueberry Compote, 245
Double Blue Blueberry Pancakes, 244
Summer Berry Bowl, 257
Breads & Spreads, 231–248
Broccoli
Grilled Broccoli, 226
Brunch Skillet Biscuits, 232
Buckwheat flour
Beer Dill Bread, 237

Butters
    Chile Garlic Butter, 247
    Double Mustard Butter, 247
    Jalapeño Cilantro Spread, 245
    Lemon-Pecan Butter, 112
    Rosemary Butter, 248
    Tri-pepper Herb Butter, 248

C
Cabbage
    Caren's Chinese Cole Slaw, West Vancouver Style, 71
Caesar Salad with Cilantro Cream Dressing, 74
Cajun Rub, 216
Cake
    Low-Fat Banana Zucchini Cake, 254
Capon
    Herb-Infused Capon or Turkey el Patio, 195
Caren's Chinese Cole Slaw, West Vancouver Style, 71
Caribbean Grilled Prawns with Salsa, 129
Carne Asada with Chipotle Rub, 185
Charcoal grills, 5–6
Charcoal smokers, 17
Cheese
    Caesar Salad with Cilantro Cream Dressing, 74
    Fresh Tomato Basil Salad with Mozzarella Cheese & Grilled Garlic Dressing, 69
    Grilled Mushroom Pizza Topping, 32
    Jan's Chile Cheese Puff, 26
    Maytag's Santa Fe Blue Cheese Barbecue Sauce, 214
    Mini-Frankfurter Reubens, 28
    Pesto Pizza Topping, 31
    Roasted Leg of Lamb with Fresh Spinach, Feta & Chipotle Stuffing, 184
    Sarah's Best Blue Cheese Smoked Potato Salad, 66
    Scott's Baked Whole Pumpkin Soup with Gruyère & Croutons, 56
    Smoked Jack with Salsa & Tortilla Crisps, 39
    Spring Asparagus Pizza Topping, 31
    Tommie's Texas Blue Cheese Dressing, 76
Cherries
    Dried Cherry Salsa, 208
Cherry-Smoked Pork Chops with Dried Cherry Salsa, 133

Chicken
    Bayou Gumbo with Roasted Tomatoes, 50
    Chicken Breasts with Lemon-Mustard Tarragon Baste, 107
    Chicken Stock, 55
    Crispy Roti Chicken with Blue Corn-Green Chile Dressing, 187
    Fruitwood-Smoked Chicken with Smoked Apple Chipotle Salsa, 148
    Gilled Chicken Adobo, 105
    Grilled Chicken Breast with Sun-Dried Tomato Vinaigrette over Fusilli, 109
    Grilled Chicken Legs with Tropical Salsa & Dipping Sauce, 106
    Grilled Chicken Stew with Piñons & Pasta, 48
    Grilled Chicken with Lemon-Pecan Butter, 112
    Grilled Chicken with Mint & Rosemary Lemon Baste and Sunny Salsa, 110
    Grilled Marinated Chicken & Pasta Salad with Garbanzos, 108
    Grilled Marinated Chicken with Harvest Vegetables, 111
    Grilled Rosemary Garlic Chicken Breasts, 104
    Herb-Infused Capon or Turkey el Patio, 195
    Hungarian-Style Roasted Chicken à la Great Southwest, 192
    Jennifer Brennan's Tandoori Chicken, 190
    Margrit's Cream of Green Chile Chicken Stew, 49
    Mayan Roast Chicken, Pibil Style, 188
    Mesquite-Smoked Chicken Breast in Red Chile Sauce, 151
    Mulligatawny Soup, 60
    Range of Satays—Chicken, Pork or Shrimp, 36
    Sage & Lemon Chile Chicken, 104
    Smoked Barbecued Chicken, 153
    Smoked Caribbean "Jerk"-Style Chicken, 152
    Smoked Chicken in Tomato Herb Sauce with Sun-Dried Tomatoes & Ripe Olives over Penne, 150
    Smoked Chicken Legs with Cabernet Cream, 149
    Smoked Chicken Roll-ups with Cabernet Cream, 25
    Southwestern Herbed Rub on Chicken Drumsticks, 113
    Spicy Quick-Smoked Chicken, 172
Chicken livers
    Hungarian-Style Roasted Chicken à la Great Southwest, 192
Chile Garlic Butter, 247

Chiles
    Aztec-Style Pico de Gallo with Chipotles, 202
    Chilied Shrimp Brochettes with Yogurt Mint Sauce, 196
    Crispy Roti Chicken with Blue Corn-Green Chile Dressing, 187
    Fresh Cranberry Salsa, 208
    Genuine Texas Armadillo Eggs, 42
    Ginger Pear Salsa, 206
    Grilled Blue Corn Polenta with Green Chile & Piñon Nuts, 226
    Grilled Corn with Green Chile Soup, 51
    Grilled Gazpacho, 58
    Grilled Green Chile Sourdough Bread, 242
    Grilled Las Cruces-Style Trout with Green Chile & Pecan Stuffing, 120
    Grilled Lobster Chili, 127
    Grilled Loin of Pork with Chipotle Marinade, 99
    Grilled Porterhouse Steak, Corpus Christi Style, 90
    Herbed Carousel Cornish Hens with Salsa Surprise Stuffing & New Potatoes, 194
    Hickory-Smoked Fresh Ham with Chipotle Sauce, 132
    Jalapeño Cilantro Spread, 245
    Margrit's Cream of Green Chile Chicken Stew, 49
    Quick-Smoked Sea Scallops with Chilied Lime-Cilantro Cream, 171
    Roasted Leg of Lamb with Fresh Spinach, Feta & Chipotle Stuffing, 184
    Sea Scallop & Shrimp Brochettes over Chipotle Rotini with Champagne Alfredo Sauce, 198
    Smoked Whole Snapper with Mushrooms & Chiles, 166
    Southwest Stack & Rack, 92
    Sunny Salsa, 205
    Tea & Chipotle Smoked Red Snapper, 172
Chilied Shrimp Brochettes with Yogurt Mint Sauce, 196
Chili
    Grilled Lobster Chili, 127
Cilantro Chicken Patties, 154
Cilantro Lime Vinaigrette, 77
Cilantro Pesto, 35
Clams
    Grilled Clams with Green Chile, Lime & Cilantro Butter, 27
Coffee Can Mushroom Bread, 236
Come Along Little Doggies, 24
Controlling temperature, 9–10

Corn
  Black Bean & Corn Salsa, 206
  Grilled Corn & Red Bell Pepper
    Salsa, 209
  Grilled Corn with Green Chile
    Soup, 51
  Southwestern Grilled Turkey
    Salad, 67
Cornbread
  Skillet Cornbread, 233
Cornish hens
  Herbed Carousel Cornish Hens
    with Salsa Surprise Stuffing &
    New Potatoes, 194
Country-style ribs
  Jamaican Jerk-Rubbed Grilled
    Pork Ribs, 95
Cranberry Salsa, Fresh, 208
Cream of coconut
  Caribbean Grilled Prawns with
    Salsa, 129
Creamy No-Fat Honey Mustard
  Dressing, 78
Crispy Roti Chicken with Blue Corn-
  Green Chile Dressing, 187
Crumble
  Strawberry Rhubarb Crumble, 250

D
Dallas-Style Grilled Flank Steak, 83
Desserts from the Grill, 249–257
Dill
  Beer Dill Bread, 237
  Horseradish Dill Cream, 210
  Smoked Dilled Salmon with
    Mustard Dill Sauce, 40
Direct and indirect grilling, 9
Doneness, 10–15
Doneness guide for grilling beef, 11
Doneness guide for grilling fish and
  seafood, 15
Doneness guide for grilling lamb, 12
Doneness guide for grilling pork, 11
Doneness guide for grilling poultry,
  14
Doneness guide for grilling veal, 13
Doneness temperatures for beef, 10
Double Blue Blueberry Pancakes,
  244
Double Mustard Butter, 247
Dried Cherry Salsa, 208
Duck
  Asian Smoked Duck Breast Salad,
    156
  Grilled Sherried Sesame Duck à la
    Bratel, 118
  Herb-Basted Duck with Seared
    Turnips, 116
  Mesquite-Smoked Duckling with
    Chile Honey Glaze & Ginger
    Pear Salsa, 155

E
Eggplant
  Grilled Salad, Italiano, 62
  Grilled Vegetable Salad with Warm
    Herb Oil Dressing, 62
  Marinated Grilled Eggplant Salad,
    72
  Smoked Eggplant, 178
Eggs
  Jan's Chile Cheese Puff, 26
  Smoked Potato Salad with Salsa
    Dressing, 65
Equipment, 16
Equipment for grilling & smoking, 6

F
Fajitas with Red Onion & Tricolored
  Peppers, 82
Family-Style Smoked Arm Roast, 137
Favorite Grilled Mushrooms, 30
Fennel
  Grilled Chicken Stew with Piñons
    & Pasta, 48
  Grilled Fennel & Fresh Mint Salsa,
    207
  Grilled Fennel, 224
  Grilled Lamb Stew with Mint &
    Barley, 46
  Grilled Leg of Lamb à la Grecque,
    86
  Grilled Pork Pinwheels with
    Fennel Salsa, 100
Fish
  Applewood-Smoked Salmon
    Steaks, 159
  Fish Stock, 53
  Gary's Smoked Sacramento Pesto
    Salmon, 158
  Grape-Smoked Trout Fillets with
    Triple Zest, 161
  Grilled Las Cruces-Style Trout with
    Green Chile & Pecan Stuffing,
    120
  Gulf Coast Grilled Seafood
    Chowder, 52
  Hickory-Grilled Salmon with
    Lemon Vermouth Butter, 122
  Hot Tuna Teriyaki with Sushi Rice,
    124
  Lemon-Basted Monkfish Nuggets
    with Tropical Salsa, 200
  Margarita-Marinated Grilled Red
    Snapper, 121
  Mesquite-Smoked Rubbed Catfish
    Fillets with Black Bean Salsa,
    167
  Mesquite-Smoked Trout with
    Cilantro Salsa, 160
  Monkfish with Hot Orange Salsa,
    126
  Red Snapper with Caribe
    Marinade, 120
  Scrod Mexicana with Orange,
    Lemon & Smoked Pineapple
    Salsa, 125
  Smoked Dilled Salmon with
    Mustard Dill Sauce, 40
  Smoked Whole Snapper with
    Mushrooms & Chiles, 166
  Tea & Chipotle Smoked Red
    Snapper, 172
  Whiskey-Marinated Grilled
    Salmon, 123
Focaccia
  My Favorite Southwestern
    Focaccia, 235
Frankfurters
  Come Along Little Doggies, 24
  Mini-Frankfurter Reubens, 28
Fresh Cranberry Salsa, 208
Fresh Lemon Zest Chile-Herb Rub,
  216
Fresh Sage & Cider Vinegar-
  Marinated Turkey Breast, 114
Fresh Tomato Basil Salad with
  Mozzarella Cheese & Grilled
  Garlic Dressing, 69
Fruitwood-Smoked Chicken with
  Smoked Apple Chipotle Salsa,
  148
Fuel selection, 3–5

G
Garlic
  Chile Garlic Butter, 247
  Fresh Tomato Basil Salad with
    Mozzarella Cheese & Grilled
    Garlic Dressing, 69
  Grilled Garlic Soup, 45
  Grilled Loin of Pork with Chipotle
    Marinade, 99
  Grilled New York Strips with
    Peppercorn-Roasted Garlic
    Baste, 87
  Smoke-Roasted Asparagus in
    Garlic à la Rominger, 220
  Ultimate Grilled Garlic Bread, 240
Gary's Smoked Sacramento Pesto
  Salmon, 158
Gas or electric grills, 6
General cooking tips, 9
General grill rack heights for
  charcoal grilling, 10
Genuine Texas Armadillo Eggs, 42
Ginger Pear Salsa, 206
Grilled Pacific Rim Steaks, 82
Gordon's Favorite Fourth of July
  Brisket, 138
Gordon's Grilled Brisket, 81
Gordon's Special New York Steak
  with Grilled Onions, Leeks &
  Mushrooms, 89
Gordon's West Texas-New Mexico
  Border Rub, 218

Grapes
  Grape-Smoked Trout Fillets with
    Triple Zest, 161
Grilled Antelope Stew with
    Tomatoes, Onion & Butternut
    Squash, 54
Grilled Barbecue Burritos, 80
Grilled Beef & Lamb, 79–92
Grilled Blackened Tomato Cream
    Soup, 44
Grilled Blue Corn Polenta with
    Green Chile & Piñon Nuts, 226
Grilled Broccoli, 226
Grilled Burgers, 84
Grilled Cajun-Style Ribs, 96
Grilled Chicken Adobo, 105
Grilled Chicken Breast with Sun-
    Dried Tomato Vinaigrette over
    Fusilli, 109
Grilled Chicken Legs with Tropical
    Salsa & Dipping Sauce, 106
Grilled Chicken Stew with Piñons &
    Pasta, 48
Grilled Chicken with Lemon-Pecan
    Butter, 112
Grilled Chicken with Mint &
    Rosemary Lemon Baste and
    Sunny Salsa, 110
Grilled Clams with Green Chile,
    Lime & Cilantro Butter, 27
Grilled Corn & Red Bell Pepper
    Salsa, 209
Grilled Corn with Green Chile Soup,
    51
Grilled Fennel, 224
Grilled Fennel & Fresh Mint Salsa,
    207
Grilled Garlic Soup, 45
Grilled Gazpacho, 58
Grilled Green Chile Sourdough
    Bread, 242
Grilled Hot Baked Pears, 253
Grilled Jicama with Lime Chile Rub,
    223
Grilled Lamb Stew with Mint &
    Barley, 46
Grilled Las Cruces-Style Trout with
    Green Chile & Pecan Stuffing,
    120
Grilled Leg of Lamb à la Grecque, 86
Grilled Lobster Chili, 127
Grilled Lobster, New Mexico Style,
    126
Grilled Loin of Pork with Chipotte
    Marinade, 99
Grilled Marinated Chicken & Pasta
    Salad with Garbanzos, 108
Grilled Marinated Chicken with
    Harvest Vegetables, 111
Grilled Mole-Marinated Turkey
    Tenders, 115
Grilled Mushroom Pizza Topping, 32

Grilled New York Strips with
    Peppercorn-Roasted Garlic
    Baste, 87
Grilled Pacific Rim Steaks, 82
Grilled Pineapple Kabobs with Mai
    Tai Baste, 250
Grilled Pork Chops with
    Caramelized Onions & Orange
    Salsa, 96
Grilled Pork Pinwheels with Fennel
    Salsa, 100
Grilled Pork, 93–102
Grilled Pork Steak with Apples &
    Onions, 98
Grilled Porterhouse Steak, Corpus
    Christi Style, 90
Grilled Poultry, 103–118
Grilled Pumpkin Pancakes, 243
Grilled Quesadillas as You Like 'Em,
    34
Grilled Salad, Italiano, 62
Grilled Salsa-Marinated Pork Chops,
    97
Grilled Seafood, 119–130
Grilled Sherried Sesame Duck à la
    Bratel, 118
Grilled Short Ribs, New Mexico
    Style, 91
Grilled Shrimp & Spinach Soup, 47
Grilled Spaghetti Squash, 230
Grilled Stuffed Peaches, 252
Grilled Tenderloin à la Houston Jet
    Set, 85
Grilled Tomato Cream, 210
Grilled Vegetable Salad with Warm
    Herb Oil Dressing, 62
Grill Roasted Leeks & Green Onions,
    228
Grilling, 3–15
Ground beef
    Grilled Burgers, 84
    Hamburger Harry's North of the
      Border Burgers, 84
    My Pecos River Cafe Burger, 84
    New Mexican Burgers, 84
    Southwest Stack & Rack, 92
Guacamole, 24
Gulf Coast Grilled Seafood Chowder,
    52

H
Ham
    Hickory-Smoked Fresh Ham with
      Chipotle Sauce, 132
    Spit-Roasted Fresh Ham with
      Raisin Bourbon Sauce, 182
Hearth Bread, 234
Hearty Grilled Sweet Potato Salad,
    64
Herb Biscuits, 233
Herb-Basted Duck with Seared
    Turnips, 116

Herb-Basted Grilled Fresh
    Vegetables, 224
Herbed Carousel Cornish Hens with
    Salsa Surprise Stuffing & New
    Potatoes, 194
Herb-Infused Capon or Turkey el
    Patio, 195
Herb-Smoked Pork Tenderloin on
    Sautéed Mushrooms, 175
Herb Vinaigrette, 77
Hickory-Grilled Salmon with Lemon
    Vermouth Butter, 122
Hickory-Smoked Fresh Ham with
    Chipotle Sauce, 132
Hickory-Smoked Turkey with Port
    Wine Mushroom Sauce, 146
Honey Whole-Wheat Bread, 238
Horseradish Dill Cream, 210
Hot Herbed Oil, 246
Hot off the Grill Biscotti, 256
Hot off the Grill Radicchio Salad, 70
Hot Orange Salsa, 204
Hot Tuna Teriyaki with Sushi Rice,
    124
Hungarian-Style Roasted Chicken à
    la Great Southwest, 192

I
Introduction, 1–22

J
Jalapeño Cilantro Spread, 245
Jamaican Jerk-Rubbed Grilled Pork
    Ribs, 95
Jan's Chile Cheese Puff, 26
Jan's Honey Nut Fruit Brochette, 255
Jane's Special Lamb Chops, 86
Jennifer Brennan's Tandoori
    Chicken, 190
Jicama
    Asian Smoked Duck Breast Salad,
      156
    Grilled Jicama with Lime Chile
      Rub, 223
Jiffy Turkey Tenders Burritos with
    Salsa, 174
Joe Azar's Lemon Herb Marinade,
    215
Just Peachy Smoked Pork Loin, 134

K
Kansas City Barbecue Sauce, 211

L
Lamb
    Grilled Lamb Stew with Mint &
      Barley, 46
    Jane's Special Lamb Chops, 86
    Grilled Leg of Lamb à la Grecque,
      86

Roasted Leg of Lamb with Fresh
  Spinach, Feta & Chipotle
  Stuffing, 184
Smoked Herbed Leg of Lamb, 141
Shashlik Shish Kabobs, 186
Leeks
  Gordon's Special New York Steak
    with Grilled Onions, Leeks &
    Mushrooms, 89
  Grill Roasted Leeks & Green
    Onions, 228
  Sea Scallops & Porcini Mushrooms
    with Leeks & Herb Baste, 197
Leg of lamb
  Grilled Leg of Lamb à la Grecque,
    86
  Roasted Leg of Lamb with Fresh
    Spinach, Feta & Chipotle
    Stuffing, 184
  Smoked Herbed Leg of Lamb, 141
Lemon-Basted Monkfish Nuggets
  with Tropical Salsa, 200
Lemon-Basted Pork Tenderloin
  Rounds with Wilted Spinach &
  Pecans, 101
Lemons
  Fresh Lemon Zest Chile-Herb Rub,
    216
  Grilled Chicken with Mint &
    Rosemary Lemon Baste and
    Sunny Salsa, 110
  Hickory-Grilled Salmon with
    Lemon Vermouth Butter, 122
  Joe Azar's Lemon Herb Marinade,
    215
  Lemon-Basted Monkfish Nuggets
    with Tropical Salsa, 200
  Sage & Lemon Chile Chicken, 104
Lime
  Aztec-Style Pico de Gallo with
    Chipotles, 202
  Herb-Infused Capon or Turkey el
    Patio, 195
  Lime-Cilantro Turkey, 116
Lobster
  Grilled Lobster Chili, 127
  Grilled Lobster, New Mexico Style,
    126
  Smoked Lobster Tail, 168
Low-Fat Banana Zucchini Cake, 254

M
Mangoes
  Grilled Chicken Legs with Tropical
    Salsa & Dipping Sauce, 106
  Tropical Salsa, 205
Margarita-Marinated Grilled Red
  Snapper, 121
Margrit's Cream of Green Chile
  Chicken Stew, 49
Marinades
  Adobo Sauce, 202

Joe Azar's Lemon Herb Marinade,
  215
Marinade, 190
Marinated Grilled Eggplant Salad, 72
Mayan Roast Chicken, Pibil Style,
  188
Maytag's Santa Fe Blue Cheese
  Barbecue Sauce, 214
Mesquite-Grilled Lemon Rubbed
  Ribs, 94
Mesquite Prime Rib Rub, 218
Mesquite-Smoked Beef Medallions &
  Salsa, 176
Mesquite-Smoked Chicken Breast in
  Red Chile Sauce, 151
Mesquite-Smoked Duckling with
  Chile Honey Glaze & Ginger
  Pear Salsa, 155
Mesquite-Smoked Mussels, 162
Mesquite-Smoked Rubbed Catfish
  Fillets with Black Bean Salsa,
  167
Mesquite-Smoked Shrimp with Pasta,
  165
Mesquite-Smoked Texas-Sized
  Turkey Legs, 147
Mesquite-Smoked Trout with
  Cilantro Salsa, 160
Mexican Oregano & Garlic Rub, 217
Mini-Frankfurter Reubens, 28
Mint
  Chilied Shrimp Brochettes with
    Yogurt Mint Sauce, 196
  Grilled Chicken with Mint &
    Rosemary Lemon Baste and
    Sunny Salsa, 110
  Grilled Fennel & Fresh Mint Salsa,
    207
  Grilled Lamb Stew with Mint &
    Barley, 46
  Mint Balsamic Cream, 210
  Smoked Herbed Leg of Lamb, 141
Mole
  Grilled Mole-Marinated Turkey
    Tenders, 115
Monkfish with Hot Orange Salsa,
  126
Mulligatawny Soup, 60
Mushrooms
  Coffee Can Mushroom Bread, 236
  Favorite Grilled Mushrooms, 30
  Gordon's Special New York Steak
    with Grilled Onions, Leeks &
    Mushrooms, 89
  Grilled Mushroom Pizza Topping,
    32
  Grilled Tenderloin à la Houston
    Jet Set, 85
  Herb-Smoked Pork Tenderloin on
    Sautéed Mushrooms, 175
  Hickory-Smoked Turkey with Port
    Mushroom Sauce, 146

Sake-Marinated Grilled Pork
  Tenderloin with Mushrooms,
  102
Sea Scallops & Porcini Mushrooms
  with Leeks & Herb Baste, 197
Shashlik Shish Kabobs, 186
Smoked Whole Snapper with
  Mushrooms & Chiles, 166
Mussels
  Mesquite-Smoked Mussels, 162
  Southwestern Mussels Vinaigrette,
    128
Mustard
  Double Mustard Butter, 247
My Favorite Southwestern Focaccia,
  235

N
New Mexico Barbecue Sauce, 213
Noodles
  Caren's Chinese Cole Slaw, West
    Vancouver Style, 71
Nuts
  Caren's Chinese Cole Slaw, West
    Vancouver Style, 71
  Cilantro Pesto, 35
  Crispy Roti Chicken with Blue
    Corn-Green Chile Dressing, 187
  Grilled Blue Corn Polenta with
    Green Chile & Piñon Nuts,
    226
  Grilled Chicken with Lemon-
    Pecan Butter, 112
  Grilled Las Cruces-Style Trout with
    Green Chile & Pecan Stuffing,
    120
  Lemon-Basted Pork Tenderloin
    Rounds with Wilted Spinach &
    Pecans, 101
  Smoked Hay & Straw, 38

O
Okra
  Bayou Gumbo with Roasted
    Tomatoes, 50
  Shashlik Shish Kabobs, 186
Onions
  Grilled Pork Chops with
    Caramelized Onions & Orange
    Salsa, 96
  Grill Roasted Leeks & Green
    Onions, 228
  Herb-Basted Grilled Fresh
    Vegetables, 224
  Rubbed Smoked Onions, 177
Orange juice
  Grilled Lobster, New Mexico Style,
    126
  Grilled Marinated Chicken with
    Harvest Vegetables, 111
  Mayan Roast Chicken, Pibil Style,
    188

Orange juice, *cont.*
Monkfish with Hot Orange Salsa, 126
Orange marmalade
Grilled Salsa-Marinated Pork Chops, 97
Oranges
Fresh Cranberry Salsa, 208
Grilled Pork Chops with Caramelized Onions & Orange Salsa, 96
Hot Orange Salsa, 204
Jan's Honey Nut Fruit Brochettes, 255
Orange, Lemon & Smoked Pineapple Salsa, 203
Raspberry Vinegar-Marinated Scallop Kabobs, 130
Rolled Pork Roast with Mexican Oregano, Orange & Garlic, 181
Summer Vegetable & Quinoa Salad, 68
Our Favorite Grilled Baking Potatoes, 220
Our Favorite Mesquite-Smoked Sirloin Tip, 136
Oysters
Gulf Coast Grilled Seafood Chowder, 52
Oysters, Ixtapa Style, 32
Smoked Oysters on the Half Shell with Horseradish Dill Cream, 163

P
Pancakes
Double Blue Blueberry Pancakes, 244
Grilled Pumpkin Pancakes, 243
Papayas
Southwestern Grilled Turkey Salad, 67
Spicy Shrimp & Papaya Bites, 33
Pasta
Asian Smoked Duck Breast Salad, 156
Grilled Chicken Breast with Sun-Dried Tomato Vinaigrette over Fusilli, 109
Grilled Chicken Stew with Piñons & Pasta, 48
Grilled Marinated Chicken & Pasta Salad with Garbanzos, 108
Mesquite-Smoked Shrimp with Pasta, 165
Sea Scallop & Shrimp Brochettes over Chipotle Rotini with Champagne Alfredo Sauce, 198
Smoked Chicken in Tomato Herb Sauce with Sun-Dried Tomatoes & Ripe Olives over Penne, 150

Peaches
Grilled Stuffed Peaches, 252
Italian Grilled Peaches, 251
Just Peachy Smoked Pork Loin, 134
Peanut butter
Dipping Sauce, 106
Peanut Sauce, 38
Pears
Ginger Pear Salsa, 206
Grilled Hot Baked Pears, 253
Pepitas
Caesar Salad with Cilantro Cream Dressing, 74
Pesto
Cilantro Pesto, 35
Gary's Smoked Sacramento Pesto Salmon, 158
Pesto Pizza Topping, 31
Pesto Vinaigrette, 77
Southwestern Pesto Bread Braid, 241
Pineapple
Grilled Chicken Legs with Tropical Salsa & Dipping Sauce, 106
Grilled Pineapple Kabobs with Mai Tai Baste, 250
Jan's Honey Nut Fruit Brochettes, 255
Orange, Lemon & Smoked Pineapple Salsa, 203
Peanut Sauce, 38
Raspberry Vinegar-Marinated Scallop Kabobs, 130
Tropical Salsa, 205
Pizza
Grilled Mushroom Pizza Topping, 32
Pesto Pizza Topping, 31
Portuguese Mini-Pizzas, 28
Spring Asparagus Pizza Topping, 31
Polenta
Grilled Blue Corn Polenta with Green Chile & Piñon Nuts, 226
Pork
Cherry-Smoked Pork Chops with Dried Cherry Salsa, 133
Grilled Cajun-Style Ribs, 96
Grilled Loin of Pork with Chipotle Marinade, 99
Grilled Pork Chops with Caramelized Onions & Orange Salsa, 96
Grilled Pork Pinwheels with Fennel Salsa, 100
Grilled Salsa-Marinated Pork Chops, 97
Herb-Smoked Pork Tenderloin on Sautéed Mushrooms, 175
Hickory-Smoked Fresh Ham with Chipotle Sauce, 132

Jamaican Jerk-Rubbed Grilled Pork Ribs, 95
Just Peachy Smoked Pork Loin, 134
Lemon-Basted Pork Tenderloin Rounds with Wilted Spinach & Pecans, 101
Mesquite-Grilled Lemon Rubbed Ribs, 94
Range of Satays—Chicken, Pork or Shrimp, 36
Rio Rancho Ribs with Barbecue Sauce, 94
Rolled Pork Roast with Mexican Oregano, Orange & Garlic, 181
Sake-Marinated Grilled Pork Tenderloin with Mushrooms, 102
Smoked Spareribs, 135
Southwestern Rubbed Pork Steaks, 173
Spit-Roasted Fresh Ham with Raisin Bourbon Sauce, 182
Pork chops
Cherry-Smoked Pork Chops with Dried Cherry Salsa, 133
Grilled Pork Chops with Caramelized Onions & Orange Salsa, 96
Grilled Salsa-Marinated Pork Chops, 97
Portuguese Mini-Pizzas, 28
Potatoes
Grilled Leg of Lamb à la Grecque, 86
Herb-Basted Grilled Fresh Vegetables, 224
Herbed Carousel Cornish Hens with Salsa Surprise Stuffing & New Potatoes, 194
Our Favorite Grilled Baking Potatoes, 220
Sarah's Best Blue Cheese Smoked Potato Salad, 66
Smoked Potato Salad with Salsa Dressing, 65
Smoked Potatoes, 221
Prime Rib Beef Bones, 140
Pumpkin
Grilled Pumpkin Pancakes, 243
Scott's Baked Whole Pumpkin Soup with Gruyère & Croutons, 56

Q
Quick 'n' Easy Satay Dipping Sauce, 37
Quick Grilled Romaine à la Romanesque Salad, 73
Quick Smoking, 169–178
Quick-Smoked Sea Scallops with Chilied Lime-Cilantro Cream, 171

Quinoa
   Quinoa with Cumin, 225
   Summer Vegetable & Quinoa
      Salad, 68

R
Radicchio
   Hot off the Grill Radicchio Salad,
      70
Raisins
   Spit-Roasted Fresh Ham with
      Raisin Bourbon Sauce, 182
Range of Satays—Chicken, Pork or
   Shrimp, 36
Raspberry Vinegar-Marinated Scallop
   Kabobs, 130
Red Snapper with Caribe Marinade,
   120
Rice
   Cilantro Chicken Patties, 154
   Hot Tuna Teriyaki with Sushi Rice,
      124
   Mulligatawny Soup, 60
Rio Rancho Ribs with Barbecue
   Sauce, 94
Roast on the Rocks, 90
Roasted Leg of Lamb with Fresh
   Spinach, Feta & Chipotle
   Stuffing, 184
Roasts
   Carne Asada with Chipotle Rub,
      185
   Family-Style Smoked Arm Roast,
      137
   Gordon's Favorite Fourth of July
      Brisket, 138
   Gordon's Grilled Brisket, 81
   Grilled Loin of Pork with Chipotle
      Marinade, 99
   Grilled Pork Pinwheels with
      Fennel Salsa, 100
   Herb-Smoked Pork Tenderloin on
      Sautéed Mushrooms, 175
   Just Peachy Smoked Pork Loin,
      134
   Lemon-Basted Pork Tenderloin
      Rounds with Wilted Spinach &
      Pecans, 101
   Mystery Marinated Chuck Roast,
      88
   Our Favorite Mesquite-Smoked
      Sirloin Tip, 136
   Roast on the Rocks, 90
   Rolled Pork Roast with Mexican
      Oregano, Orange & Garlic, 181
   Sake-Marinated Grilled Pork
      Tenderloin with Mushrooms,
      102
   Smoked Prime Rib Roast with
      Horseradish Dill Cream, 139
   Smoked Venison, Antelope or Elk,
      142

Rolled Pork Roast with Mexican
   Oregano, Orange & Garlic, 181
Romaine lettuce
   Quick Grilled Romaine à la
      Romanesque Salad, 73
Rosemary
   Grilled Chicken with Mint &
      Rosemary Lemon Baste and
      Sunny Salsa, 110
   Grilled Rosemary Garlic Chicken
      Breasts, 104
   Rosemary Butter, 248
   Smoked Herbed Leg of Lamb, 141
Rotisserie Cooking, 21–22
**Round 'n' Round She Goes,
   179–200**
Rubbed Smoked Onions, 177
Rubs
   Cajun Rub, 216
   Chipotle Rub, 218
   Fresh Lemon Zest Chile-Herb Rub,
      216
   Gordon's West Texas-New Mexico
      Border Rub, 218
   Mesquite Prime Rib Rub, 218
   Mexican Oregano & Garlic Rub,
      217

S
Safety tips, 8
Sage
   Fresh Sage & Cider Vinegar-
      Marinated Turkey Breast, 114
   Herb-Infused Capon or Turkey el
      Patio, 195
   Hungarian-Style Roasted Chicken
      à la Great Southwest, 192
   Sage & Lemon Chile Chicken, 104
Sake-Marinated Grilled Pork
   Tenderloin with Mushrooms,
   102
Salad dressings
   Cilantro Cream Dressing, 74
   Cilantro Lime, 77
   Creamy No-Fat Honey Mustard
      Dressing, 78
   Herb Vinaigrette, 77
   Lime Vinaigrette, 67, 68
   Pesto Vinaigrette, 77
   Sesame Dressing, 156
   Tommie's Texas Blue Cheese
      Dressing, 76
   Warm Herb Oil Dressing, 63
   Wine-Based Low-Fat Vinaigrette,
      77
Salads from the Grill, 61–78
Salsas
   Aztec-Style Pico de Gallo with
      Chipotles, 202
   Black Bean & Corn Salsa, 206
   Cilantro Salsa, 160
   Dried Cherry Salsa, 208

Fresh Cranberry Salsa, 208
Ginger Pear Salsa, 206
Grilled Corn & Red Bell Pepper
   Salsa, 209
Grilled Fennel & Fresh Mint Salsa,
   207
Hot Orange Salsa, 204
Orange, Lemon & Smoked
   Pineapple Salsa, 203
Tropical Salsa, 205
Tropical Fruit Salsa, 106
Salsa Dressing, 65
Smoked Apple Chipotle Salsa, 148
Sunny Salsa, 205
Sarah's Best Blue Cheese Smoked
   Potato Salad, 66
**Sauces, Salsas, Marinades, Bastes
   & Rubs, 201–218**
Sauces
   Adobo Sauce, 202
   Champagne Alfredo Sauce, 198
   Chilied Lime-Cilantro Cream, 171
   Chipotle Sauce, 132
   Dipping Sauce, 106
   Fresh Lime Ginger Cream, 164
   Grilled Tomato Cream, 210
   Horseradish Dill Cream, 210
   Mint Balsamic Cream, 210
   Mustard Dill Sauce, 40
   Peanut Sauce, 38
   Port Wine Mushroom Sauce, 146
   Quick 'n' Easy Satay Dipping
      Sauce, 37
   Raisin Bourbon Sauce, 182
   Thai Sweet Hot Sauce, 37
Sauerkraut
   Mini-Frankfurter Reubens, 28
Sausage
   Genuine Texas Armadillo Eggs, 42
   Hearty Grilled Sweet Potato Salad,
      64
   Southwest Stack & Rack, 92
Scallops
   Quick-Smoked Sea Scallops with
      Chilied Lime-Cilantro Cream,
      171
   Raspberry Vinegar-Marinated
      Scallop Kabobs, 130
   Sea Scallop & Shrimp Brochettes
      over Chipotle Rotini with
      Champagne Alfredo Sauce, 198
   Sea Scallops & Porcini Mushrooms
      with Leeks & Herb Baste, 197
   Smoked Scallops with Fresh Lime-
      Ginger Cream, 164
Scott's Baked Whole Pumpkin Soup
   with Gruyère & Croutons, 56
Scrod Mexicana with Orange, Lemon
   & Smoked Pineapple Salsa, 125
Sea Scallop & Shrimp Brochettes
   over Chipotle Rotini with
   Champagne Alfredo Sauce, 198

Sea Scallops & Porcini Mushrooms
with Leeks & Herb Baste, 197
Sesame seeds
Caren's Chinese Cole Slaw, West
Vancouver Style, 71
Shashlik Shish Kabobs, 186
Sherry
Grilled Sherried Sesame Duck à la
Bratel, 118
Short ribs
Grilled Short Ribs, New Mexico
Style, 91
Shrimp
Bayou Gumbo with Roasted
Tomatoes, 50
Caribbean Grilled Prawns with
Salsa, 129
Chilied Shrimp Brochettes with
Yogurt Mint Sauce, 196
Grilled Shrimp & Spinach Soup,
47
Gulf Coast Grilled Seafood
Chowder, 52
Mesquite-Smoked Shrimp with
Pasta, 165
Range of Satays—Chicken, Pork
or Shrimp, 36
Spicy Shrimp & Papaya Bites, 33
Simply Perfect Smoked Turkey, 144
Skillet Cornbread, 233
Smoke-Roasted Asparagus in Garlic
à la Rominger, 220
Smoked Barbecued Chicken, 153
Smoked Caribbean "Jerk"-Style
Chicken, 152
Smoked Chicken in Tomato Herb
Sauce with Sun-Dried Tomatoes
& Ripe Olives over Penne, 150
Smoked Chicken Legs with Cabernet
Cream, 149
Smoked Chicken Roll-ups with
Cabernet Cream, 25
Smoked Chile-Sparked Game Jerky,
26
Smoked Cumin Coriander Oil, 246
Smoked Dilled Salmon with Mustard
Dill Sauce, 40
Smoked Eggplant, 178
Smoked Hay & Straw, 38
Smoked Herbed Leg of Lamb, 141
Smoked Jack with Salsa & Tortilla
Crisps, 39
Smoked Lobster Tail, 168
Smoked Meats, 131–142
Smoked Oysters on the Half Shell
with Horseradish Dill Cream,
163
Smoked Potatoes, 221
Smoked Poultry, 143–156
Smoked Prime Rib Roast with
Horseradish Dill Cream, 139

Smoked Scallops with Fresh Lime-
Ginger Cream, 164
Smoked Seafood, 157–168
Smoked Spareribs, 135
Smoked Venison, Antelope or Elk,
142
Smoked Whole Snapper with
Mushrooms & Chiles, 166
Smoking, 15–21
Smoking Techniques, 17–18
Smoking tips, 19–20
Snow peas
Asian Smoked Duck Breast Salad,
156
Soups & Stews, 43–60
Sourdough Starter, 241
Southern Barbecue Sauce, 212
Southwest Stack & Rack, 92
Southwestern Grilled Turkey Salad,
67
Southwestern Herbed Rub on
Chicken Drumsticks, 113
Southwestern Mussels Vinaigrette,
128
Southwestern Pesto Bread Braid, 241
Southwestern Rubbed Pork Steaks,
173
Soy sauce
Mystery Marinated Chuck Roast, 88
Spareribs
Grilled Cajun-Style Ribs, 96
Mesquite-Grilled Lemon Rubbed
Ribs, 94
Rio Rancho Ribs with Barbecue
Sauce, 94
Smoked Spareribs, 135
Spicy Apple Barbecue Sauce, 214
Spicy Quick-Smoked Chicken, 172
Spicy Shrimp & Papaya Bites, 33
Spinach
Grilled Shrimp & Spinach Soup, 47
Lemon-Basted Pork Tenderloin
Rounds with Wilted Spinach &
Pecans, 101
Roasted Leg of Lamb with Fresh
Spinach, Feta & Chipotle
Stuffing, 184
Summer Vegetable & Quinoa
Salad, 68
Spit-Roasted Fresh Ham with Raisin
Bourbon Sauce, 182
Spring Asparagus Pizza Topping, 31
Squash
Grilled Antelope Stew with
Tomatoes, Onion & Butternut
Squash, 54
Grilled Marinated Chicken with
Harvest Vegetables, 111
Grilled Salad, Italiano, 62
Grilled Spaghetti Squash, 230
Grilled Vegetable Salad with Warm
Herb Oil Dressing, 62

Herb-Basted Grilled Fresh
Vegetables, 224
Low-Fat Banana Zucchini Cake,
254
Summer Vegetable & Quinoa
Salad, 68
Starting charcoal fire, 7–8
Steaks
Dallas-Style Grilled Flank Steak,
83
Fajitas with Red Onion &
Tricolored Peppers, 82
Gordon's Special New York Steak
with Grilled Onions, Leeks &
Mushrooms, 89
Grilled Barbecue Burritos, 80
Grilled New York Strips with
Peppercorn-Roasted Garlic
Baste, 87
Grilled Pacific Rim Steaks, 82
Grilled Pork Steak with Apples &
Onions, 98
Grilled Porterhouse Steak, Corpus
Christi Style, 90
Grilled Tenderloin à la Houston
Jet Set, 85
Mesquite-Smoked Beef Medallions
& Salsa, 176
Stocks
Beef Stock, 57
Chicken Stock, 55
Fish Stock, 53
Vegetable Stock, 59
Strawberries
Jan's Honey Nut Fruit Brochettes,
255
Strawberry Rhubarb Crumble, 250
Summer Berry Bowl, 257
Suggested smoking times, 20–21
Summer Berry Bowl, 257
Summer Vegetable & Quinoa Salad,
68
Sun-dried tomatoes
Grilled Chicken Breast with Sun-
Dried Tomato Vinaigrette over
Fusilli, 109
Grilled Mushroom Pizza Topping,
32
Roasted Leg of Lamb with Fresh
Spinach, Feta & Chipotle
Stuffing, 184
Smoked Chicken in Tomato Herb
Sauce with Sun-Dried Tomatoes
& Ripe Olives over Penne, 150
Sunny Salsa, 205
Sweet potatoes
Baked Sweet Potatoes with
Bourbon Butter, 222
Hearty Grilled Sweet Potato Salad,
64
Sweet Potato Rounds with Honey
Butter, 223

T

Tamarind pulp
  Tropical Salsa, 205
Tarragon
  Chicken Breasts with Lemon-
    Mustard Tarragon Baste, 107
Tea & Chipotle Smoked Red
  Snapper, 172
Tea-Smoked Tomatoes, 176
Tequila
  Margarita-Marinated Grilled Red
    Snapper, 121
Texas Baked Beans with Bourbon,
  227
Thai Sweet Hot Sauce, 37
Tomatoes
  Fresh Tomato Basil Salad with
    Mozzarella Cheese & Grilled
    Garlic Dressing, 69
  Grilled Blackened Tomato Cream
    Soup, 44
  Grilled Gazpacho, 58
  Grilled Tomato Cream, 210
  Herb-Basted Grilled Fresh
    Vegetables, 224
  Sunny Salsa, 205
  Tea-Smoked Tomatoes, 176
  Winter's Pleasure Grilled
    Tomatoes, 229
Tommie's Texas Blue Cheese
  Dressing, 76
Tortillas
  Caesar Salad with Cilantro Cream
    Dressing, 74
Grilled Barbecue Burritos, 80
Grilled Garlic Soup, 45
Grilled Quesadillas as You Like
  'Em, 34
Jiffy Turkey Tenders Burritos with
  Salsa, 174
Smoked Chicken Roll-ups with
  Cabernet Cream, 25
Smoked Jack with Salsa & Tortilla
  Crisps, 39
Tortilla Crisps, 40
Tri-pepper Herb Butter, 248
Tropical Salsa, 205
Turkey
  Applewood-Smoked Turkey with
    Honey Glaze, 145
  Fresh Sage & Cider Vinegar-
    Marinated Turkey Breast, 114
  Grilled Mole-Marinated Turkey
    Tenders, 115
  Hickory-Smoked Turkey with Port
    Wine Mushroom Sauce, 146
  Jiffy Turkey Tenders Burritos with
    Salsa, 174
  Lime-Cilantro Turkey, 116
  Mesquite-Smoked Texas-Sized
    Turkey Legs, 147
  Simply Perfect Smoked Turkey,
    114
  Southwestern Grilled Turkey
    Salad, 67
Turnips
  Herb-Basted Duck with Seared
    Turnips, 116

U

Ultimate Grilled Garlic Bread, 240

V

Vegetable Stock, 59
**Vegetables & Side Dishes,
  219–230**
Venison
  Smoked Chile-Sparked Game
    Jerky, 26
  Smoked Venison, Antelope or Elk,
    142

W

Weather, 18
Which type of grill to choose?, 5
Which type smoker to choose?, 16
Whiskey
  Baked Sweet Potatoes with
    Bourbon Butter, 222
  Our Favorite Mesquite-Smoked
    Sirloin Tip, 136
  Roast on the Rocks, 90
  Spit-Roasted Fresh Ham with
    Raisin Bourbon Sauce, 182
  Texas Baked Beans with Bourbon,
    227
  Whiskey-Marinated Grilled
    Salmon, 123
Wine-Based Low-Fat Vinaigrette,
  77
Winter's Pleasure Grilled Tomatoes,
  229

About the Author

JANE BUTEL, a native of New Mexico, is the author of more than a dozen cookbooks including *Hotter Than Hell*, *Jane Butel's Southwestern Grill*, and *Jane Butel's Southwestern Kitchen*. She runs Jane Butel's Southwestern School in Albuquerque, named a best vacation cooking school by *Bon Appétit* magazine, and is the founder of the Pecos Valley Spice Company, a trusted source for chiles, spices, and other ingredients for authentic Southwestern fare. Jane also hosts the public television show *Jane Butel's Southwestern Kitchen*. Visit her websites, www.janebutel.com and www.pecosvalley.com.